Third Eye Chakra 101: Intuition, Vision, Insight
Copyright © 2025 by Dr. Constance Santego.

Copy Editor & Interior Design: Constance Santego
Book Layout: ©2017 BookDesignTemplates.com

Ordering Information:
Quantity sales. Special discounts are available on quantity purchases by corporations, associations, and others. For details, contact the "Special Sales Department" at the address above.

Trade Paperback ISBN: 978-1-997907-02-2
Ebook ISBN 978-1-997907-03-9
Created and published In Canada. Printed and bound in the United States of America

First Edition
Published by Maximillian Enterprises
Kelowna, BC Canada
www.constancesantego.ca

Third Eye Chakra 10: Intuition, Vision, Insight

"The wisdom to see clearly, the intuition to trust deeply, the vision to awaken within."

(Vol VI)

Dr. Constance Santego

Maximillian Enterprises
Kelowna, BC

Dedication

To those who dare to see beyond what is visible,
who listen to the quiet voice within,
and trust the light that needs no proof.
— Dr. Constance Santego

ALSO BY DR. CONSTANCE SANTEGO

NOVELS
Illegitimate Grace
Ashcroft Hollow

Okanagan Trilogy:
Beneath the Vineyards
Under the Okanagan Sun
Guardian of the Lake

The Nine Spiritual Gifts Series:
Journey of a Soul – (Vol 1 Michael)
Language of a Soul – (Vol 2 Gabriel)
Prophecy of a Soul – (Vol 3 Bath Kol)
Healing of a Soul – (Vol 4 Raphael)
Miracles of a Soul – (Vol 5 Hamied)
Knowledge of a Soul – (Vol 6 Raziel)
Wisdom of a Soul – (Vol 7 Uriel)
Faith of a Soul – (Vol 8 Pistis Sophia)

NONFICTION
The Intuitive Life, The Gift Of Prophecy, Third Edition
Fairy Tales, Dreams And Reality… Where Are You On Your Path? Second Edition
Your Persona… The Mask You Wear
Archangel Michael's Soul Retrieval Guide
Tesla And The Future Of Energy Medicine
Beyond Tesla: Advancing The Science Of Energy Healing
Tesla's Code: Mastering Energy, Frequency, And Creative Power
Beyond The Mind: Harnessing The Power Of Astral Projection For Creative Awakening
Bend, Don't Break: Finding Your Way Back To Abundance
Ring Therapy: A Guide To Healing And Balance
Ring Therapy Pocket Guide
Floraopathy™: The Art And Science Of Vibrational Healing With Essential Oils
Dear Older Me: A Memoir… Of Sorts
It's Just Like Poker: A Spiritual Guide To Playing The Cards Life Deals You
Signs And Meanings: What The Feet Reveal About Health, Stress, And The Body's Story
Auricions: Unlocking Subconscious Healing Through Quantum Medicine
Quick Fix Acupressure Method
Manifestation – The DREAM Method in 5 Steps
Confidence- Mastering the Dream Method

REIKI WISDOM, SERIES:
Angelic Lifestyle, a Vibrant Lifestyle
Angelic Lifestyle 42-Day Energy Cleanse
Reiki and the Power of The Joint Points: Unlocking Energy Pathways for Healing (Vol I)
Reiki and Karmic Healing: Releasing Patterns From Past Lives (Vol II)
Reiki and the Five Elements (Vol III)
Secrets of a Healer, Magic Of Reiki
The Reiki Master's Manual

CHAKRA SERIES:
Heart Chakra 101: The Bridge
Root Chakra 101: Building Safety, Survival, Foundation
Sacral Chakra 101: Creativity, Pleasure, Emotions
Solar Plexus Chakra 101: Power, Confidence, Will
Throat Chakra 101: Truth, Voice, Self-Expression
Third Eye Chakra 10: Intuition, Vision, Insight
Crown Chakra 10: Spiritual Connection, Transcendence.

SECRETS OF A HEALER, SERIES:
Magic Of Aromatherapy (Vol I)
Magic Of Reflexology (Vol II)
Magic Of The Gifts (Vol III)
Magic Of Muscle Testing (Vol IV)
Magic Of Iridology (Vol V)
Magic Of Massage (Vol VI)
Magic Of Hypnotherapy (Vol VII)
Magic Of Reiki (Vol VIII)
Magic Of Advanced Aromatherapy (Vol IX)
Magic Of Esthetics (Vol X)
The Reiki Master's Manual (Vol XI)

ADULT COLORING JOURNALS
SERIES-ZEN COLORING:
Quantum Energy and Mindful Living Journal (Vol 1)
Reiki Energy Journal (Vol 2)
Nine Spiritual Gifts Journal (Vol 3)
I Forgive Journal (Vol 4)

FOR CHILDREN
I am Big Tonight. I Don't Need the Light
The Magic Elf Book: 25 Days of Surprises

COOKBOOK
My Favorite Recipes, with a Hint of Giggle

BUISNESS
How To Use ChatGPT For Authors: From Idea To Published Book
Scaling Beyond 6 Figures: Strategies For Health & Wellness Professionals
The Academypreneur's Playbook: Turn Knowledge Into A
Revenue-Generating School

HUMOR/GIFT BOOK
How Do You Like Your Eggs? Crack Into Your Personality, Yolk and All

Contents

Third Eye Chakra 10: Intuition, Vision, Insight

"The wisdom to see clearly, the intuition to trust deeply, the vision to awaken within."

Dr. Constance Santego

(Vol VI)

Preface

SEEING BEYOND THE VEIL

The journey of awakening continues — ever upward, ever inward.
From the vibration of truth in the Throat Chakra, our awareness now ascends into the subtle realms of perception — to the Third Eye Chakra (Ajna), the seat of intuition, vision, and insight.

Here, energy no longer seeks expression through words or form; it turns inward to perceive the invisible. This is the domain of the inner eye, the place where thought becomes knowing, and knowing becomes wisdom. While the lower chakras teach us to build, feel, act, and speak, Ajna invites us to see — not with the physical eyes, but with the mind illuminated by soul.

The Third Eye is the meeting point of duality — the synthesis of logic and intuition, masculine and feminine, sun and moon. When this chakra awakens, our perception shifts from separation to unity. We begin to understand that the outer world is a reflection of the inner one, and that clarity arises not from sight, but from insight.

Its element is light, symbolizing illumination and consciousness. Just as light reveals form, intuition reveals truth. When balanced, the Third Eye brings inner vision, imagination, and spiritual discernment. We trust our instincts and perceive the subtle patterns that guide our path. When clouded, confusion and illusion take hold — we doubt our intuition or become trapped in fantasy, unable to see reality as it is.

Ajna is both the lens and the light through which we experience spiritual clarity. It governs the pineal gland, the biological doorway to higher awareness, and acts as the bridge between mind and spirit. Through this chakra, dreams, visions, and revelations arise — not as escapes from the physical world, but as insights that bring greater meaning to it.

In this book, we will explore the sacred art of inner seeing — awakening intuition through meditation, visualization, Reiki, and mindfulness practices. You will learn to cultivate stillness, interpret symbols and synchronicities, and trust the wisdom that emerges from silence.

As you enter this realm of light, remember: true vision is not about seeing more, but about seeing clearly. It is the moment when the veil of illusion lifts and the deeper harmony of existence comes into focus.

The Third Eye is not a window to another world — it is the mirror of your own soul.

ABOUT THE CHAKRA 101 SERIES

The Chakra 101 Series is a journey through the seven primary energy centers of the human body — a guided exploration of how spirit expresses itself through matter, and how healing unfolds layer by layer. Each book in this series blends ancient wisdom with modern energy practices, bridging spirituality, psychology, and embodiment to help readers rediscover balance and wholeness.

The series began with Heart Chakra 101: The Bridge, where love and compassion opened the way for inner transformation. From there, Root Chakra 101: Building Safety, Survival, Foundation grounded that love into the physical world, teaching stability, trust, and the sacredness of belonging. Sacral Chakra 101: Creativity, Pleasure, Emotions then carried the journey forward — from stability to movement, from survival to creation, from love as an ideal to love as an experience felt through the body.

Next, Solar Plexus Chakra 101: Power, Confidence, Will ignited the inner fire — the energy of purpose, determination, and self-mastery. It taught how to transform fear into courage, uncertainty into action, and self-doubt into radiant confidence. Through this center, we learned what it means to stand in our power and direct our lives with intention and grace.

From this place of strength, Throat Chakra 101: Expression, Authenticity, Truth opened the gateway between the inner and outer worlds — where energy becomes vibration and truth finds its voice. It is the realm of communication, sound, and resonance, where we learn that to speak from the heart is to heal, to listen is to understand, and to express is to create. When balanced, the Throat Chakra becomes the conduit through which our higher wisdom takes form, shaping reality through the purity of sound and the honesty of expression.

Now, the journey ascends into Third Eye Chakra 101: Intuition, Vision, Insight, the realm of light and inner knowing. Here, perception expands beyond the physical, unveiling the deeper patterns that shape reality. This is where intuition awakens, imagination becomes illumination, and clarity arises through stillness. The Third Eye teaches us that true sight is not about looking outward, but inward — to perceive the unity and wisdom that already exist within.

Each book in this series builds upon the last, guiding you upward through the chakra system:

1. Heart Chakra 101 – The Bridge of Love and Compassion
2. Root Chakra 101 – Building Safety, Survival, Foundation
3. Sacral Chakra 101 – Creativity, Pleasure, Emotions
4. Solar Plexus Chakra 101 – Power, Confidence, and Will
5. Throat Chakra 101 – Expression, Authenticity, and Truth
6. Third Eye Chakra 101 – Intuition, Vision, and Insight
7. Crown Chakra 101 – Spirit, Consciousness, and Unity

While each volume stands on its own, together they form a complete map — a journey from earth to sky, from the physical to the divine. This path through the chakras mirrors the process of awakening itself: beginning with love, rooting into safety, awakening creative flow, discovering purpose, speaking truth, seeing clearly, and ultimately remembering our oneness with all that is.

Whether you are a student of energy medicine, a healer, or a seeker of self-understanding, the Chakra 101 Series is designed to guide you home — to your body, your energy, and your divine essence.

Chapter 1 – The Light of Perception

The Role of the Third Eye Chakra in the Chakra System

Every journey of energy is a movement from form to formless, from sound to silence, from expression to pure awareness. After grounding in the Root, flowing through the Sacral, igniting purpose in the Solar Plexus, and giving voice through the Throat, energy now ascends into the Third Eye Chakra (Ajna) — the sacred gateway of vision, intuition, and higher understanding.

Though our series began at the Heart, where love first awakened consciousness, it is here, in the Third Eye, that consciousness learns to *see itself.* The truths we have spoken through Vishuddha now return inward, seeking reflection and illumination. The Third Eye is the center of perception — where the invisible becomes visible, and insight transcends intellect.

If the Root whispers, "You are safe," the Sacral flows, "You may feel," the Solar Plexus declares, "You may act," and the Throat sings, "You may speak," then the Third Eye reveals, "Now you may see."

Ajna governs perception beyond the physical senses — the subtle ability to discern truth through intuition, imagination, and inner vision. It is not the eye that sees form, but the awareness that perceives meaning. When Ajna opens, the mind no longer seeks answers outside itself; it recognizes that wisdom arises from within.

The Third Eye's element is light, representing illumination and consciousness. Its color, indigo, reflects the depth of the night sky — the mystery from which all creation emerges. Its symbol, a lotus of two petals encircling an inverted triangle, represents duality merging into unity — the union of intuition and intellect, seen and unseen, soul and self. This is the portal of perception, where thought dissolves into knowing and knowledge becomes wisdom.

In the chakra system, Ajna builds directly upon Vishuddha. Without the clarity of communication and the resonance of truth, the inner eye becomes clouded by illusion or denial. Likewise, without the grounding of the lower chakras, intuitive insight may drift into fantasy or confusion. But when energy flows freely from root to throat, the Third Eye becomes a radiant lens — precise, luminous, and clear.

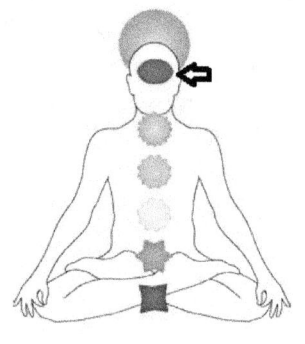

Think of Ajna as the bridge of light. The Root provides foundation, the Sacral gives movement, the Solar Plexus fuels intention, the Heart refines compassion, the Throat expresses truth — and the Third Eye receives illumination. It is the alchemy of awareness — where vibration becomes vision, and vision becomes realization.

When Ajna is balanced, perception becomes lucid and insight profound. You begin to see patterns within chaos, meaning within mystery. Intuition strengthens, imagination deepens, and dreams become messages of guidance. When blocked, perception narrows, and we become lost in logic, disbelief, or fear of the unseen. When overactive, the mind may become overstimulated — detached from reality, projecting illusions rather than perceiving truth.

In the great ascent of consciousness, the Third Eye represents the will to *see beyond.* It is the bridge between the personal mind and the universal mind — where individual awareness touches the infinite field of consciousness. Ajna teaches that to perceive clearly, one must first become still; that vision is born not from effort, but from surrender.

Balanced, the Third Eye Chakra brings clarity, imagination, and spiritual discernment. Imbalanced, it clouds perception with confusion or doubt. In its highest expression, it becomes the *Eye of Wisdom* — the awakened light within that perceives truth in all things.

The Third Eye invites you to open your inner sight — to trust what you feel beyond reason and to see the divine pattern woven through your life. For when your perception aligns with your soul, vision becomes illumination, and you begin to see not just with your eyes, but with the light of consciousness itself.

TRADITIONAL SANSKRIT NAMES

Ajna (आज्ञा) – The most common Sanskrit name for the Third Eye Chakra, meaning "command," "perception," or "to know." The term derives from the root *ajñā*, signifying both *knowledge* and *authority.* Ajna is the energetic command center of inner vision — the place where perception directs energy and consciousness obeys insight. It represents the power to discern truth beyond illusion, to receive guidance, and to see from the perspective of higher wisdom.

In ancient yogic texts, Ajna is described as a luminous lotus with two petals, glowing with the deep indigo light of dawn — the threshold between night and day, darkness and illumination. The two petals symbolize duality and its ultimate reconciliation: intuition and intellect, masculine and feminine, self and spirit. Within this lotus lies the sacred syllable Om, the sound of creation, resonating as the light of awareness that dissolves all boundaries of thought.

Ajna is associated with the element of light (tejas), the essence of illumination and consciousness. Just as light reveals what was hidden in shadow, Ajna reveals the truth concealed beneath illusion. It governs the subtle organs of perception — particularly the pineal gland, often called the "seat of the soul," which bridges physical and spiritual awareness. When Ajna is balanced, perception becomes luminous and clear; we see not only with the eyes but with the inner understanding that transcends them.

In the *Upanishads* and *Tantric texts*, Ajna is called the "Eye of Wisdom" — the portal through which the yogi perceives the unity behind diversity. It is the eye that looks inward rather than outward, reflecting the eternal truth that all reality begins in consciousness. When this chakra is awakened, thought and vision merge, intuition sharpens, and the individual becomes attuned to divine intelligence.

Ajna purifies through *clarity* rather than sound — transforming confusion into understanding, illusion into insight. Its awakening marks the shift from intellectual reasoning to intuitive knowing, where awareness perceives not through effort but through light itself.

COMMON ENGLISH NAMES

- Third Eye Chakra – The most familiar English name, referring to its location between the eyebrows and its function as the inner eye of intuition and higher perception. It symbolizes seeing beyond the physical world into the realm of spirit and consciousness.
- Brow Chakra – Emphasizes its anatomical placement at the brow point, where subtle energy converges with the physical senses to create awareness.
- Eye of Wisdom – Highlights Ajna's role as the center of insight and illumination — the eye that perceives truth beyond appearances and recognizes the unity within diversity.
- Seat of Intuition – Describes Ajna's function as the source of intuitive knowledge, where guidance arises from silence and trust replaces analysis.
- Gateway of Light – A poetic reflection of Ajna's elemental nature. It is the threshold where duality dissolves into awareness and consciousness reveals itself as radiant clarity.
- Mind's Eye – Represents the bridge between imagination and perception. Through the mind's eye, we visualize, dream, and create reality before it takes form.

Balanced, the Third Eye Chakra awakens the gift of true sight — the ability to see through illusion and perceive the divine intelligence guiding every experience. It is both the command center and the window of the soul, uniting knowing and being in one luminous point of awareness.

ELEMENTAL & SYMBOLIC ASSOCIATIONS

Light Chakra – Associated with the element of light (tejas), representing illumination, perception, and the clarity of consciousness. Light reveals form, yet itself is formless — it is both the means and the manifestation of awareness. Within Ajna, light symbolizes the awakening of inner sight — the ability to perceive truth beyond illusion. Through this element, the Third Eye governs vision, imagination, and insight — not only what is seen with the eyes, but what is *known* through intuition.

- Center of Perception – Linked to the principle of *jnana*, or higher knowledge, Ajna is the field of awareness where observation becomes understanding. Just as light reveals what was hidden in shadow, this chakra unveils the deeper patterns beneath experience. It teaches that perception is not passive — it is an act of creation. What we focus on becomes illuminated; what we ignore remains unseen.
- Indigo Chakra – Identified by its deep indigo hue, symbolizing mystery, depth, and the night sky — the cosmic canvas where stars (insights) are revealed against the backdrop of stillness. Indigo embodies wisdom, intuition, and the merging of opposites. It reflects the moment before dawn, when darkness begins to surrender to light — symbolizing awakening and spiritual clarity.
- Lotus of Two Petals – Depicted as a lotus with two petals, each representing the dual forces of logic and intuition, masculine and feminine, ida and pingala — the lunar and solar currents of consciousness. At the center of this lotus lies an inverted triangle and the sacred syllable Om (Aum), the vibration of pure awareness. The convergence of these symbols signifies the dissolution of duality and the emergence of unity —

where all opposing forces meet in harmony within the light of the higher mind.

- Seat of Intuition – The Third Eye is often called the *ajna mandala* — the command center through which inner vision directs the flow of energy throughout the subtle body. Here, imagination becomes a tool of manifestation, and dreams carry messages from higher consciousness. It is both the receiver and the projector of perception — the lens through which the soul experiences creation.
- Bridge of Light – Serving as the link between mind and spirit, Ajna unites the rational intellect with divine intuition. It is the inner sun that illuminates the path ahead, guiding us through life not by logic alone, but through the radiance of inner knowing. When this light is clear, awareness expands. When it dims, perception contracts into illusion.

Balanced, the Third Eye Chakra radiates clarity and discernment — perception becomes insight, and vision becomes truth. It reminds us that enlightenment is not a destination, but a *way of seeing* — the light within, perceiving the light in all things.

CULTURAL / ESOTERIC NAMES

- The Command Center – Derived from the Sanskrit *Ajna*, meaning "command" or "to perceive," this title reflects the Third Eye's role as the inner seat of direction and perception. It is here that consciousness issues its subtle commands, guiding thoughts, actions, and intuition through alignment with higher will. Ajna governs both vision and volition — the insight to see and the authority to act upon what is seen.
- Eye of Wisdom – Revered across mystical traditions as the "eye that sees within," the Third Eye represents awakened consciousness — perception free from

illusion. In Hindu, Buddhist, and Gnostic symbolism, it is the gateway to gnosis, the direct knowing of truth beyond sensory reality. The Eye of Wisdom does not look outward but inward, illuminating the divine spark that exists in all beings.

- Gateway of Light – In yogic and Tantric systems, Ajna is regarded as the luminous threshold between the personal and universal mind. It is through this gateway that the seeker perceives the subtle worlds of vision, dream, and revelation. The light of Ajna does not shine from without, but from within — a spiritual radiance that transforms perception into understanding.

- Lotus of Illumination – A poetic name describing the two-petaled lotus of Ajna, symbolizing the merging of duality into unity. Just as two eyes create depth of vision, the two petals create depth of understanding. This lotus opens when the soul unites intellect and intuition, revealing the inner light of truth that transcends thought.

- Temple of Vision – In esoteric and hermetic teachings, the Third Eye is the sacred temple of divine imagination — the place where thought becomes image and image becomes manifestation. It is through this temple that mystics receive visions, seers interpret symbols, and creators translate the unseen into art, philosophy, and innovation. The Temple of Vision is both a sanctuary and a laboratory of the soul.

- Sixth Gate of Ascension – Within alchemical, Qabalistic, and mystery school traditions, Ajna is known as the sixth gate — the portal through which consciousness ascends from personal identity into universal awareness. It marks the passage from perception limited by ego to vision expanded by spirit. Here, duality dissolves into unity, and the initiate learns to see through the eyes of the divine.

METAPHORICAL NAMES

- The Mirror of the Soul – Representing the reflective nature of consciousness, the Third Eye is the mirror in which the soul perceives itself. It reveals not just what is seen, but *who is seeing*. In this mirror, illusion dissolves, and true self-recognition begins — where awareness becomes both observer and observed.
- The Lamp of Insight – Symbolizing the inner light that guides the seeker through darkness. Like a lantern in the night, Ajna illuminates the unseen path, revealing clarity where confusion once reigned. It teaches that enlightenment is not the absence of shadow, but the wisdom to see through it.
- The Horizon of Mind – Portraying Ajna as the meeting point between intellect and intuition, where thought expands into vision. Just as the horizon blends earth and sky, the Third Eye unites the rational and the mystical — bridging logic with revelation, analysis with understanding.
- The Window of Light – Describing the Third Eye as a transparent opening through which higher consciousness enters. When perception is clear, light flows effortlessly through this window, illuminating insight and spiritual truth. When clouded, the window distorts reality, reflecting fear and illusion.
- The Inner Observatory – A metaphor for the vastness of perception. Within this sacred observatory, the mind becomes a telescope of awareness, capable of gazing into both the cosmos and the depths of the soul. It is here that visions, dreams, and intuition converge, offering glimpses into the infinite design of existence.
- The Indigo Flame – Evoking the transformative fire of illumination. This flame does not burn — it reveals. It represents the spark of divine intelligence that lives within all beings, igniting understanding and dissolving

ignorance. The more it is tended through meditation and mindfulness, the brighter it shines.

- The Eye of Revelation – Depicting the Third Eye as the organ of spiritual sight — not to look outward, but to see through the surface of things into their essence. It reminds us that true vision perceives beyond form and that wisdom is not found in seeing *more*, but in seeing *clearly*.

Balanced, the Third Eye Chakra becomes the light of discernment, guiding perception toward truth, unity, and purpose. It teaches that vision is not confined to the eyes — it is the radiance of consciousness recognizing itself in all things.

AJNA: THE EYE OF WISDOM

The Sanskrit name for the Third Eye Chakra is Ajna (आज्ञा) — a term rich with sacred meaning. *Ajna* translates as "command," "perception," or "to know," derived from the root *ajñā*, implying both *authority* and *understanding.* Together, these meanings reveal Ajna as the seat of inner direction — the energy center through which insight commands awareness and consciousness obeys wisdom.

If the Throat Chakra teaches us to express, Ajna teaches us to perceive. It is the sanctuary of awareness where knowledge becomes understanding and perception becomes illumination. Here, vibration from the Throat transforms into light — refined, still, and knowing. Through Ajna, the mind rises beyond words into vision, where silence speaks through insight and truth is recognized, not reasoned.

From the moment we awaken to self-awareness, we begin to interpret the world — not merely through the eyes, but through meaning. This power to perceive, to imagine, and to know lies at the heart of Ajna. The grounding of Muladhara roots us in the material world, Svadhisthana allows us to feel, Manipura grants us will, Anahata opens us to love, Vishuddha gives voice to truth — and Ajna reveals the light behind them all. It is the center of understanding, where perception turns inward to contemplate the divine source of all experience.

Ajna represents the energetic intelligence of illumination. It governs the eyes, the brow, the brain, and the pineal gland — the subtle organ of spiritual sight. It is the command hub of consciousness, guiding the senses, interpreting reality, and connecting intuition with intellect. Through this chakra, imagination becomes revelation, and thought becomes vision.

When Ajna is balanced, awareness expands beyond the limits of logic. We perceive patterns within chaos, clarity within confusion, and meaning within mystery. Intuition sharpens, dreams carry insight, and imagination becomes a tool of wisdom rather than escapism. The mind is neither restless nor rigid but tranquil — luminous, observant, and wise.

When imbalanced, Ajna may close or distort perception. Too little energy, and the inner sight dims — we lose direction, doubt intuition, and cling to the seen world for security. Too much energy, and we may become lost in fantasy, illusion, or over-analysis, confusing imagination for truth. In both extremes, clarity is veiled, and perception becomes fragmented.

Ajna is the dawn of the subtle body — the meeting place between mind and spirit, darkness and light. It draws illumination from the truth expressed through Vishuddha and directs consciousness toward Sahasrara, the Crown of Unity. Without the awakening of Ajna, knowledge remains unilluminated, and vision lacks guidance. But when Ajna shines in balance, it becomes the eye of wisdom — perceiving all things with clarity, compassion, and divine insight.

Just as the rising sun dissolves the shadows of night, the Third Eye dispels the fog of illusion. It transforms confusion into clarity, ignorance into awareness, and belief into knowing. It reminds us that vision is not about seeing more — but about *seeing truly*.

It is here, in the indigo light of Ajna, that your journey into intuition, vision, and insight begins.

WHAT IS SANSKRIT AND WHY DOES IT MATTER FOR CHAKRAS?

The chakras are rooted in the wisdom traditions of ancient India, and the language most intimately woven into their understanding is Sanskrit — often called *the language of vibration*. Every Sanskrit syllable carries a living frequency, a pulse of energy that transcends meaning to activate consciousness itself. Its sounds are not merely spoken; they are experienced as resonance within the subtle body, harmonizing the layers of being — physical, mental, emotional, and spiritual.

For the Third Eye Chakra, the Sanskrit name is Ajna (आज्ञा). The word means "command," "perception," or "to know." It arises from the root *ajñā*, signifying both *authority* and *understanding*. Thus, Ajna represents the command center of awareness — the place where insight directs energy, and consciousness responds through vision and understanding.

Unlike ordinary languages, Sanskrit is a *vibrational technology*. Each sound embodies the essence of the reality it describes. To speak *Ajna* is to invoke clarity, perception, and inner authority. The vibration of its very syllables awakens the energy behind the brow — clearing mental fog and activating intuitive intelligence.

Each chakra is also associated with a bīja mantra, or *seed sound*, that resonates with its specific frequency. For Ajna, this mantra is OM (or AUM) — the primordial vibration from which all sound and creation arise. OM is not simply a word; it is the cosmic hum, the sound of consciousness knowing itself.

When chanted softly, *OM* begins as a deep vibration in the chest, ascends through the throat, and blossoms into the forehead, where it expands like a wave of light. This sacred syllable harmonizes both hemispheres of the brain, balances thought and intuition, and stills the mind into lucidity. Chanting *OM* attunes you to the rhythm of the cosmos — the same vibration from which galaxies, breath, and awareness are born.

In the Ajna mandala, two luminous petals unfold from a central circle, within which rests the symbol ॐ (Om) — the eternal sound. These two petals represent duality and its merging into unity: intellect and intuition, logic and inspiration, the seen and the unseen. Together, they form the perfect symmetry of awakened perception.

Why does this matter today? Because vibration is the bridge between energy and consciousness. When you chant in Sanskrit, you are aligning yourself with frequencies that have harmonized the human spirit for millennia. Sanskrit mantras awaken coherence between mind and soul, returning awareness to its natural state of clarity.

When you chant *OM*, you are not simply making a sound. You are remembering your connection to infinite consciousness. You are declaring: I see. I understand. I am one with all that is.

OM dissolves confusion, clears illusion, and awakens spiritual insight. It opens the mind's eye and unites perception with truth. The vibration radiates through the brow and crown, illuminating the inner landscape and allowing wisdom to flow unobstructed.

In the traditional visualization, the two petals of Ajna radiate streams of indigo light — waves of awareness emanating from the center of consciousness. This light represents perception in motion, truth in awareness, and insight in form. Every vibration of *OM* resonates through this field, activating the luminous intelligence that lives within you.

Why does this matter now? Because when you give sound to silence, you awaken vision. Sanskrit offers not only a language for the chakras but a *frequency of remembering.* It is the voice of consciousness returning to its source — the vibration of unity expressed as light.

When you chant *OM*, you are not merely repeating an ancient sound — you are becoming it. You are affirming: I see beyond illusion. I perceive with wisdom. I am the light of awareness.

The Third Eye Chakra and Maslow's Hierarchy of Needs

In the mid-20th century, psychologist Abraham Maslow introduced his *Hierarchy of Needs*, a model describing the progressive stages of human motivation and fulfillment. Beginning with basic survival and ascending toward self-actualization, it illustrates how human consciousness evolves from physical necessity to spiritual realization.

Long before modern psychology, yogic philosophy outlined a nearly identical model through the chakra system. Each chakra represents a layer of human development — physical, emotional, mental, and spiritual — each one supporting the next. When lower needs are balanced and integrated, energy naturally rises to awaken higher levels of awareness.

- Root Chakra ↔ Physiological & Safety Needs
  Muladhara corresponds to Maslow's foundational levels

— food, water, shelter, and security. It provides the stability and grounding from which all growth arises.

- Sacral Chakra ↔ Belonging, Intimacy & Emotional Flow
  Once safety is secured, *Svadhisthana* awakens, governing connection, pleasure, and creativity. It reflects the human need for relationships, affection, and a sense of belonging.

- Solar Plexus Chakra ↔ Esteem, Confidence & Personal Power
  Manipura ignites self-worth and the drive for mastery. Here, Maslow's esteem needs — achievement, independence, and confidence — find energetic expression.

- Heart Chakra ↔ Love & Compassion
  Anahata represents love that transcends possession. It is the bridge between personal and transpersonal awareness, shifting motivation from self-centered desire to empathy, service, and connection.

- Throat Chakra ↔ Authentic Expression & Truth
  Vishuddha governs authenticity and creative expression. It is the passage where inner awareness takes voice — where individuality harmonizes with universal truth. Maslow would call this the domain of *self-actualization* — the freedom to express one's true nature without fear or repression.

- Third Eye Chakra ↔ Vision, Intuition & Inner Guidance
  When expression flows freely, perception evolves into insight. The Third Eye Chakra, Ajna, corresponds to the movement beyond self-actualization toward *self-transcendence* — a concept Maslow began exploring near the end of his life.

At this stage, awareness is no longer driven by personal achievement or outward success, but by inner knowing and connection to a higher intelligence. Ajna represents the awakening of *meta-awareness* — the ability to observe the self with clarity, perceive patterns in experience, and receive intuitive guidance beyond rational thought.

Just as Maslow's later writings described "peak experiences" — moments of unity, revelation, and profound understanding — Ajna embodies this same capacity for expanded consciousness. It is where the seeker begins to *see as the soul sees*, interpreting life not through fear or ego, but through wisdom and light.

In both systems, this level marks the transition from *doing* to *being*. The mind becomes a lens for illumination rather than a mechanism for control. Perception refines into understanding; vision transforms into revelation.

- Crown Chakra ↔ Self-Realization & Divine Union
  At the summit of both models lies unity — *Sahasrara*, the realization of oneness with all existence. Here, awareness dissolves into pure consciousness, completing the ascent from matter to spirit.

The Third Eye Chakra thus represents the *integration of perception* — the point where knowledge becomes wisdom and awareness expands beyond the boundaries of the self. While the lower chakras fulfill our human needs, Ajna reveals the spiritual context behind them, showing that growth is not a climb toward something external, but an awakening within.

Both Maslow's hierarchy and the chakra system remind us that evolution is an ascent of awareness. When Ajna opens, we move beyond survival, belonging, and even expression — into *insight*, *clarity*, and *illumined understanding*.

The Third Eye marks a pivotal threshold in this journey — the passage from intellect to intuition, from knowledge to wisdom, from seeing with the eyes to *seeing through the soul.*

It is here that both psychology and spirituality converge to reveal a profound truth:

True fulfillment arises not from what we achieve, but from what we perceive — when awareness itself becomes the light that guides us.

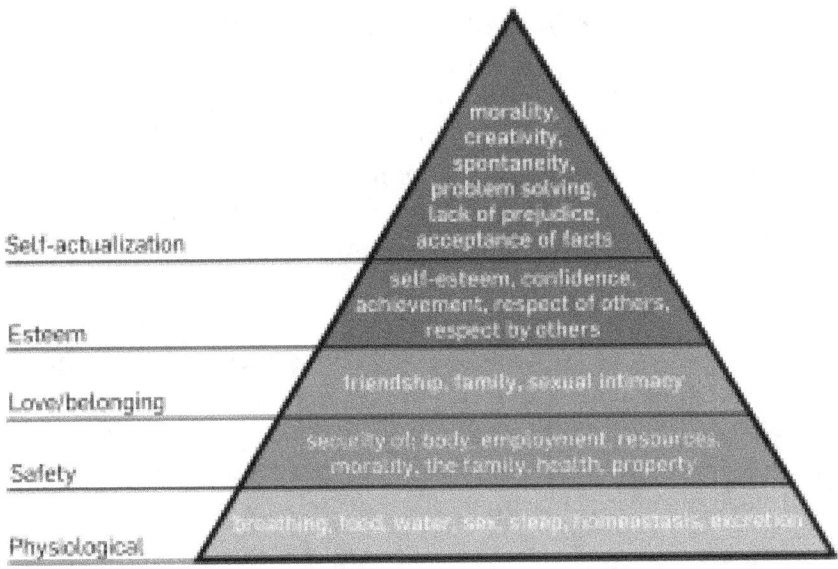

Mazlow's Hierarchy of Needs

Third Eye Chakra ↔ Vision, Intuition & Insight

The Third Eye Chakra (Ajna) is the sixth energy center in the chakra system, corresponding to the stage of human evolution beyond expression and communication. Once authenticity and resonance are established through the Throat Chakra, awareness naturally turns inward — seeking perception, wisdom, and illumination.

Just as *self-actualization* marks the summit of Maslow's Hierarchy of Needs, Ajna represents the awakening of higher consciousness — the ability to see beyond appearances and understand the deeper truth behind all experiences. Without intuitive perception, our understanding of reality remains fragmented; but when Ajna is open, awareness becomes whole.

VISION: THE HUMAN DESIRE TO SEE CLEARLY

At its essence, Ajna governs the inner eye of perception — the capacity to interpret reality not through fear or assumption, but through insight and clarity. It teaches that knowledge alone is incomplete without understanding, and that true vision comes from inner stillness rather than outer effort.

- Clarity of Perception: When Ajna is balanced, we see reality as it is, rather than as we wish it to be. Perception becomes lucid, unbiased, and reflective of truth. We discern illusion from intuition, fantasy from wisdom, and recognize patterns that were once hidden.
- Imagination as Illumination: The Third Eye transforms imagination from escape into creation. Here, visual thought becomes a spiritual instrument — a bridge between the unseen and the seen. Visualization, dreaming, and creative thinking are all tools through

which the soul perceives possibilities before they manifest.

- Symbolic Awareness: Ajna interprets meaning through intuition, synchronicity, and symbolism. The external world becomes a mirror of consciousness — every event, color, or image reflecting something within. This awareness invites a shift from judgment to understanding.
- Presence of Mind: When the Third Eye is active, awareness remains centered even amid uncertainty. We observe thoughts as they arise, detached yet compassionate, perceiving the flow of life with serenity and insight.

INTUITION: THE VOICE OF INNER KNOWING

Beyond thought and logic, Ajna represents direct knowing — the inner sense that transcends reasoning. Intuition is not a mysterious gift; it is a natural function of a quiet and balanced mind. When we cultivate stillness, the wisdom of the soul can finally be heard.

- Inner Guidance: Ajna connects us to our inner teacher — the aspect of self that knows what the conscious mind has yet to understand. When balanced, this guidance is calm, clear, and consistent, directing us toward alignment and truth.
- Discernment: This chakra refines perception into understanding. It sharpens the ability to distinguish between intuition and projection, inspiration and illusion. Discernment transforms intuition into wisdom.
- Dreams and Visions: Ajna is the realm of the subconscious — the space where dreams carry messages from the higher self. Through meditation, journaling, or energy healing, these visions become tools of transformation, revealing insights that lead to awakening.

- Trust in Awareness: Intuition requires faith in perception. When Ajna is open, we trust the subtle nudges, feelings, and symbols that guide us — understanding that insight is not separate from reason, but the light that illumines it.

INSIGHT: THE UNION OF KNOWING AND BEING

Beyond the need for understanding, the Third Eye represents the fusion of knowledge and experience — where seeing transforms into being. It is the seat of wisdom, where intellect surrenders to illumination and perception merges with unity.

- Illumined Awareness: Ajna reveals that enlightenment is not a distant state but a way of perceiving. When light shines through the mind's eye, life itself becomes meditation — every moment infused with awareness.
- Integration of Mind and Spirit: The Third Eye harmonizes analytical thought with intuitive wisdom. This balance brings depth to logic and structure to insight, allowing both to serve consciousness rather than control it.
- Visionary Consciousness: When Ajna is fully awakened, perception extends beyond time and form. We begin to see the interconnectedness of all things — past, present, and potential — as facets of a single infinite intelligence.
- Illusion and Reality: Ajna's greatest teaching is that clarity dissolves illusion. As awareness expands, fear fades, and we perceive truth as the natural state of being. Reality ceases to be something to decipher and becomes something to *witness.*

When Ajna is balanced, we no longer seek truth outside ourselves — we perceive it within. The mind becomes the canvas of awareness, the heart the mirror of vision, and consciousness the artist painting all experience.

When blocked, perception clouds into confusion, skepticism, or over-intellectualization. When overstimulated, imagination runs unchecked, leading to delusion or mental fatigue. Both are distortions of vision.

Ultimately, the Third Eye Chakra represents the freedom to see beyond illusion.
When we perceive through stillness, trust our inner knowing, and allow light to guide awareness, our vision becomes insight — and insight becomes wisdom.

True awakening begins not when we look outward, but when we finally see within.

AUTHENTIC VISION: THE ENERGY OF PERCEPTION

Ajna's element is light, symbolizing illumination, awareness, and clarity. It governs both the physical eyes and the subtle sight of intuition — the ability to perceive the truth beyond appearances. When balanced, it allows us to see life through the lens of understanding rather than judgment, transforming perception into wisdom and awareness into revelation.

- Boundaries in Perception: Authentic vision includes the ability to observe without absorbing and to perceive without projecting. It is knowing when to look deeply and when to rest the mind's eye — allowing perception to arise from stillness rather than assumption. Healthy vision honors both insight and reality, recognizing that to see clearly, one must also know when to close the eyes and listen within.
- Influence Through Clarity: A balanced Third Eye radiates serenity that naturally inspires trust. Just as light reveals without force, clarity influences without control. True vision does not seek to persuade — it illuminates. When awareness shines through humility, others are drawn to its calm radiance.

- Responsibility of Perception: With inner sight comes responsibility. Ajna teaches that what we focus on expands — that attention itself is a creative act. To see consciously is to direct the flow of energy; to perceive through love rather than fear is to transform reality. Every thought, belief, or image we hold projects subtle energy into the collective field.
- Transformation Through Insight: This chakra refines experience into understanding. When emotions and events are observed without attachment, they dissolve into wisdom. Perception becomes purification — where confusion turns to clarity, and darkness becomes light. Seeing truth becomes an act of healing, freeing both self and world from illusion.

When Ajna is balanced, your perception aligns with higher awareness. You no longer view life through the filters of fear or expectation but through the calm presence of understanding. Authentic vision is not about seeing more — it is about seeing truly, recognizing the divine pattern beneath all form.

WHY THIS MATTERS FOR ENERGY FLOW

Just as blocked communication limits self-expression, distorted perception restricts consciousness itself. The chakra system teaches that Ajna is the gateway through which awareness ascends into unity. When the Third Eye is clouded by illusion, the connection between the individual mind and the universal mind weakens, and light cannot flow freely through the system.

If Ajna is weak or unstable:

- The Throat Chakra (Vishuddha) may struggle to express truth with clarity. When perception is unclear, communication becomes confused, and words lose their resonance. Clear seeing supports clear speaking.

- The Crown Chakra (Sahasrara) may lose its direct link to divine wisdom. The mind becomes restless or skeptical, seeking meaning but doubting revelation. Illumination requires a steady flame of awareness.
- The Heart Chakra (Anahata) may lose its deeper discernment in love, mistaking emotional intensity for truth. When perception is clouded, compassion can turn into projection or attachment.

When Ajna is balanced, the entire chakra system harmonizes through illumination. Energy flows upward as consciousness expands, guided by inner light rather than external influence. The Third Eye affirms:
"I see with clarity. I perceive with love. I understand through light."

With this alignment, perception becomes revelation. Thought becomes knowing. Awareness becomes creation. A clear Ajna transforms light into wisdom and vision into truth — turning perception into a sacred act of awakening.

When you see through the soul's eye, reality no longer divides; it reveals.

Chapter 2 – Foundations of Ajna

Third Eye Chakra Basics: A Gentle Recap

If you are new to chakra study, the Third Eye Chakra, or Ajna, is the sixth of the seven primary energy centers. It is located between the eyebrows, extending through the forehead, temples, and brain, and energetically governs the pineal gland, the "seat of intuition," as well as the eyes and nervous system.

Ajna acts as the bridge between the mind's perception and the soul's knowing — transforming knowledge into wisdom and vision into understanding. Where the Throat Chakra gives truth its voice, the Third Eye allows that truth to be *seen*. It is the center of intuition, imagination, and inner sight — guiding how we perceive reality, interpret meaning, and align thought with spiritual awareness.

The energy of Ajna is luminous and subtle, like starlight reflected on still water. It governs perception, clarity, and the synthesis of dualities — intellect and intuition, self and spirit, reason and revelation. When this chakra is balanced, we perceive life through expanded awareness, recognizing patterns, synchronicities, and the deeper harmony behind events. When blocked, perception becomes clouded — intuition weakens, the mind grows restless, and we lose sight of the wisdom that resides within.

KEY QUALITIES OF AJNA

- Element: Light (*Tejas*) — representing illumination, perception, and awareness. Light is the essence of consciousness itself, revealing what is hidden and dissolving illusion.
- Color: Indigo — symbolizing intuition, insight, and the merging of mind and spirit. It is the hue of night just before dawn — the threshold of awakening.
- Symbol: A two-petaled lotus enclosing a downward-pointing triangle within a circle, representing duality and its unification through higher awareness. At its center rests the sacred syllable Om (ॐ) — the vibration of pure consciousness.
- Sound (Bīja Mantra): OM or AUM — the primordial sound of creation and dissolution. Chanting OM resonates through the skull and brow, harmonizing both hemispheres of the brain and awakening intuitive sight.
- Location in the Body: Forehead, brow point, eyes, temples, brain, and upper spinal cord.
- Organs and Systems: Pineal gland, pituitary gland, eyes, sinuses, and the central nervous system — all processes linked to perception, hormonal balance, and circadian rhythm.
- Core Themes: Intuition, imagination, perception, clarity, insight, wisdom, visualization, discernment, and spiritual vision.

THE EYE OF INSIGHT

When Ajna is balanced, perception becomes luminous and steady. You see beyond appearances, discerning truth from illusion with calm clarity. Intuition flows effortlessly, and your imagination becomes a tool of creation rather than escape. You trust your inner guidance, recognizing it as the voice of higher awareness.

When this chakra is blocked or weak, perception narrows and confusion arises. Doubt, overthinking, or cynicism cloud intuition, while attachment to logic or external validation can silence inner knowing. Physical signs may include eye strain, headaches, tension in the brow, or disrupted sleep cycles linked to pineal imbalance. Emotionally, it may manifest as indecision, skepticism, or disconnection from one's spiritual path.

When Ajna is overactive, the mind may drift into illusion or fantasy — confusing imagination with intuition. Excessive mental activity, obsessive thinking, or spiritual escapism can distort perception. The goal is not to see *more*, but to see *clearly* — balancing inner sight with grounded presence.

BALANCING THE INNER LIGHT

Ajna reminds us that seeing clearly requires both focus and surrender. True vision arises not from effort, but from stillness — the quiet mind reflecting the light of consciousness. When we balance the Third Eye Chakra, we awaken our natural capacity for insight and understanding. Thought becomes perception, and perception becomes wisdom.

To balance Ajna:

- Meditate on Light: Visualize an indigo flame glowing between your brows. With each breath, let it grow brighter, illuminating your thoughts with clarity and calm.
- Trust Intuition: Begin to honor your first instincts. Keep an intuitive journal to record impressions, dreams, and insights.
- Reduce Overstimulation: Limit external noise — screens, information, distractions — to create mental stillness.
- Practice Visualization: Strengthen creative imagination through guided imagery, art, or mindful dreaming.

- Connect with Silence: Rest the mind daily in meditation or contemplative prayer. Vision arises from inner quiet, not external effort.

When Ajna is clear, energy flows effortlessly upward to the Crown Chakra, where individual awareness merges with divine consciousness. Light becomes wisdom, and wisdom becomes unity.

The Third Eye Chakra is your invitation to see beyond illusion — to perceive the truth that underlies all form, and to awaken the light of awareness that has always been within you.

When you see with clarity, life itself becomes the reflection of your inner vision.

Cross-Cultural Perspectives on the Third Eye Chakra

The concept of inner sight — the ability to perceive truth beyond the physical senses — transcends geography, language, and era. Across civilizations, the Third Eye has symbolized wisdom, illumination, and the awakening of spiritual vision. Whether described as divine perception, enlightenment, or inner knowing, this archetype represents humanity's timeless aspiration to see beyond illusion and glimpse the reality of the soul.

Though expressions vary, the essence of Ajna is universal: perception is not limited to the eyes but arises from consciousness itself. True vision comes not from seeing outwardly, but from recognizing inwardly — from the light that reveals rather than the light that shines.

YOGIC TRADITION

In the yogic chakra system, Ajna is the sixth chakra — the command center of awareness and perception. Its Sanskrit name means *"to perceive"* or *"to command,"* reflecting both intuitive authority and clarity of vision. Symbolized by a two-petaled lotus and illuminated by indigo light, Ajna represents the merging of dualities — the unification of intellect and intuition, masculine and feminine, self and spirit.

Ancient yogic texts such as the *Shat-Chakra-Nirupana* describe Ajna as the "Eye of Wisdom," where the sacred syllable OM (AUM) resonates eternally. This is the eye through which the yogi perceives truth directly, beyond thought or illusion. Its element is light (tejas) — the medium through which consciousness recognizes itself.

When awakened, Ajna grants insight into the subtle workings of reality. It is said to reveal the patterns behind cause and effect, allowing perception of the divine order underlying all creation. Through meditation, breath, and inner stillness, practitioners learn to quiet the outer senses so that the inner eye may open, seeing the unity behind all forms.

SHAMANIC TRADITIONS

In shamanic and animistic cosmologies, vision is the bridge between worlds. The shaman — the "seer" or "one who knows" — enters altered states of awareness to receive guidance from spirit realms. This practice mirrors the function of Ajna: perceiving the unseen, interpreting symbols, and translating intuitive insight into wisdom for the community.

Shamanic vision quests, plant medicine journeys, and dreamwork all engage the same inner faculty the yogic tradition calls the Third Eye. Through rhythmic drumming, fasting, or isolation, the shaman shifts consciousness to access the "world behind the world." The visions received are not mere hallucinations but teachings encoded in symbolic language — messages from the collective soul.

Just as Ajna refines thought into insight, the shaman refines experience into understanding. Both paths honor the luminous thread connecting human awareness to universal intelligence — the inner guidance that reveals itself through stillness, vision, and communion with the unseen.

INDIGENOUS PERSPECTIVES

Across Indigenous cultures, *seeing* is deeply spiritual. Vision is not limited to physical sight but includes the ability to perceive energy, emotion, and spirit. To "see clearly" is to understand the interconnectedness of all life — to look through the eyes of the heart.

In many First Nations and Aboriginal teachings, vision quests are sacred rites of passage where individuals seek guidance through solitude and communion with nature. These journeys mirror the activation of Ajna: a period of inner reflection that awakens insight, purpose, and clarity of path. The visions received are considered gifts from Spirit, carrying personal and communal meaning.

Among Indigenous healers and wisdom keepers, dreams are viewed as messages from the ancestors or the Great Spirit — much like Ajna's role as the gateway between the conscious and the subconscious, the seen and the unseen. In storytelling traditions, the visionary is not simply one who sees beyond — but one who *understands* what is seen and lives in harmony with that understanding.

Just as the drum represents the heartbeat of Mother Earth in the Throat Chakra's teachings, the visionary fire represents the light of awareness in the Third Eye. Both are tools of connection —

one through sound, the other through sight — uniting the physical and the spiritual in a single act of perception.

MYSTICAL AND RELIGIOUS SYMBOLISM

Across the world's wisdom traditions, the Third Eye appears as a shared symbol of divine perception:

- In Hinduism, it is the eye of Shiva, the destroyer of illusion and revealer of truth.
- In Buddhism, it represents enlightenment — the awakening that transcends ignorance and duality.
- In Christian mysticism, it corresponds to the "single eye" of the Gospel of Matthew: *"If thine eye be single, thy whole body shall be full of light."*
- In Egyptian spirituality, it is the Eye of Horus, symbolizing protection, healing, and the all-seeing awareness of the divine.
- In Taoist philosophy, it resonates with the "Heavenly Eye," cultivated through meditation to perceive the subtle flows of chi and the harmony of the cosmos.

Across all these perspectives, the message remains the same: when the inner eye opens, perception becomes sacred. Awareness no longer divides the world into seen and unseen, good and bad, self and other — it recognizes the unity that underlies all things.

The Third Eye Chakra is not bound to one culture, religion, or era. It is a universal symbol of awakening — the remembrance that we are not separate from the light we seek. Through meditation, prayer, art, or vision, every tradition points toward the same truth:

To see clearly is to know oneself as light.

LIGHT AND VISION DEITIES

Across world mythologies, deities associated with light, vision, and divine wisdom embody the essence of Ajna, the Third Eye Chakra. Their symbols — radiant eyes, flaming lamps, shining suns — represent illumination, perception, and the awakening of consciousness. Though their names differ, they all express the same truth: light reveals, and through that revelation, we understand.

- Hinduism: In the yogic and Tantric traditions, Ajna is often associated with Shiva, whose opened third eye burns away illusion (*maya*) and reveals cosmic truth. The goddess Durga, sometimes depicted with a third eye, represents intuitive clarity — the power to perceive deception and discern truth.
- Buddhism: The Buddha's "Eye of Wisdom" symbolizes enlightenment — direct perception of reality as it is. The urna, a small dot on the forehead of Buddha statues, represents the opening of this eye of compassion and insight.
- Egyptian Tradition: The Eye of Horus (or *Udjat*) embodies protection, perception, and restoration. It is the eye that sees all, the symbol of divine awareness that guards against ignorance and fragmentation.
- Greek and Roman Mysticism: The sun gods Apollo and Helios personify illumination — both the physical light that nourishes and the intellectual light that reveals truth. The Oracle of Delphi, devoted to Apollo, served as an earthly reflection of Ajna's function — channeling divine insight into human understanding.
- Indigenous and Shamanic Cosmologies: The Sun Spirit or Sky Watcher represents the all-seeing intelligence of nature — the awareness that guides cycles, seasons, and spirit journeys. The shaman, like the Third Eye itself, acts as the intermediary between worlds, perceiving what others cannot see.

- Christian Mysticism: The "Eye of God," often depicted within a radiant triangle, mirrors the symbolism of Ajna's downward-pointing triangle within a circle. It represents divine omniscience — the light that observes all things from the stillness of perfect awareness.

Across these traditions, vision is sacred — not merely the act of seeing, but of *understanding through illumination.* Just as Ajna governs the union of intellect and intuition, these deities and symbols remind us that wisdom is both a light we perceive and a light we become.

LIGHT-BASED SPIRITUALITY

Light-based spiritual traditions — from the meditative gaze of yogis to the illumination practices of mystics — express the same reverence for the divine nature of perception. Light reveals what sound initiates: consciousness in motion.

From the lamps of Diwali to the candles of Advent, from Buddhist butter lamps to Zoroastrian fire temples, the lighting of flame symbolizes the awakening of awareness — the victory of vision over darkness. In all these, Ajna's essence shines: the realization that enlightenment is not bestowed from above but awakened from within.

Meditation on light — whether through visualization, sun gazing at dawn, or contemplating the flame of a candle — activates the inner sight. Light purifies thought, clarifies emotion, and dissolves the veils that obscure truth. To see with the Third Eye is to experience existence illuminated by consciousness itself.

Vision-based practices across cultures include:

- The Vedic trataka — fixed gaze meditation on a flame or sacred image to awaken concentration and clarity.

- Christian contemplative prayer — "The Light of Christ" as inner illumination.
- Tibetan Buddhism's "Clear Light" meditation — resting awareness in its purest, most luminous form.
- Islamic Sufi mysticism — perceiving the "Light upon Light" described in the Qur'an, the radiant essence of divine presence.
- Indigenous sun ceremonies — greeting the first light as a renewal of the sacred covenant between humanity and creation.

Each of these practices honors light as both symbol and substance of consciousness — the unifying principle through which all beings awaken to truth.

ORIGINS & HIDDEN HISTORY OF AJNA

The Third Eye Chakra, or Ajna, arises from the yogic and Tantric traditions of India, where the chakra system was first described in the ancient Tantras and later codified in the *Shat-Chakra-Nirupana* (circa 16th century).

In these texts, Ajna is depicted as a two-petaled lotus, luminous with indigo light. Within its circle lies a downward-pointing triangle — symbol of divine awareness descending into human consciousness — and the sacred syllable OM (ॐ), representing the eternal vibration of unity.

Ajna is governed by light (tejas), the most refined of the subtle elements. Where Vishuddha refines sound into resonance, Ajna refines perception into realization. It governs both intuition and intellect, harmonizing them into wisdom. Yogic adepts describe it as the *command center* — the point where thought is transmuted into insight and awareness perceives without distortion.

VEDIC INDIA

In the early Vedas, the idea of the "seer" (*rishi*) embodies Ajna's archetype. The rishis were not merely poets or philosophers — they were visionaries who perceived sacred truths through inner sight. Their hymns, recorded as revelation (*shruti*), were said to be "seen" rather than composed.

The *Upanishads* echo this understanding: "The Self, luminous and pure, is seen by the mind made still." This reflects Ajna's essence — perception purified through meditation. The Gayatri Mantra, invoking the divine light of the sun (*Savitur*), is one of the earliest articulations of Third Eye consciousness: illumination that awakens wisdom and aligns the human mind with cosmic order (*rta*).

EGYPTIAN MYSTERIES

In ancient Egypt, the Eye of Horus symbolized the restoration of divine sight — awareness healed and made whole. Myth tells that Horus lost his eye in battle, but it was restored by Thoth, the god of wisdom. This restoration mirrors the awakening of Ajna: the reclaiming of inner vision after the loss of spiritual clarity.

The Egyptian priests practiced forms of inner seeing through sacred geometry, astronomy, and initiation rites in which light was both literal and symbolic. The temple architecture itself was designed to align with celestial light — a living reflection of the cosmic order perceived through awakened awareness.

GREEK PHILOSOPHY & WESTERN ESOTERICISM

In Greek philosophy, the concept of *noesis* — intuitive understanding — corresponds closely with Ajna's energy. Pythagoras taught that numbers and harmonies were divine patterns, perceived through mental vision. Plato's Allegory of the Cave depicts humanity's awakening from illusion to the light of truth — a direct parallel to the Third Eye's role in perceiving the Real beyond shadow.

Later, in Hermetic philosophy and Western mysticism, this idea evolved into the "Eye of the Mind" — the capacity to perceive divine forms through contemplation. In Christian Gnosticism, Christ is described as the "Light of the World," symbolizing the illumination of consciousness that dissolves ignorance. The mystic's goal, whether yogic or Christian, was the same: *union through illumination.*

CHINESE MEDICINE

In Traditional Chinese Medicine (TCM), the Third Eye corresponds with the Upper Dan Tian, located at the brow — the energetic center of spirit (*shen*). This is the seat of consciousness and insight, where thought becomes awareness. Practices such as Qigong, Tai Chi, and Daoist meditation cultivate this center to refine perception, awaken intuition, and restore harmony between Heaven (spirit) and Earth (form).

Through the practice of inner alchemy (neidan), light is circulated through the meridians, uniting yin and yang energies into one luminous field — a mirror of Ajna's balancing of duality into unity.

KABBALISTIC MYSTICISM

In Kabbalah, the Third Eye's qualities align with the sefirah Tiferet, the "Beauty" or radiant harmony that mediates between divine wisdom (*Chokhmah*) and understanding (*Binah*). Located symbolically at the center of the Tree of Life — near the heart and head — Tiferet reflects the illuminated consciousness that perceives unity within multiplicity.

The Zohar describes enlightenment as the moment when the "eyes of the heart" open — when perception turns inward and the divine light reveals itself. Similarly, the Hebrew phrase *"Yehi or"* ("Let there be light") marks not only the creation of the physical world but the awakening of awareness itself — an echo of Ajna's illumination.

Across all cultures — from the solar hymns of the Vedas to the light temples of Egypt, from the philosophical revelations of Greece to the inner alchemy of China — humanity has revered the Eye of Wisdom as the symbol of awakened consciousness.

Ajna embodies this universal remembrance: that the light we seek is the light we are.
To awaken the Third Eye is to perceive the divine not as something distant, but as the radiance already shining within.

When the eye of vision opens, the world is not transformed — *we are.*

THE HIDDEN HISTORY OF AJNA

Throughout history, the Third Eye has represented more than intuition or foresight — it has symbolized *illumination, awareness,* and *spiritual sovereignty.* Yogic sages taught that when the light of Ajna is awakened, perception transcends illusion, revealing the underlying unity between the inner and outer worlds. It is the center where intellect meets insight, where seeing becomes knowing, and where consciousness commands its own evolution.

The "hidden history" of Ajna is not found in temples or texts alone, but in humanity's shifting relationship with vision — how we perceive truth, wisdom, and reality itself.
In ages where intuition was revered, societies were guided by visionaries — shamans, prophets, seers, and mystics — those who could see beyond appearances into the invisible pattern of

life. These were cultures of connection, where inner knowing was valued as much as outer knowledge.

Yet as materialism rose and empirical thought became the sole authority, humanity's inner sight dimmed. The unseen was dismissed as superstition; the intuitive mind, silenced. The age of intellect brought clarity, but also fragmentation — a reliance on the external eye at the cost of the inner one.

This imbalance continues today in the tension between logic and intuition, technology and consciousness, information and wisdom.

Ajna's reawakening invites the reconciliation of these opposites — a return to *seeing with wholeness*. It calls for perception that unites reason with revelation, evidence with empathy, and intellect with insight.

To understand Ajna is not only to study light, symbol, or gland — it is to reclaim the sacredness of *vision itself*. True seeing is not observation — it is revelation. It is the illumination that dissolves separation and restores coherence between mind and spirit.

Ajna reminds us that perception is sacred when it flows from stillness. To awaken this chakra is to remember that intuition and intellect, imagination and discernment, are not adversaries — they are the twin flames of the same inner light. When balanced, they purify perception, heal delusion, and restore harmony between self and Source.

THE SYMBOLISM OF THE THIRD EYE CHAKRA

Ajna is associated with the element of light (tejas) — the essence of illumination, clarity, and higher awareness. Light reveals what shadow conceals. It is the bridge between consciousness and form, shining through the lens of perception to illuminate truth. Just as light allows the eye to see the world, awareness allows the soul to perceive reality.

Its color is indigo, the hue of twilight — that mystical threshold between day and night, seen and unseen, waking and dreaming. Indigo represents deep insight, spiritual maturity, and the merging of intellect with intuition. It is the color of contemplation, stillness, and the infinite expanse of mind illuminated by awareness.

The symbol of Ajna is a two-petaled lotus, representing the unification of duality — sun and moon, logic and intuition, masculine and feminine, self and Spirit. Each petal symbolizes one aspect of perception, and their merging reflects the transcendence of polarity into wisdom.
Within the lotus lies a downward-pointing triangle enclosed in a circle, signifying the descent of divine light into human consciousness. This symbol echoes the inner geometry of vision — the meeting of higher illumination with embodied awareness, forming the "Eye of Wisdom."

At the center of Ajna rests the sacred syllable OM (ॐ) — the primordial vibration from which all perception arises. While Vishuddha governs the sound of truth, Ajna perceives the light of that truth. Together, they form the continuum of communication between soul and cosmos: *vibration becoming vision, sound becoming sight.*

Ajna's symbolism reminds us that the Third Eye is not a physical organ, but a spiritual faculty — a lens of consciousness itself. Through it, the invisible becomes known, the infinite becomes intimate, and the divine reveals itself in every reflection.

To awaken this chakra is to let your mind become light — clear, discerning, and illuminated by the radiance of inner wisdom.

When Ajna opens, the world is not merely seen — it is *understood.*

THE INDIGO LOTUS

The lotus of Ajna, the Third Eye Chakra, is always depicted as deep indigo, radiant like the night sky before dawn — that mystical moment when darkness gives way to the first light of understanding. It is the lotus of light and awareness, symbolizing the awakening of *inner sight, intuition,* and *spiritual perception.*

Where the Throat Chakra's blue lotus opens through sound and expression, the Indigo Lotus of Ajna opens through silence and perception — not the silence of emptiness, but the stillness that sees. Its light reveals rather than speaks, transforming reflection into revelation.

Unlike the many-petaled lotuses of the lower chakras, Ajna's lotus has only two petals — simple, balanced, and profound. These petals represent duality and its reconciliation: the left and right hemispheres of the brain, intuition and intellect, moon and sun, inner and outer sight. Within their union, perception transcends polarity, and awareness expands into wisdom.

At the center of the indigo lotus glows a white circle containing a downward-pointing triangle, symbolizing the descent of divine illumination into human consciousness. The circle represents the infinite expanse of awareness — the boundless field of mind in its purest form — while the triangle signifies the channel through which higher vision flows into embodied experience.

Inside this sacred geometry rests the eternal syllable OM (ॐ) — the vibration of pure consciousness. Where Vishuddha transforms vibration into sound, Ajna refines that sound into light. Together they complete a sacred progression: truth becomes resonance, and resonance becomes revelation.

The Indigo Lotus teaches the art of *seeing within*. It is not the eye of imagination or fantasy, but of clarity and insight. Through its light, illusions dissolve, and the unity behind all appearances is revealed. It is the flower of discernment, the bloom of insight — where awareness no longer seeks outward but reflects inward to recognize its own radiance.

Each petal of Ajna embodies a quality of awakened perception:

- Intuition — seeing without reasoning.
- Clarity — perceiving without distortion.
- Imagination — envisioning the possible from the unseen.
- Wisdom — interpreting vision through compassion. Together, they form the sacred architecture of consciousness — the harmonious balance between seeing and knowing, between mind and spirit.

If the blue lotus of Vishuddha teaches us to *speak our truth*, the indigo lotus of Ajna teaches us to *see the truth that cannot be spoken*.
Where the heart teaches us to love and the throat teaches us to

express, the Third Eye teaches us to understand — to perceive the divine pattern that underlies every form of existence.

The Indigo Lotus of Ajna invites us to *see through the illusion* of separation and awaken to the light within all things. It reminds us that vision is not limited to eyes but arises from consciousness itself. When the Third Eye opens, every face becomes a mirror, every moment a revelation, and every breath a beam of light returning to its source.

To awaken Ajna is to let your awareness become radiant — to see with the eye of wisdom and to recognize that all you perceive is the divine perceiving itself.

When the Indigo Lotus blossoms, there is no more searching — only seeing, and knowing that you have always been the light you sought.

THE COLOR INDIGO OF AJNA

When you close your eyes and focus on the space between your brows, a deep, velvety indigo often begins to appear — a color both mysterious and luminous, like twilight descending over still waters or the night sky revealing its first stars. This is no mere visualization; it is the frequency of Ajna, the Third Eye Chakra — the center of inner vision, wisdom, and illumination.

Indigo carries the vibration of light transformed into insight, the meeting point between shadow and radiance, form and formlessness. It is the color of awareness — the hue of perception turned inward to behold the infinite within.

INDIGO: INTUITION, LIGHT, AND AWARENESS
• *The Color of Night and Knowing*

Indigo is the color of mystery and depth — the hue of the unseen, where knowledge becomes wisdom. Just as twilight marks the transition between day and night, indigo represents the threshold between conscious thought and superconscious awareness. It is the bridge between what is known through the senses and what is perceived through the soul.

Where blue expands outward into space, indigo turns inward, drawing awareness into the luminous vastness of the inner world.

• *The Light of Perception*

Associated with the element of light (tejas), indigo symbolizes illumination through understanding. It refines perception, sharpening intuition and dissolving illusion. When Ajna is open, this color reveals not just what is seen, but *what it means*.

Indigo light is the lamp of consciousness — it does not shine upon objects but reveals the seer behind all seeing.

It invites us to perceive reality not through logic alone, but through direct awareness — a knowing that comes from within.

• *The Vibration of Insight*

Indigo resonates with the frequency of truth realized rather than spoken. It is the silent wisdom that arises from deep reflection, meditation, and trust in one's inner guidance. This color carries the vibration of discernment — the ability to see patterns, decode symbols, and perceive the harmony hidden beneath life's surface.

When the Third Eye is balanced, indigo light fills the mind like a calm, starry sky — clear, infinite, and awake.

• *The Stillness of Vision*

Indigo awakens the peace of pure perception. It slows the restless mind, dissolves distractions, and deepens focus. In its presence, the distinction between the observer and the observed fades away, leaving only awareness itself — vast and serene.

When we dwell in Ajna's indigo light, our inner sight becomes steady, our thoughts luminous, and our intuition effortless. Seeing becomes meditation; knowing becomes being.

• *The Frequency of Illumination*

Indigo carries the vibration of unity — the merging of intellect and intuition, logic and love, the human and the divine. It is the light of integration, reminding us that vision and understanding are not separate paths but facets of the same illumination. When the Third Eye radiates indigo light, the world no longer appears fragmented. Every form, color, and experience reveals itself as part of a greater whole — consciousness perceiving itself in motion.

Indigo is the color of truth realized, light embodied, and consciousness awakened.
It invites you to look not outward for clarity but inward, where light meets stillness and awareness blooms into wisdom.

To live in the radiance of Ajna's indigo is to dwell at the meeting point of knowing and mystery — to see with both eyes open and the soul illuminated.

When your perception rests in this luminous hue, you no longer seek the light — you become it.

WHY INDIGO BELONGS TO THE THIRD EYE CHAKRA

Each chakra color corresponds to a frequency of light within the visible spectrum, representing a stage in the soul's ascent from matter to spirit. Indigo vibrates just above blue — the hue of expression — marking the transition from *sound to sight*, from *communication to comprehension*, from *truth spoken to truth seen.*

Where blue gives voice to understanding, indigo gives vision to wisdom. It belongs to Ajna, the Third Eye Chakra, because it embodies the still light of awareness — the luminous frequency through which consciousness perceives itself.

• The Sixth Color of the Rainbow

Just as indigo follows blue in the visible spectrum, Ajna follows Vishuddha in the energetic ladder of the chakras. Once truth is spoken, it seeks to be seen. The calm blue of expression deepens into the rich indigo of perception — the color of inner sight, reflection, and intuitive knowing.

Indigo symbolizes the mind turned inward toward illumination. Where the Throat communicates with others, the Third Eye communes with the infinite — translating light into understanding and perception into insight.

• A Frequency of Light and Awareness

Indigo vibrates at a frequency that bridges the personal and the universal, the finite and the infinite. It is subtler than blue yet denser than violet — the threshold between reason and revelation.

This frequency refines thought into vision and transforms intellect into intuition. It resonates with light (tejas) — the element of perception and illumination — inviting the mind to see beyond appearance into essence.

Indigo energy calms mental turbulence, heightens awareness, and opens consciousness to subtle realities. It is the color of clarity without noise — awareness without attachment.

• The Color of Illumination and Insight

Indigo is the light of inner vision — the radiance that shines from within the mind when it is still. Just as blue mirrors the open sky, indigo mirrors the night sky — vast, infinite, and filled with hidden stars.

Within Ajna, indigo represents illumination born of stillness — the capacity to perceive what lies beyond the surface of things. It carries the vibration of deep wisdom, the quiet knowing that comes not from study but from presence.

Where blue listens, indigo *sees*. It is the color of intuitive revelation — perception that flows directly from consciousness itself.

• Integrative and Transcendent

Indigo harmonizes all colors that come before it, gathering their lessons into vision. From red's vitality to green's compassion to blue's truth, every frequency converges in Ajna's indigo light — unified, clarified, and illuminated.

It is the hue of integration — the space where dualities dissolve and awareness perceives oneness. Indigo belongs to Ajna because it represents the merging of intellect and intuition, thought and understanding, light and shadow.

When the Third Eye is awakened, indigo radiance surrounds the being like a field of clarity — a living aura of awareness and peace.

Indigo belongs to Ajna because it is the color of consciousness perceiving itself — the vibration of illumination moving through the mind.

It signifies the awakening of inner sight, the calm radiance that transforms observation into wisdom and vision into truth.

To live in the indigo of Ajna is to perceive with the soul — to see through illusion into essence, to understand without words, and to recognize that light does not merely illuminate the world… it reveals the divine within it.

INDIGO IN DAILY LIFE

• **When you feel uncertain or disconnected from intuition:**

Wear indigo or deep violet clothing, shawls, or gemstones to awaken inner guidance and trust in your insight. The color indigo activates the Third Eye's frequency of awareness, quieting overthinking and strengthening your connection to higher wisdom. It helps you see the bigger picture and make choices with clarity and confidence.

• **When the mind feels cluttered or overwhelmed:**

Close your eyes and visualize breathing in indigo light — cool, deep, and steady like twilight. Let it fill the space between your brows, dissolving tension and clearing mental fog. Indigo light calms scattered thoughts, integrates logic with intuition, and restores stillness to the inner mind.

• **When seeking clarity or spiritual vision:**

Hold or wear stones that resonate with Ajna's indigo vibration, such as lapis lazuli, amethyst, or azurite. These crystals heighten intuitive perception, strengthen focus during meditation, and assist in dream recall or visualization practices. They remind you to trust what you *feel and know*, not only what you see.

• In rituals of insight and awareness:

Light indigo or purple candles to invoke wisdom and inner illumination. Burn resins or incense such as frankincense, myrrh, or sandalwood to quiet the mind and open perception. Meditate facing the rising sun or under the night sky — times when light and darkness meet — to attune your consciousness to Ajna's subtle balance of vision and surrender.

Surround yourself with indigo fabrics, celestial imagery, or soft ambient tones that evoke spaciousness and depth. Allow silence to be part of your ritual; in stillness, perception expands.

Indigo energy in daily life reminds you to look beyond appearances — to sense the truth beneath the surface. When you invite this color into your awareness, you cultivate clarity, calm, and confidence in your inner knowing.

To live in the indigo of Ajna is to walk with eyes open to both worlds — the visible and the unseen — guided by the luminous wisdom of your own higher vision.

MEDITATION WITH INDIGO

1. Close your eyes and visualize a radiant indigo lotus at the center of your forehead, between your brows — glowing like the night sky just before dawn.
2. See its deep indigo light expanding outward, softening your temples, eyes, and forehead — releasing tension, thought loops, and mental strain.
3. With each breath, feel this luminous indigo energy illuminating your mind, harmonizing your thoughts, and quieting the inner noise as you silently repeat:

"I see with clarity. I trust my intuition. I am guided by the light within."

Indigo invites stillness and awareness — the perfect balance between seeing and knowing.
To live in its frequency is to perceive without distortion, to listen to the voice of inner guidance, and to recognize truth not by evidence, but by resonance.

WANT TO EXPERIENCE IT IN ACTION?...
Watch this video for the Third Eye Chakra Meditation.
Watch it here: https://youtu.be/kyR06ttM9VE

THE DEEPER LESSON OF INDIGO

Indigo teaches us that wisdom, intuition, and perception are sacred expressions of consciousness. To see with clarity, to discern truth, and to live guided by inner vision — these are acts of devotion when anchored in awareness.
Just as darkness allows the stars to shine, the still mind reveals the light of the soul.

The Third Eye's indigo light is both a gift and a revelation. It is the gaze of Spirit through the lens of the human mind, whispering:

"You are awareness. You are light. You are the vision of truth itself."

Ajna reminds us that sight was never meant only for observation, but for understanding — to perceive the sacred pattern woven through all existence. When we honor the indigo vibration within, we remember that perception is prayer, and seeing clearly is a form of divine participation.

To awaken the Third Eye is to let light itself become our guide — not the light that blinds, but the one that reveals. When perception aligns with wisdom, every moment becomes an act of sacred seeing, and every insight becomes a bridge between the human and the divine.

THE TWO-PETALED LOTUS OF AJNA

At the center of Ajna's symbolism lies a two-petaled indigo lotus — elegant and balanced, representing the union of duality and the awakening of inner vision. These petals symbolize the meeting of opposites: sun and moon, logic and intuition, masculine and feminine, seen and unseen. When they unfold in harmony, perception transcends polarity and becomes wisdom.

This lotus marks the threshold where energy moves from vibration (Throat Chakra) into illumination (Third Eye Chakra). It is the lotus of light and insight, where thought dissolves into awareness and perception becomes pure consciousness.

Each of Ajna's two petals carries a sacred sound — the seed syllables "HAM" and "KSHAM."
Together, they represent the fusion of wisdom and compassion, intellect and intuition, structure and surrender. In meditation, chanting these syllables awakens equilibrium within the mind, bringing balance to the left and right hemispheres of the brain and aligning human perception with divine understanding.

At the heart of this lotus lies the OM (ॐ) — the eternal vibration of awareness. When contemplated, it reveals the essence of Ajna's teaching: that all sight arises from consciousness itself.

THE TWO SEED SYLLABLES OF VISION

The vibrations HAM and KSHAM (pronounced "hum" and "kshum") are not just sounds — they are frequencies of awakening.

- HAM represents the active principle — awareness expanding outward, the impulse to understand and illuminate.

- KSHAM represents the receptive principle — awareness turning inward, embracing the vast stillness of the soul.

When balanced, these vibrations unify thought and intuition, producing insight that is both wise and compassionate.

Chanting these syllables or visualizing them as radiant symbols within the forehead activates the Third Eye's subtle field, dissolving illusion and awakening inner sight. Each tone resonates through the head and mind, clearing density and restoring the natural luminosity of awareness.

When sound becomes light within, vision becomes revelation. Ajna is the eye of wisdom — the silent witness within every act of seeing, dreaming, and understanding.

To meditate upon the indigo lotus is to awaken your inner light — the awareness that sees without eyes and knows without thought.
The Third Eye does not simply observe the world; it illuminates it.

THE TWO QUALITIES OF VISION

The two petals of Ajna represent the merging of dual perception — the meeting of opposites within consciousness. Where Vishuddha refines sound into truth, Ajna refines thought into light. These two sacred currents — perception and discernment — must be purified before vision becomes wisdom.

They are the twin eyes of inner sight: one looks outward upon creation, the other looks inward upon consciousness. When they act separately, confusion and illusion arise. When they unite, clarity dawns, and awareness perceives truth beyond polarity.

THE DUAL CURRENTS OF AJNA

Each petal corresponds to a quality of awareness that must evolve from human perception into divine insight:

- The Left Petal (Moon / Receptive / Feminine): Represents intuition, imagination, receptivity, and reflection. When unbalanced, it may express as fantasy, emotional projection, or spiritual confusion. When refined, it becomes inner knowing — perception guided by peace and compassion.
- The Right Petal (Sun / Active / Masculine): Represents logic, intellect, structure, and clarity. When unbalanced, it may manifest as skepticism, rigidity, or dominance of reason over intuition. When refined, it becomes discernment — wisdom guided by understanding and light.

When these two forces are harmonized, the Third Eye opens — neither emotional nor analytical, but radiant with the calm awareness that simply *is*. Vision becomes illumination; perception becomes unity.

THE TWO DIRECTIONS OF AWARENESS

The two petals also symbolize the two directions of sight — inward and outward.

- Inward vision reveals the infinite within, guiding the soul toward realization.
- Outward vision perceives the divine reflected in the external world.

Ajna's awakening is the moment these two directions merge — where the seer, the seen, and the act of seeing become one. This convergence marks the transcendence of duality and the birth of holistic awareness.

Just as Vishuddha radiates in sixteen directions of sound, Ajna radiates in two beams of light, forming a single ray of insight. Its perception is not scattered but focused — clear, centered, and unwavering.

THE TWO STREAMS OF LIGHT

In Tantric symbolism, the two petals also represent the Ida and Pingala — the lunar and solar channels of energy that spiral around the spine. Their currents converge at the Third Eye, where dual energy merges into a single current called Sushumna, the central pathway of enlightenment.

This union marks the end of polarity and the beginning of integration — the awakening of consciousness that perceives without preference or distortion.
Where Ida cools and nourishes, Pingala warms and activates; their harmony ignites the light of inner vision.

To meditate on the two-petaled lotus is to unite breath, mind, and awareness — allowing perception to flow in perfect balance between stillness and illumination.

THE SACRED GEOMETRY OF TWO

In sacred geometry, the number two represents polarity, reflection, and relationship — the first division of unity, and the necessary tension through which consciousness knows itself. Within Ajna, two becomes one again: duality dissolves back into awareness.

This geometry teaches that all opposites are mirrors — that every darkness holds the seed of light, every thought the essence of silence.
When the two petals of Ajna unfold in harmony, they form the vesica piscis, the almond-shaped window of divine vision —

symbol of the sacred intersection between heaven and earth, soul and matter, seen and unseen.

Ajna's twofold symmetry reminds us that perception is not achieved through force but through balance — through the meeting of intuition and intellect, surrender and awareness, night and dawn.

THE TWO PETALS AS COSMIC EYES

The two petals of the Third Eye are often seen as the eyes of the soul — one perceiving the manifest world, the other the unmanifest source. Together, they form the gateway to true sight — where the observer and the observed become one continuum of light.

When consciousness stabilizes at Ajna, all perception becomes sacred. The illusion of separation dissolves, and what remains is pure awareness — luminous, unbroken, eternal.

When Ajna is awakened, perception is no longer divided between "I" and "other."
Awareness becomes the single field of vision through which the universe sees itself.
This is the alchemy of indigo — the transformation of dual sight into divine knowing.

To see with the Third Eye is to realize that all wisdom already exists within the still center of being — where both petals open toward infinity, and light becomes the language of the soul.

THE TRIANGLE OF LIGHT: AJNA'S CORE GEOMETRY

At the center of Ajna's indigo lotus lies a downward-pointing triangle of luminous light, framed within a radiant circle. This sacred geometry represents the convergence of duality into unity — the fusion of wisdom and intuition, mind and spirit,

human perception and divine vision.
Where Vishuddha's triangle brings sound into form, Ajna's
triangle transforms form into insight.
It is not the vibration of expression, but the illumination of
awareness — the alchemy of perception itself.

Unlike Vishuddha's open ether or Manipura's fiery energy,
Ajna's light is cool, refined, and eternal — the flame of
consciousness burning without smoke or shadow.
This triangle does not descend; it expands inward — a beacon
within the mind that illuminates all worlds, inner and outer.

THE TRIANGLE

• The three sides represent the sacred triad of *perception,
intuition, and wisdom* — the process by which awareness
observes, understands, and transcends.
• The downward point signifies the descent of divine vision into
human understanding — insight filtering through the mind as
revelation.
• The three corners symbolize the seer (*drashta*), the seen
(*drishya*), and the act of seeing (*darshana*) — unified in the still
point of pure awareness.
• In meditation, this triangle becomes the window of
consciousness — the portal through which illusion dissolves
and truth is revealed.

Ajna's triangle teaches that true sight is not achieved through
effort but through surrender — through resting so deeply in
awareness that light reveals itself.

THE CIRCLE

• The circle surrounding the triangle represents the infinite field
of consciousness, the boundless awareness in which all
perception arises and subsides.
• It signifies wholeness and eternity, the continuum of

awareness that is never interrupted by time or thought.
• The circle also represents the *eye itself* — not the physical
organ, but the mystical aperture through which consciousness
observes its own reflection.

Together, the triangle and circle form the Eye of the Soul — the
balance of structure and infinity, focus and surrender, awareness
and emptiness.
Ajna's circle is the mirror of the cosmos; its triangle is the ray
of light that awakens within it.

THE UNION OF LIGHT AND AWARENESS

Where Vishuddha refines sound into resonance, Ajna refines
perception into illumination.
Sound purifies; light reveals.
Through Ajna's geometry, consciousness no longer seeks to
express truth — it becomes truth itself.

When meditated upon, the Triangle of Light reveals the still
radiance that exists beyond thought.
This is the place where intuition arises effortlessly, where
knowing precedes words, and where the divine perceives
through the human.

It teaches that clarity does not come from analysis but from
alignment — the stilling of the inner waters until reflection
becomes revelation.

TRIANGLES IN TAROT SYMBOLISM

In esoteric tradition, triangles of light symbolize revelation,
vision, and the direct perception of truth.
Within the Tarot, Ajna's principles appear in cards where
illumination replaces interpretation — where insight dissolves
illusion and consciousness awakens to unity.

THE MAJOR ARCANA

• **The Hermit (IX):**
His lantern forms the upward-pointing triangle of illumination
— wisdom guiding from within. The Hermit embodies Ajna's
light: seeing in darkness, perceiving from silence.

• **The Hanged Man (XII):**
Suspended upside-down, his head forms the glowing triangle of
enlightenment — surrender leading to revelation. This is Ajna's
initiation: perception inverted until truth is seen from a higher
plane.

• **The Moon (XVIII):**
Two towers, a path, and the full moon create a triangle of
unfolding awareness — the movement from illusion to
intuition. Ajna's domain is here: navigating shadows to find
inner sight.

• **The Sun (XIX):**
The rays of the sun form radiating triangles — illumination and
joy through clarity. This is the Third Eye fully open — light
expressed as consciousness itself.

• **The Judgment (XX):**
The trumpet's sound awakens vision; the souls rise toward light.
In Ajna, hearing becomes seeing, vibration becomes
illumination — awareness reborn through revelation.

• **The World (XXI):**
Encircled by the wreath of wholeness, the dancer stands within
the cosmic mandala — the perfect integration of vision and
embodiment. This is the geometry of enlightenment itself.

THE MINOR ARCANA

• The Suit of Swords (Air):
Represents thought refined into awareness. Triangular
arrangements often depict insight after struggle — Ajna's
lesson that clarity comes through stillness, not conflict.

• The Suit of Cups (Water):
When two vessels or figures form a triangle, it reflects intuition
flowing between heart and mind. These cards embody
emotional perception evolving into intuitive wisdom.

• The Suit of Wands (Fire):
The triangle of flame symbolizes inner vision made manifest —
the spark of divine inspiration that ignites conscious creation.

• The Suit of Pentacles (Earth):
When pentacles align to form upward or downward triangles,
they mirror the embodiment of vision — the grounding of
spiritual insight into practical understanding.

THE EYE OF LIGHT IN SYMBOLISM

Throughout mysticism, the Eye within the Triangle appears as
the symbol of awakened consciousness — from the Egyptian
Udjat Eye of Horus to the Christian *Eye of Providence.*
It represents the awareness that perceives all, not as separate,
but as sacred.

In Ajna, this geometry becomes internalized: the triangle
becomes the lens through which we perceive truth, and the
circle becomes the infinite field of that perception.
It is the bridge between duality and divinity — where the
human mind becomes the instrument of cosmic vision.

THIRD EYE REFLECTIONS IN TRIANGULAR IMAGERY

• Perception:
Triangles in Tarot and mysticism symbolize the moment of revelation — when hidden truth becomes visible, when consciousness turns inward to recognize itself. This is Ajna's sacred act: awakening through seeing.

• Integration:
Unlike circles that expand endlessly or squares that hold form, the triangle directs energy toward insight — focusing awareness into illumination. It is the geometry of realization, of energy converging to a single point of knowing.

• Revelation:
Ajna's downward-pointing triangle represents divine truth descending into perception. It teaches that insight is not created but received — unveiled when the mind becomes clear, still, and receptive.

The triangle is the sacred geometry of awareness and illumination.
It is the form through which consciousness recognizes itself — the shape of awakening.

KEY CARDS TO MEDITATE ON FOR THE THIRD EYE CHAKRA

• The Hermit (IX):
Inner illumination — light that guides from within.

• The Hanged Man (XII):
Surrender of ego — vision through inversion.

• The Moon (XVIII):
Navigating illusion — awakening intuitive sight.

• The Sun (XIX):
Radiance and clarity — the light of awakened mind.

• The Star (XVII):
Hope as vision — divine light pouring through human
awareness.

• The Judgment (XX):
Awakening through revelation — sound becoming light,
awareness reborn.

• The World (XXI):
Integration and unity — vision realized in embodiment.

Ajna is not merely the organ of sight — it is the witness of
seeing itself.
It is the luminous center where silence becomes light, and
perception becomes wisdom.
To awaken the Third Eye is to remember that awareness was
never blind — only waiting for the mind to grow still enough to
see.

The Third Eye does not look outward. It shines inward.
And in that eternal illumination, everything is revealed as one.

AJNA IN YOGIC PRACTICE

In the earliest Tantric and yogic teachings, the chakras were not
conceived as physical organs but as luminous centers of
consciousness — subtle vortices where divine energy and
human awareness meet. Each chakra serves as a gate to a
specific frequency of realization.
Ajna, the Third Eye Chakra, is the seat of intuition, insight, and
inner perception — the luminous bridge between the personal
mind and universal intelligence.

The Sanskrit word *Ajna* (आज्ञा) means "command" or "perception", referring to the higher directive of the soul — the point where the individual self receives guidance from the inner guru, the light of consciousness itself.
Its element is light (tejas) — not the physical flame of fire, but the radiant intelligence that reveals truth and dispels illusion.

The bīja mantra or seed sound of Ajna is OM (ॐ) — the primordial vibration of all creation.
When chanted with awareness, OM awakens the field of subtle perception and harmonizes the dual hemispheres of the mind. It aligns intellect and intuition, transforming thought into clarity and awareness into illumination.
Just as Vishuddha purifies through sound, Ajna enlightens through vision — not the sight of the eyes, but the light of knowing.

Yogic adepts regarded Ajna as the command center of consciousness — the junction where the dual currents of energy, *Ida* (lunar, receptive) and *Pingala* (solar, active), merge into *Sushumna*, the central channel of spiritual ascent. When these energies unite at Ajna, duality dissolves and the practitioner enters *dhyāna* — meditative absorption in pure awareness.

Traditional practices for awakening Ajna included trāṭaka (fixed gazing) on a flame or sacred symbol, antar darshan (inner visualization), and OM meditation, all designed to still the fluctuations of the mind (*chitta-vritti-nirodha*).
By focusing attention on the space between the brows, the yogi trains perception to turn inward — from the objects of sight to the essence of seeing itself.
In this inward gaze, thought gradually subsides, revealing the silent witness within — the eternal observer untouched by form or change.

For the yogi, vision was never limited to the eyes. True sight was an act of revelation — an awakening of the inner light that perceives all worlds.

Mastery of Ajna requires discipline, devotion, and detachment. One must refine the intellect without clinging to thought, and trust intuition without falling into illusion.

When the Third Eye opens, perception becomes pure awareness — direct, unmediated, and radiant with wisdom.

In its awakened state, Ajna dissolves the veil between the seer and the seen.

Dreams become lucid, intuition becomes accurate, and understanding transcends intellect.

Perception is no longer filtered through fear or desire; it becomes luminous — the soul's own reflection in the mirror of consciousness.

THE INNER SYMBOL OF AJNA

At the center of Ajna's indigo lotus rests a downward-pointing white triangle, radiant within a field of deep blue light.

This triangle represents the convergence of wisdom, will, and insight — the trinity of divine intelligence that governs perception and awareness.

It points downward to signify the descent of intuition into intellect, the translation of divine knowing into human comprehension.

Surrounding this luminous core are two petals, representing the twin aspects of perception: intuition and reason, sun and moon, Ida and Pingala. When harmonized, these two merge into one — illuminating the unified field of consciousness.

At the heart of the triangle vibrates the bīja mantra OM (ॐ) — the soundless sound, the vibration of creation and dissolution.

When chanted or meditated upon, OM reverberates throughout the subtle body, quieting the chatter of the mind and awakening

the flame of insight.
It is said that when the practitioner truly hears the inner OM, all outer sound falls away — for this vibration is the source of all that is.

Ajna's geometry reveals a profound truth:
Light itself is the voice of consciousness.
When thought is still and vision is clear, awareness reflects its own divinity — perception becomes prayer, and knowing becomes liberation.

The Third Eye symbol teaches that illumination is not attained by striving, but by surrendering to stillness.
When the gaze turns inward and awareness rests in itself, the mind becomes a crystal — transparent, steady, and luminous. Through this clear lens, the infinite shines through the finite, and the yogi perceives the universe as one unbroken field of light.

To awaken Ajna is to awaken remembrance — the recognition that wisdom has always been within.
Through meditation on OM and contemplation of the inner light, the yogi enters the boundless clarity where thought, vision, and being dissolve into pure consciousness.

WHAT OM REPRESENTS
• **Vibrational Key:**

OM (ॐ) is the sacred sound that awakens the Third Eye Chakra — the gateway of perception, wisdom, and divine vision.
Known as the Primordial Sound, OM embodies the total vibration of existence — the beginning, the continuation, and the dissolution of all creation.
When chanted, OM opens the inner ear of consciousness, aligning the practitioner with universal intelligence. It is the sound of light itself — the vibration through which awareness recognizes its infinite nature.

• Sound of Light and Consciousness:

Where HAM resonates through the throat, OM vibrates through the skull and mind's eye, radiating clarity through the frontal lobes and crown.
It creates a subtle pressure between the brows — the pulse of awakening — while soothing the nervous system and illuminating the inner pathways of awareness.
OM carries the frequency of *Tejas*, the luminous fire of insight. It does not merely vibrate in the air; it resounds in consciousness. Through this mantra, the practitioner experiences stillness as radiant light, silence as revelation.

• Dissolver of Illusion and Duality:

Ancient yogic texts describe OM as the sound that bridges the finite and the infinite. It dissolves the illusion of separateness, melting the boundaries between subject and object, thought and thinker, self and spirit.
OM refines the chatter of the mind into one pure tone of awareness. In its vibration, illusion (*Maya*) softens, ego quiets, and the seeker awakens to the truth: all perception is one consciousness observing itself.
Through OM, duality becomes unity — light recognizing light.

• Link to the Element of Light (Tejas):

Each chakra corresponds to one of the five elements (*tattvas*). Ajna aligns with light — not the physical flame, but the inner radiance of awareness that illumines both inner and outer worlds.
Light (*Tejas*) reveals form and truth alike; it is both energy and understanding.
By meditating on OM, the practitioner attunes to this inner luminosity — perceiving thoughts as waves of light, emotions as patterns of radiance, and consciousness as infinite brilliance.

OM unites the perceiver and the perceived in a single field of clarity.

THE SEED SOUND OF AJNA: OM

At the center of Ajna's two-petaled lotus lies not only sacred geometry, but sacred sound — the eternal vibration of OM.
In Tantric and yogic philosophy, each chakra holds a bīja mantra, or "seed sound," containing its essential frequency.
For Ajna, that sound is OM (pronounced "AUM"), representing the trinity of existence: creation (*A*), preservation (*U*), and dissolution (*M*).

OM is not merely a sound — it is a cosmic vibration, the voice of consciousness itself. When chanted, it harmonizes every energy center, connecting the individual to the universal.
It is said that the yogi who meditates upon OM no longer sees with the eyes, but through the soul.

THE POWER OF OM

• Resonance in the Mind and Beyond:
When chanted, OM begins in the navel as *A*, rises through the chest as *U*, and culminates in the skull as *M*.
The vibration then dissolves into silence — the fourth stage, *Turiya* — representing pure awareness beyond sound.
This journey mirrors the ascent of Kundalini through the chakras, culminating in the illumination of the Third Eye.

• Purifying the Channel of Perception:
Ajna can become clouded by overthinking, self-doubt, and attachment to sensory impressions.
OM clears these distortions, stilling the mind's surface so intuition may arise from its depths.
It refines thought into vision, transforming perception into direct knowing.

• Awakening the Inner Vision:
OM opens the gateway of intuition, revealing the subtle
dimensions of reality.
It awakens clairvoyance, insight, and higher guidance — not as
supernatural gifts, but as natural states of consciousness
unveiled through purity of mind.
Through OM, we learn that true seeing does not occur with the
eyes, but with awareness itself.

• Honoring the Element of Light (Tejas):
Just as Vishuddha aligns with ether, Ajna aligns with light —
the pure intelligence that illuminates both thought and
emptiness.
Light is not merely energy; it is consciousness made visible.
Through OM, the yogi becomes the lamp of awareness, shining
through all experience with equanimity and grace.

THE MYSTERY OF OM

In the *Mandukya Upanishad*, the sages declared:

"OM is this imperishable sound — the past, the present, and the
future.
All that is, all that was, all that will be, is OM."

When meditated upon, OM reveals the silence beyond sound —
the space where thought ceases and awareness shines.
It is both the path and the destination, the mantra and the
realization, the vibration and the void.

OM is the Third Eye's eternal instruction:
Be still and know that you are light.

CHANTING OM

Chanting OM is a practice of awakening and remembrance.
It is the vibration of unity — the resonance that merges silence and sound, mind and soul, self and spirit.
Through OM, awareness expands beyond thought, returning to its natural radiance.
Each repetition illuminates the inner sky of consciousness, dissolving confusion, fear, and fragmentation.

OM does not belong to any one tradition; it is the hum of existence itself — the echo of creation and the pulse of awareness.
When you chant OM, you align your energy with the rhythm of the cosmos.
It opens the Third Eye, calms the nervous system, and reveals the stillness that was always within.

OM is the vibrational key to illumination — the soundless sound through which the soul recognizes itself as light.
It is the mantra of awakening — the voice of consciousness remembering its infinite source.

HOW TO CHANT OM
Step 1 – Prepare the Body

• Sit comfortably with your spine tall and the crown of your head lifted toward the sky.
• Rest your hands lightly on your knees or over your heart.
• Take several slow, deep breaths. With each exhale, release the tension in your face, jaw, and eyes.
• Feel your awareness settling gently into the space between your eyebrows — the gateway of insight.

Step 2 – Focus on the Third Eye

• Visualize a deep indigo light glowing between your brows —
serene, radiant, and infinite.
• See this light expanding into a luminous lotus with two petals,
representing intuition and wisdom.
• Imagine each breath brightening this lotus, filling your mind
with calm awareness and inner clarity.

Step 3 – Chant the Sound

• Inhale slowly. As you exhale, chant with full awareness:
Aaaa…Uuuu…Mmmm…
• Let the *A* begin in the lower abdomen, the *U* rise through the
heart and throat, and the *M* vibrate in the head and crown.
• Feel the sound expand like ripples of light radiating from the
Third Eye, connecting every cell with the rhythm of the cosmos.

Step 4 – Repeat Rhythmically

• Chant OM 7, 12, or 108 times.
• With each repetition, feel your awareness becoming more
spacious, the light between your brows glowing brighter and
clearer.
• Allow the vibration to dissolve into silence — a silence that
feels alive, luminous, and infinite.

Step 5 – Rest in Silence

• After chanting, remain still and present.
• Feel the subtle hum lingering in your skull, the gentle
pulsation behind your forehead, the peace within your mind.
• Rest in this awareness — the silence beyond sound — and
inwardly affirm:

"I see with clarity.
I know with peace.
I am the light within all things."

WAYS TO USE OM IN PRACTICE
• **Morning Alignment:**

Begin your day by chanting OM three times to center your mind
and awaken intuitive awareness.
Let the sound clear mental fog and attune your thoughts to
wisdom and calm.

• **Before Meditation or Study:**

Chant OM to quiet inner noise and focus the mind before
spiritual practice, learning, or creative work.
It steadies concentration and heightens perception.

• **Emotional Clarity:**

When overwhelmed or uncertain, close your eyes and chant OM
until your breath and heartbeat synchronize.
Let the vibration melt tension and restore inner balance.

• **Healing or Energy Work:**

Practitioners may chant OM softly or internally during Reiki,
meditation, or third-eye activation to harmonize subtle energies.
Its resonance clears stagnation and opens intuitive pathways.

• **Movement & Breath Integration:**

Combine OM chanting with poses that stimulate Ajna — such
as Child's Pose (Balasana), Forward Fold (Uttanasana), or
Dolphin Pose (Ardha Pincha Mayurasana).
As you breathe, visualize each sound wave radiating indigo
light through the forehead and crown.

• Group Meditation:

Chanting OM together creates a luminous field of unity and peace.
Collective resonance amplifies awareness, attuning every participant to the vibration of divine consciousness.

LIGHT-CENTERED AFFIRMATION WITH OM

"As I chant OM, my mind becomes still.
My thoughts dissolve into light.
I see clearly. I know deeply.
I am the awareness that shines through all creation."

THE ANIMAL SYMBOL OF AJNA: THE BLACK ANTELOPE (GAZELLE OF LIGHT)

At the base of every chakra lotus lies a sacred guardian — an animal symbolizing the instinctual force that animates its energy.
For the Third Eye Chakra, this guardian is the Black Antelope, also called the Gazelle of Light (*Krishnasāra* in Sanskrit).
Agile, alert, and luminous, the antelope embodies the essence of perception, the purity of focus, and the swift grace of intuitive awareness.

It represents the element of light (tejas) — radiant consciousness that moves effortlessly through space, illuminating truth with clarity and discernment.
The antelope's fluid movement mirrors the quality of awakened perception: ever-aware, yet serene; in motion, yet centered in stillness.

WHY THE BLACK ANTELOPE?
• *Light Element and Awareness:*

The antelope's dark, glistening coat reflects light like a mirror — symbolizing the mind's ability to perceive truth even in darkness.
Its alert gaze represents heightened awareness, the refined intuition that sees beyond illusion.
Just as light reveals what shadow conceals, Ajna transforms ignorance into insight through the radiance of consciousness.

• *Vision and Intuition:*

In ancient Vedic imagery, the Black Antelope was sacred to Vayu (the wind) and Soma (the elixir of wisdom), both deities of subtle perception.
Its keen senses symbolize the precision of intuition — awareness that pierces veils and reads the language of energy.
Where Vishuddha listens through vibration, Ajna sees through stillness — perceiving not form, but essence.

• *Agility of Mind:*

The antelope's movement is fluid and precise, embodying the balance between instinct and intellect.
It reminds us that perception must be agile — flexible enough to follow insight, yet steady enough to remain focused.
Just as the gazelle leaps without hesitation, the awakened mind moves intuitively through the landscape of experience, unbound by fear or doubt.

• *Purity and Illumination:*

In Indian and Buddhist symbology, the Black Antelope is often depicted beneath the Wheel of Dharma, representing pure awareness guiding the cycle of life.
Its presence at the feet of divine teachers symbolizes the mind

tamed by meditation — no longer scattered by illusion, but luminous and still.

Where the White Elephant purifies expression, the Black Antelope refines perception — turning the restless mind into a vessel of light.

• *The Messenger of Insight:*

The antelope is a creature of both earth and ether — moving silently, yet seeing far.

It carries the message of inner vision: that wisdom is not gained by chasing truth, but by standing so still that truth reveals itself.

Its quiet alertness mirrors the discipline of meditation — perception without pursuit, awareness without attachment.

THE SHADOW OF THE ANTELOPE

The Black Antelope symbolizes intuitive clarity and effortless awareness.

Yet, when Ajna is clouded or overactive, its gifts can cast shadows — intuition turns to illusion, clarity to confusion.

• *Illusion and Overthinking:*

When the Third Eye is overstimulated or misaligned, imagination overtakes insight.

Perception becomes distorted — one sees through projection rather than intuition.

The mind creates mirages, mistaking thoughts for truth.

• *Spiritual Arrogance:*

True intuition is humble, but ego may claim the gifts of vision as superiority.

When Ajna's light becomes self-centered, discernment gives way to delusion.

The seeker begins to believe rather than perceive, closing the inner eye through pride.

• *Doubt and Blindness:*

When Ajna is underactive or blocked, faith in one's inner knowing fades.
The gaze turns inward but finds only darkness — confusion replaces confidence, and decision-making becomes paralyzed.
This is the antelope caught in its own shadow — hesitant, fearful, unable to trust the path it once saw clearly.

• *Disconnection from Reality:*

An ungrounded Third Eye may float in abstraction — lost in thought, detached from embodiment.
Intuition becomes escapism; vision becomes fantasy.
The challenge of Ajna is to balance transcendence with truth, to keep both feet on the earth even as the gaze lifts to the heavens.

THE LESSON OF THE ANTELOPE

The Black Antelope teaches us that awareness must be both still and alert, luminous yet humble.
It reminds us that vision is not a chase for meaning, but a return to seeing clearly.
Its grace lies in precision — each movement deliberate, each perception pure.

In meditation, the antelope becomes the guide of the inner eye — leading consciousness from distraction to discernment, from duality to direct knowing.
It whispers:

"Run not toward truth — stand still, and let light find you."

The antelope embodies the awakened Third Eye — where perception becomes wisdom, and wisdom becomes illumination.
Gentle yet perceptive, swift yet serene, it moves through the mind's wilderness as a guardian of insight, reminding us that true vision is not about seeing more — but seeing clearly.

THE WISDOM OF THE ANTELOPE

When balanced, the Black Antelope embodies the stillness of alert awareness — perception guided by insight, and intuition expressed through clarity.
Its wisdom lies not in pursuit, but in presence: a reminder that true vision is born from quiet observation.
Where the Elephant listens through sound, the Antelope sees through stillness.

• Grace in Perception:

Like the Antelope that moves lightly across vast terrain, we are called to move through thought with fluid grace — neither chasing ideas nor resisting them.
Clarity comes not from control, but from allowing awareness to flow unobstructed.
Through mindful perception, we learn that insight, when guided by gentleness, illuminates without burning.

• Stillness as Strength:

The Antelope's strength lies in its poise — in the still moment before the leap.
It teaches us that stillness is not inactivity but *presence in readiness.*
The awakened Third Eye holds this same energy — silent power, ever-aware, yet untouched by restlessness.
Through this stillness, intuition awakens, and wisdom becomes natural vision.

• Purity of Vision:

When the inner gaze aligns with truth, perception becomes revelation.
The Antelope's eyes, wide and luminous, see what lies beyond illusion — discerning essence within form, spirit within matter.
To see purely is to look without judgment, to perceive without distortion.
In Ajna's wisdom, seeing becomes knowing, and knowing becomes peace.

• The Power of Awareness:

True awareness does not grasp — it receives.
The Antelope reminds us that perception is not about acquiring knowledge, but about recognizing the unity behind all experience.
The mind that is calm becomes a mirror — reflecting light without claiming it.
Ajna's gift is this power of reflection — vision that enlightens without attachment, awareness that perceives without distortion.

The Antelope's wisdom is the dance of awareness — movement within stillness, perception within silence.
Its grace bridges the earthly and the divine, just as the Third Eye bridges mind and spirit.
When we honor Ajna's energy with mindfulness, we discover that vision is not for seeing more, but for seeing truly — the light within light, the awareness within all things.

THE ANTELOPE IN TANTRIC SYMBOLISM

In Tantric imagery, the Black Antelope (Krishnasāra) rests at the base of the two-petaled lotus of Ajna as its *vāhana* — the sacred vehicle of perception.
It is the carrier of the awakened mind, the messenger of light traveling between the seen and unseen worlds.

Just as Airavata, the White Elephant, carries the voice of Indra through ether, the Black Antelope carries the radiance of intuition through light.

In the *Shat-Chakra-Nirupana* and other yogic texts, the Antelope symbolizes lightness, agility, and transcendence — the ability of consciousness to leap beyond the senses.
Its blackness is not darkness but depth — the infinite field of awareness into which all visions dissolve and from which all insight arises.
Where Vishuddha refines expression, Ajna refines perception — transforming sensory experience into spiritual vision.

The Antelope's effortless movement mirrors the fluidity of awareness when freed from attachment.
It traverses the boundless landscape of the mind, alert yet unburdened, carrying the light of intuition into every corner of consciousness.
It reminds us that perception, like the Antelope's leap, is both spontaneous and precise — guided not by effort, but by instinct aligned with wisdom.

In Tantric wisdom, the Black Antelope stands as the guardian of Mahat-Tattva — the principle of pure intelligence, the threshold between thought and realization.
Its silent grace whispers of discernment: to see clearly without clinging, to know without claiming, to move without losing stillness.

Thus, the Antelope becomes the embodiment of spiritual sight — the vision as offering, awareness as prayer, and illumination as the bridge between matter and consciousness.

MEDITATING ON THE ANTELOPE
• Visualization:

Close your eyes and envision a Black Antelope standing upon a field of deep indigo light.
Its sleek form glows with quiet luminescence, its eyes reflecting the infinite expanse of the night sky.
A ray of light shines gently from its brow, extending outward like a calm horizon of awareness.
With every breath, the antelope becomes more radiant — poised, still, alert.
This is your inner vision — clear, tranquil, and awake.
It sees without grasping and understands without words.

• Affirmation:

"I trust the light within me.
I see with wisdom and clarity.
My intuition guides me in peace and truth."

• Integration:

Work with the element of light — gaze softly at the flame of a candle, the reflection of moonlight on water, or the space behind closed eyes.
Let this light become a mirror for your awareness.
With each inhalation, draw that light into your forehead; with each exhalation, let it radiate outward as calm understanding.

Visualize light waves flowing gently through your mind — dissolving confusion, illuminating insight.
Feel your awareness expanding like the night sky — still, infinite, luminous.

The Antelope teaches that true vision is not found through striving, but through stillness. It is the light of consciousness —

awareness moving freely through the open sky of being, where perception becomes peace and insight becomes illumination.

THE DEITIES OF THE THIRD EYE CHAKRA

In the Tantric tradition, each chakra is animated by divine energies — archetypal expressions of consciousness that guide awakening.
These deities are not external gods, but living principles of awareness within us — forces of light and perception that unfold as we evolve in understanding.

For Ajna, the Third Eye Chakra, these energies represent intuition, wisdom, and the union of dualities through insight.
They teach that *true vision is not with the eyes, but through awareness itself* — the inner sight that perceives beyond illusion.

HAKINI – THE GODDESS OF THE THIRD EYE

• Hakini, radiant and serene, is the presiding goddess of Ajna. She embodies the awakened intuition that bridges thought and transcendence.
Her name derives from the Sanskrit root *hā*, meaning "to breathe" or "to illuminate," symbolizing the breath of consciousness and the light of awareness.

• In Tantric imagery, Hakini is depicted as six-faced and six-armed, seated upon a luminous white lotus.
Her faces represent multidimensional perception — the ability to see all directions and all truths simultaneously.
She holds a book, a skull, a drum, a rosary, a human head, and a gesture of blessing, symbolizing knowledge, transcendence, vibration, time, awareness, and liberation.

• Hakini governs the mind purified by meditation, the awakened intellect that no longer divides but unites.

She is intuition made luminous — awareness that perceives not through logic, but through clarity of being.

• When meditated upon, Hakini awakens the eye of wisdom (jnana chakshu) — the faculty of direct knowing.
Her blessing is illumination: the power to discern truth from illusion, to see with the eyes of the soul rather than the senses.

ARDHANARISHVARA – THE LORD OF UNITY

• The masculine energy of Ajna is Ardhanarishvara, the fusion of Shiva and Shakti — divine consciousness and creative energy united as one.
Half male, half female, Ardhanarishvara represents the *transcendence of polarity* — the merging of intuition and intellect, logic and emotion, inner and outer vision.

• Seated within a radiant field of indigo light, Ardhanarishvara is the eternal equilibrium — the eye that sees without duality. He embodies the perfect harmony of opposites, revealing that all perception flows from the same source: the single awareness behind all experience.

• In meditation, this form teaches that enlightenment is not escape from duality, but the recognition of unity within it. Ardhanarishvara's gaze dissolves the illusion of separation, reminding us that both the seer and the seen are expressions of the same consciousness.

TOGETHER: HAKINI AND ARDHANARISHVARA

Together, Hakini and Ardhanarishvara form the sacred polarity of Ajna — *the perceiver and the perceived united through awareness.*
Hakini is the awakened mind — insight, imagination, illumination.

Ardhanarishvara is the cosmic eye — consciousness witnessing itself through all forms.

• Hakini is the light that reveals.
• Ardhanarishvara is the stillness that perceives.

Their union opens the Third Eye — not as a mystical organ, but as a state of pure perception where thought, feeling, and knowing converge.
When these deities awaken within, the boundaries between subject and object dissolve, and the soul begins to see as spirit sees — without fear, without distortion, without separation.

In this awakened vision, perception becomes prayer, and awareness becomes communion with the infinite.

DEITIES OF VISION AND WISDOM IN OTHER TRADITIONS

While Tantra names Hakini and Ardhanarishvara as the presiding energies of Ajna, countless cultures throughout time have revered divine figures of *sight, wisdom, and revelation.* Though the symbols differ, each reflects the essence of the Third Eye — the light of insight and the path of inner knowing.

• **Saraswati (Hindu Tradition):**

Beyond her role as the goddess of speech, Saraswati also governs perception and divine intellect.
Her swan symbolizes discernment — the ability to separate truth from illusion.
Through her, wisdom flows like a clear river of consciousness, guiding seekers toward understanding.

• Athena (Greek Tradition):

The goddess of wisdom and strategy, Athena embodies the *clarity of thought and precision of vision* associated with Ajna. Her owl, the nocturnal seer, perceives what the day conceals. She reminds us that wisdom requires both intellect and intuition — the calm mind that sees all sides before acting.

• Isis (Egyptian Mysticism):

The mother of magic and insight, Isis embodies the mysteries of hidden knowledge and spiritual sight.
Her crown, adorned with the sun disk, mirrors Ajna's radiance — the illumination that guides through darkness.
Isis teaches that seeing clearly requires compassion as much as intelligence.

• Odin (Norse Tradition):

Having sacrificed one eye for wisdom, Odin symbolizes the opening of the inner eye — vision exchanged for insight.
He teaches that true seeing comes not through sight but through surrender, and that enlightenment requires both sacrifice and trust in the unseen.

• The Oracle of Delphi (Greek Mysticism):

Seated in trance, the Pythia channeled the divine through stillness and surrender.
She is the voice of inner knowing — intuition speaking in symbols rather than words.
Her message echoes Ajna's gift: that clarity arises when the mind becomes the vessel of truth, not its source.

• The Buddha (Buddhist Tradition):

The Buddha's "eye of wisdom" (*prajna chakshu*) represents complete insight into reality — seeing the world as it truly is, beyond illusion and ignorance.
This is the awakened Third Eye — awareness perceiving itself in all things, free from craving or aversion.

• Archangel Raziel (Jewish and Christian Mysticism):

Known as the "Keeper of Divine Secrets," Raziel governs spiritual insight and the mysteries of the universe.
His presence opens intuitive understanding, granting the seeker access to higher wisdom and the remembrance of divine truth.

THE ELEMENT OF AJNA: LIGHT (JYOTI / TEJAS)

Each chakra corresponds to one of the five great elements (*Pancha Mahabhutas*).
For the Third Eye Chakra, that element is Light — Jyoti or Tejas in Sanskrit.

More than the physical light of sun or flame, *Tejas* is the light of consciousness — the inner radiance that illuminates perception, reveals truth, and awakens wisdom.
It is the essence of Ajna: luminous, discerning, and pure — the element of vision between the known and the infinite.

LIGHT AS THE FIELD OF PERCEPTION

Light is not merely what we see — it is what allows us to see.
It is both the revealer and the revealed, the bridge between object and awareness.
Where Ether carries sound through space, Light carries consciousness through perception.

Through *Jyoti*, thought becomes insight, and insight becomes revelation.
Light is the flame of discernment — the spark through which awareness recognizes itself.

QUALITIES OF LIGHT

• Clarity and Illumination:
Light dispels obscurity and reveals truth as it is.
When balanced, the element of Light brings mental clarity, intuitive understanding, and the calm knowing that arises from direct perception.
Through Tejas, confusion dissolves, and awareness shines unobstructed.

• Awareness and Insight:
Light is consciousness perceiving itself — the awareness that observes thought without being bound by it.
It reveals patterns, unveils illusions, and transforms knowledge into wisdom.
When Ajna is awakened, perception becomes multidimensional — you no longer see from the mind, but through it.

• Radiance and Purification:
Just as sunlight clarifies water, the inner light of Ajna purifies thought and emotion.
It burns away distortion, illuminating the subtle truth hidden within every experience.
This is not the consuming fire of Manipura, but the gentle, steady flame of realization.

• Unity and Vision:
Light unites the seen and the unseen.
It travels through every element — earth, water, fire, air, and ether — connecting all forms within one field of awareness.
In Ajna, this element reveals that perception is not separate

from creation; to see clearly is to participate consciously in existence.

BALANCE AND IMBALANCE

When the element of Light is dimmed, perception becomes clouded — intuition fades, imagination narrows, and vision turns outward rather than inward.
You may feel lost in thought, unable to discern truth from illusion, mistaking mental projection for insight.

When Light is overstimulated, awareness can burn too bright — leading to mental strain, over-analysis, or detachment from the body.
The mind races faster than the soul can guide, and intuition becomes fragmented into ideas without grounding.

When balanced, *Tejas* radiates as steady awareness — bright but not blinding, focused but not rigid.
It is calm clarity — the mind illuminated by the soul's quiet flame.

THE SACRED TEACHING OF LIGHT

Light teaches that perception is sacred.
To see truly is not to judge or define, but to witness with awareness.
It reveals that knowledge is not accumulation, but illumination — a remembering of what has always been.

Light is both the lamp and the gaze — it shows that the seer, the seen, and the act of seeing are one.
When we honor Light, we no longer search outward for clarity; we awaken the luminous awareness that was within us all along.

WHY LIGHT BELONGS TO THE THIRD EYE CHAKRA

The chakras rise through the elements — earth (Root), water (Sacral), fire (Solar Plexus), air (Heart), ether (Throat), and finally Light (Ajna) — the refined essence of perception itself.

After the resonance of Ether in Vishuddha, Light is the next subtle evolution — the illumination that allows consciousness to perceive its own reflection.
It is the element of intuition, discernment, and wisdom — the awareness that sees without needing to look.

Light belongs to Ajna because this chakra governs vision and insight — the illumination of truth beyond sensory perception. Just as Ether transforms sound into meaning, Light transforms awareness into understanding.
It is the revelation of consciousness recognizing itself through form.

Ajna asks us to:
• See beyond appearances into essence.
• Perceive with compassion, not comparison.
• Let awareness be the guide rather than thought.

Light is the element of spiritual sight — the power to know through stillness, to see through the heart, and to perceive unity within all.
It reminds us that every thought is a reflection, every perception a mirror, and every moment a window into the divine.

MEDITATING ON LIGHT

Bringing the element of Light into Third Eye practice awakens inner vision and clarity of mind.

1. Light Visualization:
Close your eyes and imagine a radiant indigo light glowing at

the center of your forehead.
With each inhale, it brightens; with each exhale, it expands —
illuminating the space behind your eyes.
Feel this light spreading through your mind, clearing fog and
revealing stillness.

2. Flame Meditation (Trataka):
Gaze softly at the flame of a candle.
Let your eyes rest without strain until the image of light remains
even when you close them.
Visualize that flame within your brow, steady and clear — the
light of awareness itself.

3. Breath & Awareness Practice:
As you breathe, imagine drawing light in through your forehead
and exhaling it through the back of your head, creating a
luminous circuit of clarity.
Whisper:

"I see truth.
I perceive with peace.
I am the light of awareness itself."

When we meditate with the element of Light, we align with the
sacred essence of Ajna:
You are the seer, the seen, and the seeing — the eternal witness
illuminated from within.
To awaken the Third Eye is to remember that you are not the
light you see, but the consciousness by which all light is known.

Light In Daily Life

• When your mind feels clouded or uncertain:
Sit quietly and visualize a soft indigo light glowing at your
forehead.
Breathe into it gently until it brightens, clearing away
confusion.

Let your thoughts pass like clouds across an illuminated sky —
transient, harmless, and transparent.

• When you seek guidance or direction:
Close your eyes and focus on the space between your brows.
Ask your question inwardly, then sit in stillness.
Do not strain to receive — allow insight to rise naturally from
the quiet light within.
Clarity always emerges when the mind rests in its own
illumination.

• When emotion overwhelms perception:
Step back from the story and bring awareness to the breath.
Imagine light filtering through every thought, softening
judgment and revealing truth without blame.
Light clarifies without burning — it sees all and forgives all.

• When you feel disconnected from intuition:
Gaze softly into a candle flame or the evening sky until your
mind grows still.
Let the light outside awaken the light within.
In the mirror of illumination, your inner guidance becomes
visible again.

• When seeking divine connection:
Meditate on the phrase:

"I am the light that perceives all light."
Feel the subtle radiance of awareness expanding beyond the
body — infinite, calm, and clear.
Here, you remember that illumination is not something you
find; it is what you are.

Light teaches that clarity is not control, but surrender.
In Ajna, this illumination becomes the lens of perception —
where every image, thought, and insight returns to its source as
wisdom.

THE LESSON OF LIGHT

Light teaches that seeing clearly requires stillness.
It is not the effort of the eyes, but the openness of awareness
that allows true vision to arise.

The mind reflects whatever shines upon it — chaos or peace,
fear or truth.
When we turn the gaze inward, the reflection becomes pure.
Through Light, Ajna reveals that knowledge does not come
from accumulation, but from illumination — awareness seeing
itself.

Balanced Light brings clarity without rigidity, understanding
without judgment, and vision without attachment.
It transforms perception into compassion, insight into peace.
Just as the sun illuminates all things equally, awakened
consciousness sees all beings as reflections of the same divine
light.

Ajna reminds us that illumination is not about seeing more, but
seeing truly.
When your inner light steadies, you perceive unity in diversity,
silence in motion, and eternity in every breath.

A Third Eye attuned to Light becomes the dawn itself:
luminous, infinite, and awake — the sky of awareness where all
things are seen and all truth is known.

BRINGING THE SYMBOLS TOGETHER

Taken together, these sacred symbols reveal the complete
essence of the Third Eye Chakra — the radiant center of
intuition, wisdom, and inner vision.

• The two lotus petals represent duality transcended — the
merging of mind and spirit, thought and awareness.

• The downward-pointing triangle signifies perception descending into manifestation — insight given form, wisdom embodied as awareness.
• The color indigo radiates depth, peace, and divine perception — the wavelength of insight and the vibration of consciousness.
• The element of Light (Jyoti) illuminates the subtle world within — transforming darkness into understanding and illusion into truth.
• The seed sound OM (ॐ) vibrates as the resonance of all creation — the soundless sound, the eternal witness of awareness itself.
• The Black Antelope, guardian of Ajna, symbolizes graceful perception and alert stillness — the soul's capacity to move through mystery with trust and calm.
• The deities Hakini and Ardhanarishvara embody the sacred union of intellect and intuition — the balance of inner knowing and divine consciousness.

To meditate upon these symbols is to awaken the inner light — the clear, unbroken awareness through which truth is both seen and lived.

Each image invites you to remember:
Vision is not found through the eyes, but through presence.
The Third Eye is the lamp of the soul, and when it shines, every shadow becomes a teacher, every moment a reflection of the infinite light within.

THE THIRD EYE CHAKRA AS THE SACRED LIGHT

Long before chakras were envisioned as radiant wheels of energy, ancient sages described Ajna as the *Sacred Light* — the inner flame of awareness that reveals truth beyond illusion. This light was not merely the light we see, but the radiance through which *seeing itself* becomes possible — the consciousness that illuminates all perception.

It is the lamp of the soul — the eternal witness that perceives both form and formlessness, both shadow and splendor, without judgment.
Where Vishuddha was the *sound of creation*, Ajna is the *sight of creation* — the light that recognizes the divine pattern woven through all things.

THE LIGHT WITHIN

Where the Throat was a sky of sound, the Third Eye is a dawn of light.
It is the inner horizon where thought yields to vision, and vision yields to knowing.

Yogic sages taught that when awareness rests in the brow, one perceives not with the eyes, but with the soul — through the *jyoti*, the sacred light that reveals reality as consciousness itself. This inner illumination is not limited by distance or direction; it shines equally through dream and waking, silence and sound, form and void.

Here resides *Tejas*, the element of light — radiant intelligence, pure awareness.
It is the medium of insight and intuition, the flame that transforms perception into wisdom.

Through this light, the mind becomes transparent; through this transparency, truth is revealed.
In Ajna, seeing and knowing merge into one: the perceiver, the perception, and the perceived dissolve into pure consciousness.

WHY THE THIRD EYE CHAKRA?

The Third Eye Chakra is the seat of inner vision and higher understanding — the subtle eye that perceives what lies beyond the limits of form.

It is the realm of illumination, the sacred lens through which awareness contemplates itself.

To enter this space is to remember that light is not separate from consciousness — it *is* consciousness, shining through the window of your being.

• In Tantra: Ajna is the command center — the *guru chakra*, where spiritual insight directs the flow of energy and awareness.
• In Yoga: It is the "eye of wisdom," the portal through which the seeker perceives truth beyond illusion (*avidya*).
• In Alchemy: Light is the quintessence refined — spirit crystallized as illumination, transforming ignorance into understanding.
• In Mystical Traditions Worldwide: Light is the first emanation of the Divine — the self-revealing presence that bridges the unmanifest and the manifest, darkness and revelation.

To meditate on Ajna is to *see* — not with the eyes, but through the eternal light of awareness.
It is to recognize that you are both the lamp and its glow, the seer and the seen — the silent radiance through which all life becomes known.

THE LIGHT AND THE THIRD EYE CHAKRA

"And God said, 'Let there be light,' and there was light."
— Genesis 1:3

Before the world took shape, there was illumination — the awakening of consciousness within the void.
This first light was not physical but spiritual — the radiant knowing that made creation visible to itself.

In yogic and Tantric philosophy, this moment of illumination mirrors the awakening of the Third Eye — *the instant*

awareness recognizes its own light.
It is the same truth expressed in the Upanishads:

"From the Self comes light; by its light, all things shine."

Light, whether divine or human, is the revelation of being —
the consciousness that transforms darkness into understanding.
Where Vishuddha expressed creation through *sound*, Ajna
beholds creation through *sight.*

AJNA: THE GATEWAY OF DIVINE ILLUMINATION

The Third Eye Chakra, Ajna, is the energetic embodiment of
divine vision — the place where consciousness perceives itself
reflected in all creation.
Just as God said, "Let there be light," and illumination arose, so
too does the seeker awaken this light within, seeing not the
world as separate, but as sacred expression.

Every realization born through Ajna is a spark of divine
awareness — the Word made visible as Light, the vibration of
truth transfigured into understanding.
When insight arises, it is the same cosmic illumination speaking
through the silence of your mind.

To see clearly is therefore, an act of devotion.
Each moment of awareness is a resurrection of light within
darkness — consciousness remembering its own brilliance.

THE SACRED PARALLEL

• In Genesis, the Word gave birth to Light — vibration became
illumination.
• In Vishuddha, we speak; in Ajna, we see.
• In Tantra, sound (nāda) precedes light (jyoti) — creation first
heard, then seen.

Thus, the Throat and Third Eye are twin gates of revelation: through sound, the Divine expresses; through light, the Divine perceives.

To awaken Ajna is to behold this eternal interplay — the sound of truth transforming into the sight of wisdom.
What was spoken through Vishuddha now becomes understood through Ajna.
What was heard as resonance is now seen as radiance.

THE INNER REVELATION

To awaken the Third Eye is to rediscover that the Light still shines — not only in the heavens, but within every breath and every act of awareness.
When your perception aligns with Spirit, vision itself becomes prayer — a silent offering of clarity, peace, and truth.

Ajna reveals that illumination is not something attained but remembered.
You do not seek light — you *are* the light, gazing upon itself through the eyes of eternity.

When you look with the Third Eye, you see as the Divine sees: through unity, through compassion, through infinite clarity.

In the beginning was the Light — and the Light still shines in you.

A SHARED WISDOM

Across traditions, the Third Eye Chakra has always been linked to light, perception, and divine vision — the inner illumination through which wisdom is revealed.
Where the Throat expresses and the Crown unites, Ajna perceives — it is the eye of understanding, the moment when awareness recognizes itself as truth.

The lesson of the Third Eye is clear: Tend your perception. See beyond appearances. Witness without judgment. Let your vision be guided by insight rather than illusion. When the light of Ajna shines clear and steady, you no longer look *at* the world — you look *through* it, perceiving the divine pattern that binds all things in harmony.

THE THIRD EYE AS SACRED LIGHT

The Third Eye's two-petaled lotus — embracing a field of indigo radiance and the seed sound OM (ॐ) — can be seen as a map of divine illumination.
The petals are duality — intellect and intuition, thought and awareness — now joined in perfect balance.
The indigo sphere is infinite consciousness, luminous yet still.
And OM is the eternal sound of light — the vibration of creation seeing itself.

Together, they reveal the sacred purpose of Ajna: to transform perception into wisdom and knowing into being.
It is not the eye that sees, but the light within it — the consciousness that illumines every thought, dream, and realization.

A PRACTICE: ENTERING THE LIGHT

1. Close your eyes. Gently focus on the space between your brows.
2. Visualize a deep indigo flame glowing within your forehead — tranquil, unwavering, and luminous.
3. Breathe slowly, allowing this light to brighten with each inhale and spread through your mind with each exhale.
4. As your breath deepens, whisper softly:

"Om… Shanti… Om…"
Let the vibration travel inward, dissolving thought into clarity.

5. Rest in stillness.
   The light continues to glow even when you cease to visualize.
   This is the inner lamp of awareness — eternal, steady, awake.

In this silence, perception expands.
You begin to see not only with the eyes, but with the heart — recognizing the unity behind diversity, the order beneath all motion.
Clarity replaces effort; knowing replaces seeking.

THE DEEPER LESSON

The vision of Ajna reminds us that spiritual awakening is not escape from the world, but illumination within it.
You are not here to withdraw from life's appearances, but to see them clearly — as mirrors of consciousness reflecting its own infinite creativity.

The world may obscure your view; illusion may cast shadows; yet within you burns a light that cannot be extinguished.
To return to this light is to remember who you are.
To live from this light is to perceive with wisdom, compassion, and grace.

When you trust your inner sight, you do not search for enlightenment — you become its radiance.

THE WESTERN ADAPTATION

When the ancient teachings of the chakras reached the West in the late 19th and early 20th centuries, their deeply symbolic and Tantric origins were reinterpreted through the lens of Western mysticism, philosophy, and psychology.
Thinkers of the Theosophical Society — such as C.W. Leadbeater, Alice Bailey, and later Carl Jung — reimagined the chakra system as a model for human consciousness, merging Eastern metaphysics with the Western quest for self-realization.

In this adaptation, the Third Eye Chakra (Ajna) came to represent intuition, perception, and the higher mind — the inner faculty of insight that transcends sensory experience.
Rather than being viewed solely as the yogic "command center" of prāṇa and awareness, Ajna became a symbol of psychic vision, imagination, and spiritual intelligence — the gateway between intellect and intuition, reason and revelation.

THEOSOPHICAL AND ESOTERIC INFLUENCE

Early Western esotericists described Ajna as the "eye of wisdom," the point at which consciousness turns inward to perceive the soul's light.
C.W. Leadbeater's clairvoyant observations equated the Third Eye with extrasensory perception and subtle sight, expanding the chakra's interpretation from inner knowing to psychic sensitivity.
Alice Bailey, in her *A Treatise on Cosmic Fire*, framed Ajna as the "organ of synthesis" — the meeting place of the spiritual will and the active intelligence, where vision directs creation.
Through such teachings, Ajna evolved from a meditative symbol into a metaphysical instrument — the *lens of spiritual awakening.*

PSYCHOLOGICAL AND HUMANISTIC PERSPECTIVES

As psychology matured in the 20th century, Carl Jung introduced the concept of the *archetypal eye* — the part of the psyche that perceives symbolic truth through dreams, intuition, and synchronicity.

Jung associated the Ajna center with the process of individuation — the awakening of inner sight that bridges the conscious and unconscious mind.

In this context, Ajna became not just a spiritual organ, but a psychological function: the capacity for self-reflection, imagination, and insight.

Vision, in Jung's framework, was the mind's way of seeing the soul.

By mid-century, the New Age movement had adopted Ajna as the emblem of intuition and enlightenment — the "third eye" that sees beyond illusion.

Meditation practices began emphasizing visualization, guided imagery, and mindfulness as tools for activating inner sight.

The mystical act of *trataka* (candle gazing) became a means of focusing the mind; *visualization* replaced ancient yantra practice; *affirmations* took the place of Sanskrit mantras.

Ajna was reimagined as the seat of psychic awareness and intuitive clarity, accessible to all who sought to "open" their spiritual perception.

AJNA IN THE MODERN ERA

In contemporary wellness and psychological healing, the Third Eye Chakra symbolizes the integration of intellect and intuition — the union of rational clarity with spiritual insight.

It represents the courage to trust inner knowing, to see beyond appearances, and to align perception with purpose.

Ajna, once reserved for yogic adepts, has become a guiding metaphor for mindfulness, visioning, and creative consciousness.

In coaching, therapy, and intuitive training, "opening the third eye" now signifies expanding awareness — not through mysticism alone, but through self-inquiry, mindfulness, and the willingness to see clearly.

BRIDGING EAST AND WEST

The Western view of Ajna, though simplified, honors its timeless essence: that true vision arises not from the eyes, but from consciousness itself.
While the original Tantric texts described Ajna as the command center of prāṇa and meditation, Western psychology reframed it as the *command center of awareness* — where insight governs thought and perception.
Thus, the Third Eye continues to serve as a bridge — between ancient mysticism and modern psychology, contemplation and cognition, seeing and knowing.

The journey of Ajna in the West reflects humanity's ongoing quest for light — both literal and symbolic.
It teaches that enlightenment is not merely mystical, but profoundly human: the capacity to perceive with wisdom, to interpret with compassion, and to live with awareness.

As this book continues, we will weave together the ancient yogic understanding of Ajna with the modern language of intuition, cognition, and spiritual insight — restoring this chakra to its true role: the light of consciousness itself — the eye through which the soul perceives eternity.

SCIENTIFIC CORRELATIONS OF THE THIRD EYE CHAKRA

While ancient yogic texts described Ajna as the seat of inner vision and divine intelligence, modern science offers striking parallels between this subtle center and the structures of the brain, endocrine, and sensory systems responsible for perception, cognition, and intuition.

The Third Eye Chakra, located between the eyebrows and extending inward to the midbrain, corresponds primarily with the pineal gland, pituitary gland, and frontal cortex — regions associated with insight, awareness, and higher states of consciousness.

THE PINEAL GLAND: THE INNER EYE OF BIOLOGY

Nestled deep within the brain, the pineal gland is a small, pine-cone-shaped organ long regarded as the *seat of the soul.*
It regulates the sleep-wake cycle through its secretion of melatonin, a hormone influenced by light and darkness.
Beyond its circadian function, the pineal is photosensitive — containing cells similar to those found in the retina — suggesting that it may act as an internal receptor of light.

This biological "inner eye" mirrors Ajna's spiritual symbolism: the capacity to *see without seeing* — to perceive inner light independent of the physical eyes.
As the pineal responds to cycles of illumination, so too does Ajna awaken as consciousness transitions from ignorance (darkness) to insight (light).

Recent research into neuro-endocrine transduction suggests that the pineal gland plays a role in mood regulation, dream states, and possibly the generation of visionary or mystical experiences.
Neuroscientists studying altered states of awareness, meditation, and lucid dreaming find that pineal activity correlates with increased coherence in brainwave patterns — a measurable reflection of the yogic description of *light-born awareness.*

THE PITUITARY GLAND: THE MASTER REGULATOR OF HARMONY

The pituitary, situated just below the hypothalamus and closely linked with the pineal, orchestrates the body's hormonal symphony — regulating growth, metabolism, reproduction, and stress response.
In yogic anatomy, Ajna is often said to bridge the masculine (pituitary) and feminine (pineal) aspects of consciousness — intellect and intuition, logic and love — achieving union through awareness.

Physiologically, the pituitary's integrative function mirrors Ajna's role as *the command center* — directing the body's responses based on signals from higher consciousness.
Balanced pituitary function ensures internal coherence; imbalanced signaling can manifest as confusion, emotional instability, or disconnection — the same symptoms described in ancient texts as disturbances of the Third Eye.

Thus, the pituitary represents the biological expression of Ajna's spiritual purpose: to unify thought and intuition, mind and matter, reason and revelation.

THE FRONTAL CORTEX AND NEURAL INTEGRATION

Modern neuroscience identifies the prefrontal cortex — located just behind the forehead — as the seat of executive function, imagination, foresight, and empathy.
It is here that humans visualize, plan, and reflect — processes deeply tied to Ajna's domain of visualization and inner knowing.

Advanced imaging studies of experienced meditators reveal increased gray-matter density and enhanced neural connectivity in this region, especially during deep meditative focus or visualization practices.

These findings mirror yogic claims that meditation at the Third Eye strengthens intuitive clarity and insight.

When the prefrontal cortex harmonizes with the limbic system (emotional center), perception becomes more balanced — a state akin to Ajna's "illumined mind."

LIGHT, PERCEPTION, AND QUANTUM AWARENESS

Light is central to both science and spirituality.

Photons carry information, and the human brain is exquisitely sensitive to light — not only through vision but through circadian and energetic pathways.

In quantum biology, biophotons (ultra-weak light emissions from living cells) are believed to facilitate cellular communication and coherence.

Researchers suggest that the brain, particularly the pineal region, emits and responds to these subtle light signals — a fascinating resonance with the yogic concept of the *inner light of awareness.*

Ajna's ancient description as a *luminous wheel between the brows* finds modern expression in this discovery: consciousness itself may operate as a coherent field of light, organizing perception and meaning across the neural network.

BRAINWAVE COHERENCE AND MEDITATION

Scientific studies using EEG and fMRI have shown that meditation focusing on the Third Eye increases alpha-theta brainwave coherence — the same frequencies associated with creativity, intuition, and deep relaxation.

This synchronization between hemispheres enhances holistic perception — where analytical and intuitive faculties operate as one.

It echoes the Tantric teaching that Ajna unites duality — the left (logic) and right (intuition) — into unified awareness.

Neuroplasticity research confirms that such practices rewire neural pathways, improving clarity, emotional regulation, and insight — demonstrating that "seeing inwardly" is a measurable transformation of the brain's architecture.

VISION, HORMONES, AND ENERGY

When the endocrine and neural systems are in balance, the mind experiences lucidity, restful alertness, and heightened creativity — the physiological signature of an awakened Third Eye. Disturbance in these systems, however, may manifest as disorientation, anxiety, or disconnection from purpose — reflections of Ajna's imbalance described in both ancient texts and modern psychology.

Just as Vishuddha's health mirrors thyroid balance, Ajna's vitality corresponds with hormonal harmony, light exposure, and cognitive clarity.
In both science and spirituality, insight arises when inner chemistry and consciousness resonate in coherence.

MODERN RESONANCE: THE SCIENCE OF INNER VISION

Emerging studies in neurotheology, cognitive science, and consciousness research explore how meditation, visualization, and prayer alter the brain's light and energy patterns.
Functional scans reveal bursts of synchrony and rhythmic light activity in the midbrain and prefrontal regions during experiences of profound insight or spiritual unity — a phenomenon yogis described centuries ago as the *flashing of the inner flame.*

Such findings affirm what the ancients intuited: perception is not merely sensory, but vibrational — a dynamic interaction of light, chemistry, and consciousness.

THE UNIFIED UNDERSTANDING

From the yogic view, Ajna refines perception — transforming thought into wisdom and awareness into illumination.
From a scientific view, it integrates the neural, endocrine, and perceptual systems, translating sensory data into meaning and coherence.
Together, they reveal a profound truth:

Vision is both biological and spiritual — light interpreted by the mind, and light remembered by the soul.

To awaken the Third Eye is to bring brain and being into resonance — where chemistry meets consciousness, where photons become perception, and where awareness itself becomes the sacred light that sees all.

ARCHETYPES OF THE THIRD EYE CHAKRA

Every chakra embodies universal archetypes — patterns of consciousness that express both the light and shadow of the soul's evolution. For the Third Eye Chakra (Ajna) — the center of perception, intuition, and wisdom — these archetypes reflect the ways we see, interpret, and understand reality.
They reveal how awareness itself becomes vision — either illuminated by insight or clouded by illusion.

Ajna's energy unfolds through two primary archetypes: The Seer and The Visionary.

THE SEER

The Seer represents Ajna's essential function — the ability to perceive truth beyond the visible, to discern patterns beneath appearances, and to see the self with clarity and compassion.
This archetype lives in each of us as the quiet witness — the

one who observes without judgment, who looks inward for truth rather than outward for validation.

The Seer reminds us that perception creates reality.
When we see clearly, life aligns with wisdom.
When vision is clouded, illusion becomes our guide.

In Balance:

The balanced Seer perceives life through the lens of awareness, not projection.
They trust intuition without abandoning reason and discern truth without fear of what it reveals.
Their insight is calm, impartial, and luminous — a mirror reflecting what *is*, not what the ego wishes to see.
They recognize symbols and synchronicities as messages of consciousness itself.

A balanced Seer knows that true vision arises from stillness — the mind silent, the heart open.

In Shadow:

When unbalanced, the Seer falls into two shadows.
In one, they become The Skeptic — trapped in intellect, dismissing intuition, believing only what the eyes can measure.
In the other, they become The Deluded — lost in fantasy or false prophecy, mistaking imagination for insight.
Both are forms of blindness: one denies inner light; the other distorts it.

The Seer's lesson is to integrate intuition with reason — to see both the mystical and the material as reflections of the same truth.

THE VISIONARY

If the Seer perceives what *is*, the Visionary perceives what *can be*.
This archetype embodies Ajna's higher expression — the creative intelligence that imagines possibility and brings vision into form.
The Visionary bridges inspiration and manifestation, revealing the divine blueprint behind innovation, art, and purpose.

They are the dreamers who see beyond the horizon, translating inner images into reality — not as fantasy, but as revelation made tangible.

In Balance:

The balanced Visionary sees with clarity and purpose.
They trust their imagination as sacred guidance and act with grounded intention.
Their visions uplift others, offering new ways of perceiving the world.
They live from the understanding that thought is creation, and vision is its first movement.
In this harmony, imagination becomes illumination.

In Shadow:

When unbalanced, the Visionary may lose discernment.
They become The Escapist — living in dreams but avoiding reality.
Or The Manipulator — using insight to control or impress rather than to enlighten.
Both shadows stem from ego-driven vision — seeing only through the self, not the soul.

The Visionary's lesson is to surrender vision to service — to create not from ambition, but from alignment with higher wisdom.

THE DEEPER LESSON

The archetypes of Ajna reveal that seeing is not merely visual — it is vibrational.
Every perception is shaped by the clarity of the observer.
When the mind is clear, truth shines effortlessly; when clouded, even light becomes shadow.

The Seer and the Visionary together teach that insight must be balanced by imagination, and imagination by insight.
To see truly is to unify intuition and intellect — the eye that perceives with the light that understands.

When these archetypes harmonize, awareness becomes illumination:
You no longer look *at* the world, but *through* it — perceiving spirit in all forms.

TOGETHER: THE SEER AND THE VISIONARY

Together, these archetypes express the full potential of the Third Eye Chakra:

- The Seer brings discernment — the wisdom to perceive truth as it is.
- The Visionary brings imagination — the courage to envision what could be.

One illuminates the present; the other shapes the future.
One anchors intuition in awareness; the other expands awareness into creation.

When they work in harmony, Ajna awakens its sacred purpose: to perceive with clarity, to imagine with integrity, and to create with consciousness.

In this union, perception becomes revelation — and the Third Eye opens not to fantasy, but to truth.

LIVING ARCHETYPALLY

Both the Seer and the Visionary dwell within us.
At times, one gazes inward — seeking understanding through stillness — while the other looks forward, dreaming new worlds into being.
Recognizing which is active allows us to balance observation and imagination, intuition and intellect, inner knowing and outer creation.

Living archetypally with Ajna means seeing life through the lens of consciousness itself — perceiving not just with the eyes, but with awareness.
It is the art of discerning truth from illusion, of trusting intuition without losing grounding, of seeing what *is* while envisioning what *can be.*

When the Seer and the Visionary unite, perception becomes revelation.
The mind no longer struggles to control or predict — it opens as a clear window for insight.
Vision becomes service, and every thought becomes a ray of illumination.
In this balance, the Third Eye is not about *seeing more* — it is about *seeing truly.*

THIRD EYE CHAKRA ARCHETYPE REFLECTION EXERCISE

Find a quiet space where light feels soft and natural.
Sit comfortably with your spine tall and your attention resting between your brows.
Breathe slowly and deeply, allowing each inhale to draw awareness inward.
With each exhale, release tension from your forehead, jaw, and mind.

Visualize a violet or indigo light radiating from the center of your brow — expanding gently through your temples, eyes, and mind.
Feel this light clearing confusion and awakening calm insight.
Let it expand until it surrounds you — a field of quiet knowing and luminous peace.

When your awareness feels still, reflect on the questions below and record your insights in your journal.

EXPLORING THE SEER

1. When do I feel most connected to my intuition or inner knowing?
2. How do I discern between perception (what I see) and projection (what I assume)?
3. What beliefs or fears may cloud my ability to see clearly?
4. How do I respond when truth challenges what I've always believed?
5. What helps me return to stillness — the space where true insight arises?

EXPLORING THE VISIONARY

1. What visions or ideas am I being called to bring into reality?
2. How can I align my imagination with compassion and purpose?
3. Do I act on my visions, or do I keep them safely unexpressed?
4. Where might I blur the line between divine inspiration and personal fantasy?
5. What creative practice — visualization, journaling, meditation, or art — helps me translate insight into form?

INTEGRATION

- Which archetype feels stronger within me right now — The Seer or The Visionary?
- Where do I notice resistance to seeing clearly — in myself, in others, or in life's unfolding?
- What gentle action can I take this week to align my inner vision with truth and purpose?

REFLECTION MANTRA

"I honor the Seer within me for perceiving truth with calm awareness.
I honor the Visionary within me for transforming insight into inspired creation.
Together, they awaken my inner light — clear, wise, and infinite."

Chapter 3 – The Energetic Blueprint of the Third Eye Chakra

The Third Eye Chakra and the Aura

The Third Eye Chakra (Ajna) is far more than the seat of intuition — it is the energetic eye of consciousness, the subtle field where perception becomes illumination and thought becomes insight.
If the Throat transforms truth into sound, and the Crown receives divine wisdom, then the Third Eye refines awareness into vision — translating vibration into light, and understanding into knowing.

When Ajna is open and balanced, the aura around the forehead and brow glows with indigo-violet radiance — deep, steady, and luminous like twilight between day and night.
This energy emanates through the head and upper face, extending into the subtle auric field like waves of soft light pulsing from an inner flame.

It carries the frequency of clarity — a vibration that feels centered, observant, and wise.
Others sense it as calm intelligence and quiet confidence — the unmistakable presence of one who *sees* rather than merely looks.
This energy communicates understanding without words — a resonance that aligns intuition, intellect, and soul.

Energetically, a balanced Third Eye Chakra expresses as mental clarity, intuitive precision, and inner vision.
You see beyond illusion and perceive the interconnectedness of all things.
Your aura expands like a halo of deep indigo light, smooth and clear — each thought refined by awareness, each insight radiating peace.
The field becomes coherent, resembling gentle waves of light moving through a vast stillness — consciousness seeing itself.

When Ajna is blocked or underactive, the aura around the brow and temples may appear dull, shadowed, or fractured.
The mind feels clouded, vision blurred — unable to distinguish intuition from imagination, or truth from belief.
Confusion, overthinking, or lack of focus often accompany this stagnation, creating a veil over perception.
The individual may feel disconnected from inner guidance, uncertain of direction, or fearful of what lies beyond the known.

When overactive, Ajna's field may appear intense or erratic — thoughts racing faster than intuition can integrate.
This can lead to psychic overwhelm, headaches, insomnia, or fixation on abstract ideas without grounding them into reality.
Energy swirls too quickly, creating an over-bright, unanchored vibration that seeks control rather than clarity.

Restoring harmony to Ajna brings both vision and peace.
When light flows evenly through this center, awareness becomes expansive yet serene — the mind quiet, the eyes soft, the soul luminous.
You no longer seek answers — you *see* them, reflected in every moment.

THE THIRD EYE AS THE RADIANT FIELD OF PERCEPTION

The Third Eye Chakra (Ajna) acts as the luminous lens of the energy field — the subtle point through which consciousness perceives and interprets vibration.
Just as the Throat refines sound into resonance, Ajna refines light into vision.
It translates intuition, thought, and awareness into perception — shaping how reality is seen and understood.

When balanced, the entire aura aligns in luminous coherence, as though illuminated from within by a steady inner flame.
This is why visualization, meditation, and focused awareness can immediately clarify the auric field — tuning perception to truth and quieting the noise of illusion.
Practices such as gazing softly into candlelight, visualizing an indigo sphere at the brow, or silently repeating the mantra OM send a clear energetic message through the mind and field:

"I see clearly. I trust my vision. I perceive truth through the light of awareness."

In response, the aura becomes radiant and still — its texture fine, luminous, and quietly pulsating.
It resembles the calm of the night sky — infinite, yet intimate; silent, yet filled with subtle light.

From an energetic practitioner's perspective, Ajna represents the blueprint of clarity within the aura — the pattern of illumination that reveals whether perception is aligned with truth or clouded by distortion.
Even when energy flows strongly through the lower chakras and the Throat expresses with power, if the Third Eye is dim or scattered, the current loses direction.
Vision becomes fragmented, insight dulled, and intention unfocused.

To clear Ajna is to restore coherence to consciousness itself — allowing thought and intuition to merge in balance.
It is the meeting point of light and mind, where awareness expands beyond logic and intuition becomes luminous understanding.
When Ajna awakens, the aura shines with indigo light — still, radiant, and precise.
This is not brightness that blinds, but light that reveals — the glow of truth recognized.

The Third Eye is the energetic blueprint of illumination — the inner sky of perception through which divine wisdom reflects itself.
Here, vision becomes vibration, and awareness becomes creation.
It is the eye through which the soul remembers itself as light.

THE AURA OF LIGHT: HOW AJNA RADIATES THROUGH THE ENERGY FIELD

When the Third Eye Chakra is balanced, its indigo radiance expands through the head and brow, forming an oval field of subtle luminosity.
Unlike the warmth of solar energy or the coolness of throat resonance, Ajna's field feels like light woven with silence — spacious, steady, and timeless.

This energy is often perceived not as movement, but as presence — a luminous stillness that both perceives and reflects.
It is the silent awareness behind the eyes, the calm intelligence that observes all without attachment.
When this vibration fills the aura, others sense it as calm insight — the quiet confidence of one who sees with the heart as much as with the mind.

In the auric field, Ajna appears as soft waves of indigo and violet light emanating from the brow and temples, pulsing

gently with the rhythm of breath.
It carries no effort, no striving — only awareness, pure and
clear.
This is perception in its highest form: the ability to see without
distortion, to understand without judgment, and to know
without fear.

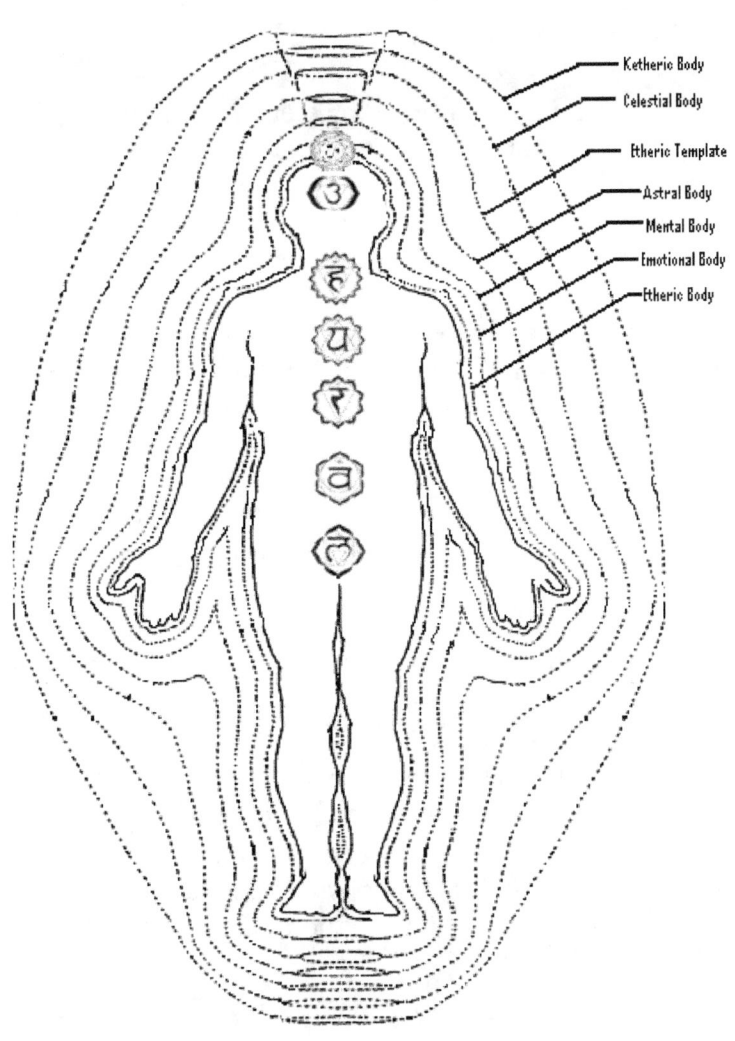

When Ajna radiates freely, the aura becomes a mirror of truth
— luminous, vast, and serene.
It is the energetic signature of clarity in motion, the light of
consciousness perceiving itself.
The Third Eye Chakra is thus the inner sun of awareness — the
radiant field where insight becomes illumination, and
perception becomes wisdom.

THE QUALITY OF LIGHT

Ajna's energy expresses through the element of light (jyoti) —
the bridge between form and formlessness, where perception
becomes illumination and consciousness reveals itself.
When balanced, this luminous field shimmers in hues of indigo,
deep violet, and soft midnight blue, often fringed with silver-
white or gold where intuition meets divine awareness.
Its presence feels quiet, expansive, and crystalline — like
standing beneath a starlit sky that both reflects and absorbs
infinity.

Others may describe sensing wisdom, serenity, or focus in your
presence — as though your very energy *sees them truly.*
This is Ajna's radiance: calm yet alert, luminous yet grounded.

When the Third Eye Chakra is underactive, the aura appears
dim or clouded around the brow and temples — thoughts may
scatter, insight dulls, and clarity fades beneath confusion or
disbelief.
When overactive, the field can become overstimulated — vision
racing faster than discernment, imagination blurring into
illusion.
True balance lies in illumination: awareness that perceives
clearly, neither blinded by intensity nor veiled by doubt.

THE FIELD OF PERCEPTION

The Third Eye governs vision and understanding — how energy becomes insight and insight becomes wisdom.
Its light in the aura reflects the harmony between intellect, intuition, and imagination.

When balanced, Ajna refines the energies of the lower chakras into *awareness* — meaning you not only think clearly, but *see* through clarity itself.
Your perception becomes a radiant mirror, neither absorbing distortion nor projecting illusion.
You recognize truth without effort, and your energy field emanates quiet lucidity — the calm of one who trusts inner knowing over outer noise.

This is the aura of perception: it does not seek to analyze; it seeks to *understand.*
It says to the world:

"I see truth. I understand beyond appearances. I am light within awareness."

INFLUENCE AND ILLUMINATION

A balanced Third Eye Chakra influences not through persuasion, but through presence.
Its radiance magnetizes insight and alignment, drawing others toward stillness and clarity.

Your vision carries frequency — it reveals, guides, and awakens simply because it arises from illumination.
When Ajna is radiant, perception flows like light through water — refracting wisdom into all it touches.
Others feel calm and seen in your presence because you perceive with compassion rather than judgment.

This is why healers, teachers, mystics, and visionaries with an awakened Third Eye often inspire transformation: they transmit *awareness*, not ideology — presence, not performance.
Their gaze becomes a portal of peace — an invitation into deeper seeing.

ENERGY EXCHANGE AND INNER LISTENING

Ajna is also the center of energetic perception — the dialogue not only of thought, but of awareness between beings.
Here, communication transcends words; understanding occurs through resonance.

When balanced, perception is reciprocal — seeing and being seen in equal grace.
When weak, one may rely too heavily on logic, dismissing intuition; when excessive, one may become lost in fantasy, detached from physical grounding.
Awareness restores balance.

Pausing before interpreting, breathing into the brow, and visualizing an indigo light between the eyes harmonizes perception — allowing intuition and intellect to merge in luminous understanding.

THE RADIANCE OF SACRED VISION

At its highest vibration, the Third Eye becomes the light of divine perception — awareness as prayer, truth as illumination, and vision as revelation.
In this awakened state, the aura expands in subtle violet-white brilliance, encompassing both insight and stillness.
Your mind becomes a clear channel of consciousness — discerning, receptive, and radiant with wisdom.

To live from this center is to perceive as the soul perceives: without distortion, without fear, and without separation.

This is the essence of a balanced Ajna — a sky of inner light that neither blinds nor darkens, but opens vast and clear — a living field of illumination where truth becomes vision, and perception becomes peace.

FLOW OF ENERGY FROM THE THIRD EYE UPWARD

The Third Eye Chakra (Ajna) is far more than the center of intuition — it is the gateway of perception, where awareness becomes vision and thought becomes illumination.
It is the bridge between intellect and spirit, refining reason into revelation and knowledge into knowing.

In yogic and Tantric tradition, Ajna represents a sacred threshold in the ascent of Kundalini through the sushumna nadi, the central current of consciousness.
Here, prana — the vital force — is transmuted into light, uniting mind and soul in radiant awareness.
It is said that when energy reaches Ajna, the inner eye opens — the self begins to *see* itself through the gaze of divine intelligence.

At this stage, the resonance of the Throat (Vishuddha) evolves into vision — sound becomes light, and vibration becomes insight.
The courage once used to speak now transforms into the stillness required to perceive; expression matures into observation, and understanding becomes illumination.

THE UPWARD FLOW OF AWARENESS

• From Ajna (Third Eye) → to Sahasrara (Crown):
Vision transcends duality. Perception merges with pure consciousness.
The seer, the seeing, and the seen dissolve into one infinite awareness — silence radiant with understanding.

• From Vishuddha (Throat) → to Ajna (Third Eye):
Sound refines into light. Expression deepens into perception.
What is spoken with clarity becomes understood with wisdom;
communication becomes communion with truth.

• From Anahata (Heart) → to Ajna (Third Eye):
Love ascends into awareness. Compassion becomes insight.
Feeling gains vision, and emotion matures into intuitive
knowing — seeing the divine pattern woven through all things.

THE PATH OF ILLUMINATION

This upward flow mirrors the journey of consciousness from
sound to silence, and from silence to light.
Expression evolves into perception; perception evolves into
realization.
Each chakra refines the energy it receives — lifting vibration
higher: from communication to intuition, from intuition to
unity, from unity to pure awareness.

When Ajna is balanced, this current flows effortlessly.
The truth spoken through Vishuddha rises into the vision of
Ajna, illuminating the pathway to the Crown.
Perception becomes peaceful, the aura steady and radiant — an
indigo light that speaks without words, knowing without
thought.

When Ajna is blocked or clouded, the current stalls.
Insight becomes confusion, intuition turns to doubt, and clarity
gives way to illusion.
If perception is obscured, wisdom cannot descend, and divine
guidance cannot rise.
The inner light dims — awareness narrows, and truth becomes
distorted through fear or disbelief.

THE EYE AS THE BRIDGE OF LIGHT

Practitioners often describe Ajna as the dawn of the subtle body
— the meeting of night and day, shadow and illumination.
Here, energy no longer vibrates or flows — it *shines*.
It radiates through the mind as vision, intuition, and insight.

When the Third Eye opens, thought becomes light, and light
becomes understanding.
Perception itself becomes prayer — each realization a ray of
consciousness piercing illusion.
Energy rises pure and clear, freed from attachment and duality.

This is the stage where seeing becomes knowing, and knowing
becomes being.
It is the awakening of the inner vision — the recognition that
truth is not observed, but *revealed.*

THE ESSENCE OF THE FLOW

Ajna does not hold light — it transmits it.
It transforms the resonance of sound into perception, and the
wisdom of the soul into insight.
Like a prism that catches sunlight and reveals its hidden
spectrum, the Third Eye refracts consciousness into
understanding.

When balanced, it radiates the pure light of awareness — calm,
focused, and luminous.
It reminds us that perception is not analysis, but alignment; that
the purpose of vision is not to interpret, but to *awaken.*

Through Ajna, the life force becomes light, and the soul learns
to see its eternal self reflected in every form.

THE THIRD EYE CHAKRA AS THE SEAT OF VISION AND WISDOM

If the Throat is the seat of truth and expression, and the Heart is the seat of love, then the Third Eye Chakra is the seat of vision and wisdom.
Ajna governs the element of light — the subtle field through which consciousness perceives and truth reveals itself.

It is the sacred space where awareness transforms into revelation, where intuition refines intellect, and where the finite meets the infinite.
This chakra represents the evolution of perception from belief to direct knowing — from the mind that seeks truth to the consciousness that *is* truth.

At Ajna, perception no longer depends on the senses but arises from within.
It is the awakening of higher intelligence — the merging of seeing and being, observer and observed.

From an evolutionary perspective, the Third Eye mirrors humanity's awakening to self-awareness — when perception expanded beyond survival and into reflection.
When early mystics closed their eyes and saw the light within, they rediscovered the power of inner sight — the vision that connects all life.

Likewise, when Ajna awakens within us, we rediscover the creative power of awareness — the light that bridges thought and spirit, self and source, the human and the divine.

BRIDGE OF PERCEPTION

The Third Eye Chakra (Ajna) serves as the energetic bridge between the clarity of the mind and the silence of the spirit. It is through this center that thought becomes vision and awareness becomes illumination.
Where the Throat gives us courage to speak, the Third Eye grants us the courage to *see* — to look beyond illusion, to perceive with wisdom, and to trust the unseen.

When Ajna is balanced, energy flows as light through a clear lens. Perception is steady and intuitive, yet rooted in discernment. You see truth without judgment and illusion without fear. Your insight is calm, precise, and compassionate — perception guided by peace rather than projection. You no longer seek certainty; you *recognize clarity.* You perceive not to control, but to understand.

When Ajna is underactive, perception narrows.
The world feels fragmented, intuition fades, and understanding becomes clouded by doubt or overthinking.
When overactive, awareness scatters into overstimulation — imagination blurs into fantasy, vision rushes faster than grounding, and clarity gives way to confusion.
In both extremes, the light of consciousness distorts: perception becomes either dim or dazzling, too faint to see truth or too bright to discern its shape.

THE BODY OF LIGHT AND CONSCIOUSNESS

Just as the Throat Chakra governs vibration and communication, the Third Eye governs illumination and comprehension.
It filters the energy of thought and perception — transforming sensory input into awareness, and awareness into wisdom.

Physiologically, this center corresponds with the pituitary and pineal glands, the optic system, and regions of the brain associated with vision, intuition, and hormonal balance. Energetically, it governs how we *interpret reality*: how we translate intuition into understanding and understanding into awareness.

When Ajna is aligned, thought becomes light — perception clear, steady, and true.
You move through life guided not by reaction, but by recognition — responding from awareness rather than instinct. Intuition and intellect harmonize, and insight flows as revelation rather than analysis.

MODERN CHALLENGES TO AJNA

In modern life, the Third Eye is often clouded by overstimulation and distraction.
Endless information floods the mind, but little of it becomes understanding.
Screens, noise, and artificial light tire the eyes and scatter attention, weakening inner vision.
Simultaneously, intuition is often dismissed as unscientific, leaving the inner sight untrusted or unused.

The result is a collective imbalance — knowledge without wisdom, perception without insight.
The mind becomes reactive, and the inner light flickers under the weight of constant mental noise.

Healing the Third Eye restores the balance between intellect and intuition.
It invites silence back into awareness, allowing perception to deepen rather than quicken.
Meditation, darkness, stillness, and contemplative practices all nourish this chakra, clearing the fog of overstimulation and reigniting the luminous calm of inner knowing.

To awaken Ajna is to remember that *seeing* is not only physical — it is spiritual.
True vision perceives not with the eyes, but through the light of consciousness itself.

THE LIGHT OF CLARITY

When balanced, Ajna radiates a tranquil indigo-violet glow — vast, silent, and deep as the night sky.
Your awareness becomes luminous and calm, your thoughts steady and precise.
You no longer chase meaning — you *see* it.
You no longer force understanding — you *receive* it.

In this state, the Third Eye becomes the temple of divine vision — the meeting place of mind and spirit within you.
Here, you remember that perception is sacred: every insight, image, or intuition is light speaking in its own language.

To honor Ajna is to perceive with integrity, to discern with compassion, and to live as a vessel of awareness.
It is to know that your sight is sacred, your silence is powerful, and your understanding is divine.

When you live from this center, you do not seek to know — you *see to understand.*
You do not analyze to prove — you *perceive to awaken.*

Ajna teaches that truth is not discovered but revealed — the radiant unfolding of consciousness seeing itself, the eternal light within whispering, "I see."

A UNIVERSAL UNDERSTANDING OF LIGHT

Though the chakra system originates in the yogic and Tantric sciences, the experience of light — both literal and symbolic — is universal.

Across cultures and eras, humanity has understood illumination as the symbol of wisdom, divinity, and awakening.

Before speech, there was silence; before sound, there was light. Light is the bridge between the visible and the invisible — the radiance through which consciousness perceives creation.

From the "Eye of Horus" in Egyptian mysticism to the "Inner Lamp" of the Upanishads, and the "Third Eye of Shiva" that burns through illusion, every tradition honors light as the essence of truth.
Mystics across time have described enlightenment as *seeing clearly*, not through the eyes, but through awareness itself — the realization that to see truly is to recognize the divine in all things.

To live in light is to live in harmony — to know that every perception, thought, and moment carries frequency and radiance.
Whether through contemplation, prayer, or meditation, humans have always turned inward to find illumination — the inner eye awakening to its own infinite brilliance.

CROSS-CULTURAL EXPRESSIONS OF LIGHT
Indigenous Traditions

For many Indigenous and First Nations peoples, light is the presence of Spirit — the fire of life dwelling in all beings.
The rising sun marks renewal; the stars map ancestry; the flame within the hearth connects the living with their ancestors.
Light ceremonies — from fire vigils to solstice rites — are not mere observances but acts of remembrance, honoring the eternal illumination that guides, protects, and teaches.
To walk in the light is to walk in truth — to live in balance with all creation.

Eastern Systems

In yogic philosophy, Ajna is the seat of *jyoti*, inner illumination
— the point where consciousness becomes self-aware.
Its element, light, represents knowledge, perception, and
awakening.
Meditation upon the inner flame (*jyoti dharana*) dissolves
illusion, revealing the light that has never known darkness.
In Buddhism, this illumination is called *prajna*, the wisdom that
sees beyond duality.
The awakened mind perceives the world as radiant — each
thought a beam of consciousness shining through form.
In Taoist alchemy, the "crystal palace" within the forehead is
where heaven's light is gathered and refined, returning the spirit
to its source.

Ancient Egypt

To the Egyptians, light was the essence of divinity — the
visible breath of the gods.
The solar deity Ra journeyed across the sky as the eternal
witness, illuminating creation with consciousness.
Initiates of the temples practiced meditations on the "Eye of
Ra" and the "Eye of Horus," symbols of perception, protection,
and higher sight.
To awaken this eye was to see through the illusions of the
material world and remember one's divine origin — the light
within the light.

Greek Philosophy

For the Greeks, light symbolized reason (*logos*) and divine
intelligence.
Plato described enlightenment as the soul's ascent from the
shadows of the cave into the radiance of truth.
Pythagoras and later Neoplatonists viewed light as the
substance of the cosmos — a spiritual energy emanating from

the One, cascading through creation as levels of awareness.
To live wisely was to align perception with this inner
illumination — to "see with the mind's eye" rather than be
deceived by appearances.

Biblical and Mystical Traditions

In Genesis, light is the first act of creation: *"And God said, Let
there be light."*
The Word and the Light are inseparable — vibration giving rise
to illumination, thought manifesting as vision.
In Christian mysticism, Christ is the "Light of the World,"
symbolizing divine awareness awakening within the human
heart.
In Kabbalistic tradition, the *Or Ein Sof* — the Infinite Light —
pours into creation, forming the Tree of Life and all levels of
consciousness.
In Sufism, *nur* (light) is both knowledge and love: the lamp of
the heart through which the Divine reveals itself.
To polish the mirror of perception is to let this light reflect
unclouded.

Eastern and Western Alchemy

Alchemy speaks of light as the *prima materia* — the hidden
radiance within matter that, when purified, becomes gold.
Just as fire transforms metal, illumination transforms
consciousness.
The alchemist's inner work mirrors the ascent through Ajna:
dissolving darkness, refining awareness, and allowing the light
of spirit to shine through the mind.
In this sacred science, the "Philosopher's Stone" is not a
mineral, but enlightened perception — the realization that
matter and spirit are one luminous field.

Western Mysticism and Tarot

The Third Eye corresponds to the Suit of Wands, symbolizing illumination, inspiration, and divine spark.
Where Vishuddha's sword cuts through illusion, Ajna's wand ignites vision — the light that reveals truth rather than divides it.
The Hermit card, holding his lantern, depicts the seeker who carries inner illumination through darkness, guiding others not by doctrine but by example.
Light, in the Western Mystery Tradition, is both the journey and the destination — the revelation of wisdom within silence.

THE SACRED LIGHT

Across time and culture, light has been revered as the essence of consciousness — the eternal witness within all that sees and is seen.
It connects matter to spirit, self to source, perception to truth.
To see is to awaken; to know is to remember; to illuminate is to love.

Light reveals that the universe is not a static creation, but a continuum of awareness — every atom, every star, every soul a spark in the infinite brilliance of being.
The Third Eye Chakra reminds us that truth is not found through the eyes, but through the light behind them.

When awareness aligns with wisdom and compassion, perception becomes sacred — the gaze becomes prayer, and the world is seen as it truly is: radiant, interconnected, and alive with consciousness.

THE UNIVERSAL LESSON OF LIGHT

In every tradition, light is the teacher of truth and vision.
It reminds us that awakening does not begin in thought, but in perception — in the still clarity that reveals what has always been.

When we close our inner eye, we lose perspective; when we misuse our vision, we cast shadows upon others.
Balance lies in sacred sight — perceiving without judgment, seeing with compassion, and letting clarity dissolve illusion.

Across all paths, one wisdom endures:

- Light awakens.
- Light reveals.
- Light unites.

Whether we call it *Jyoti*, *Prajna*, or *Ein Sof*, or the *Eye of Horus*, the essence is the same: When our inner light shines clear and unwavering, we awaken the radiance of Ajna — the power to perceive, to understand, and to live in the illumination of Spirit.

To honor light is to honor awareness.
To perceive with clarity is to shape reality through understanding.
To see deeply is to witness the divine — shining through sky, flame, and the eyes of all beings.

When our perception is pure and our mind still, we become instruments of illumination — reflecting not confusion or fear, but the eternal brilliance of consciousness itself.

HOW PRACTITIONERS WORK WITH THE THIRD EYE CHAKRA

For healers and energy practitioners, the Third Eye Chakra — Ajna — is recognized as the center of perception, intuition, and spiritual insight.
Located between the eyebrows, it governs clarity of thought, inner vision, and the ability to perceive truth beyond the physical senses.
It is where awareness becomes illumination — where thought transforms into understanding, and understanding into wisdom.

When Ajna is balanced, a person perceives with calm discernment. Their intuition is clear, their thinking focused, and their inner guidance steady and trustworthy.
When blocked, perception becomes clouded — thoughts feel scattered, decisions uncertain, or intuition disconnected. The person may experience confusion, self-doubt, or a tendency to overanalyze.

ASSESSMENT

Practitioners begin by tuning into a client's relationship with clarity, intuition, and perception.
They may explore questions such as:

- Do you trust your inner guidance, or often second-guess yourself?
- Do you experience mental overactivity or difficulty focusing?
- Are you open to insight and imagination, or do you dismiss intuition as "unreal"?
- Do you find yourself lost in thoughts, worries, or mental images that feel overwhelming?
- Do you experience pressure, headaches, or tension between the eyebrows or temples?

Energetically, healers sense Ajna as a field of deep indigo or violet light radiating from the center of the forehead and extending into the temples, eyes, and crown.

- A balanced Ajna feels luminous, steady, and expansive — like still water reflecting light.
- An underactive Ajna may appear dim or clouded, reflecting doubt, confusion, or overreliance on logic.
- An overactive Ajna may feel sharp or overstimulated — mental chatter, vivid but fragmented visions, or difficulty grounding intuitive impressions.

Practitioners also observe how Ajna interacts with the Throat and Crown Chakras — the centers most closely linked to its function.

When Vishuddha (Throat) expresses clearly and Sahasrara (Crown) receives divine inspiration, Ajna becomes the bridge — translating the language of spirit into insight that the mind can understand.

When these centers are misaligned, perception may distort — intuition becomes fear, or intellect overpowers awareness.

ENERGY HEALING TECHNIQUES

- Reiki & Hands-On Healing:
  Energy is channeled into the forehead, temples, and pineal region to clear mental fog and awaken inner sight. Practitioners visualize an indigo or violet light pulsing between the brows, radiating through the mind and nervous system. The intention is not to "see more," but to *see truly* — harmonizing intuition with intellect.
- Light and Visualization Healing:
  Visualizing a luminous indigo flame or star between the eyebrows helps to focus scattered thoughts and activate perception. Some practitioners guide clients to imagine breathing light into this point, expanding awareness outward until it merges with universal consciousness.

- Sound & Frequency Healing:
  The bija mantra OM (AUM) resonates with Ajna,
  aligning its frequency to higher consciousness. Chanting
  or toning OM — alone or with a singing bowl tuned to
  indigo frequencies — harmonizes the hemispheres of the
  brain and calms mental restlessness.
- Crystal Healing:
  Indigo and violet stones such as lapis lazuli, amethyst,
  sodalite, azurite, and fluorite are placed upon the
  forehead or worn as jewelry to enhance clarity, intuition,
  and spiritual connection. These crystals encourage
  mental stillness, insight, and connection to higher
  wisdom.
- Aromatherapy:
  Oils such as sandalwood, frankincense, myrrh, lavender,
  and clary sage promote meditation, focus, and spiritual
  awareness. Diffused during healing or applied to the
  brow, these oils quiet the analytical mind and invite
  inner illumination.

BODYWORK PRACTICES

Because Ajna governs sight, perception, and the mind-body
connection, bodywork for this chakra focuses on stillness,
clarity, and balance between the hemispheres of the brain.

- Head, Neck, and Face Release:
  Gentle massage around the temples, jaw, and forehead
  releases stored tension and mental fatigue. The
  relaxation of these muscles allows intuitive energy to
  flow more freely through the pineal region.
- Eye Movement & Focus Practices:
  Slow, circular eye movements or focusing on a candle
  flame (*Trataka*) train the mind to sustain attention.
  These exercises strengthen concentration and awaken
  the inner eye.

- Meditative Breathwork:
  Practices such as Nadi Shodhana (alternate nostril
  breathing) or slow rhythmic breathing balance the brain
  hemispheres, purify energy channels, and promote a
  tranquil mind — a key precursor to intuitive insight.
- Yoga Poses for Ajna:
  Forward folds and gentle inversions — such as Child's
  Pose (Balasana), Downward-Facing Dog (Adho Mukha
  Svanasana), or Dolphin Pose (Ardha Pincha
  Mayurasana) — increase circulation to the head and
  quiet the nervous system. These postures encourage
  introspection and balance between thought and
  awareness.
- Meditative Stillness:
  Unlike the expressive movement of Vishuddha, Ajna's
  healing often arises in silence and focus. Sitting quietly,
  eyes closed, attention turned inward, one learns to
  witness rather than react.
  In that stillness, perception refines — the inner eye
  opens, and the outer world becomes a mirror of
  consciousness.

INTEGRATION AND PRACTICE

Working with Ajna teaches practitioners that true sight is not
about what is seen, but how it is seen.
Healing this chakra is less about stimulation and more about
purification — releasing illusion, mental tension, and egoic
interference so that wisdom can arise naturally.

When Ajna is open and balanced, perception becomes luminous
and steady.
Thought and intuition merge in harmony, and understanding
flows effortlessly from silence.
The practitioner's presence itself becomes a lens of clarity —
reflecting truth without distortion, light without shadow.

To awaken Ajna is to live in conscious perception — to think with light, to see with love, and to know that every insight is the universe remembering itself through you.

SPIRITUAL AND ANCESTRAL HEALING

Practitioners working at the Third Eye Chakra (Ajna) often focus on releasing ancestral, karmic, or collective patterns related to distorted perception, illusion, or spiritual disconnection.
Across generations, many have inherited energetic imprints of fear, denial, or misuse of vision — lineages where intuition was suppressed, insight punished, or inner knowing dismissed. Healing Ajna restores the sacred gift of sight — not only the ability to see clearly, but to *see truly.*

It is an awakening from illusion — freeing the mind from inherited veils of confusion, fear, or false belief so that wisdom may shine unobstructed.
Common practices include:

• Ancestral Clearing and Timeline Meditation:
Visualizing a line of ancestors behind you, practitioners guide clients to send indigo light through the lineage — dissolving old beliefs that cloud perception and reclaiming the gift of intuitive sight for all generations.

• Third Eye Illumination:
A guided visualization using indigo or violet flame energy to dissolve karmic veils and awaken the pineal "eye of light." This opens the channel for divine insight unfiltered by ego or fear.

• Dream and Vision Retrieval:
Through trance, meditation, or light hypnotherapy, clients revisit dreams, visions, or memories that hold ancestral messages. These symbolic insights often reveal unresolved patterns that seek to be understood and released.

• Karmic Belief Rewriting:
Practitioners help clients identify limiting beliefs inherited through family or past lives — such as fear of the unknown, distrust of intuition, or dependency on external authority — and replace them with affirmations of clarity and faith in inner truth.

• Light Rituals:
Candles, mirrors, or crystals are used as tools of reflection and illumination. Gazing softly into a flame or crystal allows energy to flow from confusion into comprehension — transforming shadow into insight, darkness into revelation.

INTEGRATION

Healing Ajna is the art of turning perception into wisdom — bridging the seen and unseen through clarity of awareness. Practitioners encourage clients to cultivate daily practices that refine inner sight, strengthen discernment, and honor intuition as sacred communication from the soul.

• Begin each day by sitting quietly in stillness, breathing light into the space between the brows. Whisper:
"I see with clarity, I trust what I know, I walk in light."

• Keep a dream or intuition journal to record images, synchronicities, and insights that arise in meditation or daily life — observing patterns without judgment.

• Practice mirror gazing for a few minutes each day, looking into your own eyes with love and recognition — acknowledging the divine witness within.

• Meditate on a flame, moon, or night sky, allowing your gaze to soften until the boundary between seer and seen dissolves.

• Chant OM (AUM) softly, feeling the vibration expand through your forehead and crown — merging personal consciousness with the universal.

• Wear or visualize indigo and violet hues to harmonize the mind and invite intuitive calm.

• Limit overstimulation — turn off devices, step into darkness, and rest your eyes in silence. The Third Eye thrives in stillness.

For healers, Ajna represents the alchemy of perception — where insight becomes illumination, and awareness becomes truth.
It reminds us that vision is not merely an act of seeing outward, but a sacred journey inward.

When the Third Eye radiates clear and luminous, we no longer seek to predict or control — we *understand*.
We see beyond fear and form into the timeless light of consciousness itself.
In this clarity, perception becomes prayer, and seeing becomes communion.

To awaken Ajna is to remember that enlightenment is not a distant state — it is the moment you open your inner eyes and realize: "I am light, and through me, light sees."

Chapter 4 – Signs of Imbalance

Shadow Aspects of the Third Eye Chakra

Every chakra holds both light and shadow.
The Third Eye Chakra — Ajna — governs perception, intuition, and the clarity of inner vision.
It is the seat of wisdom where insight merges with awareness, where truth is seen rather than merely known.

When balanced, Ajna radiates lucidity — perception becomes clear, thought becomes calm, and intuition flows effortlessly.
When misaligned, its energy either dims into confusion or over-activates into illusion.
Vision clouds, thoughts distort, and imagination detaches from grounding.

These shadows are not failures but *invitations* — doorways to deeper understanding.
Each imbalance reveals where the mind has become overrun by fear, illusion, or false perception.
They call us to clear the lens of awareness, to remember that true sight arises from stillness, not from striving.

CONFUSION AND MENTAL FOG

When Ajna is underactive, perception dulls.
You may struggle to focus, trust your intuition, or see the bigger picture.

Life feels hazy — decisions unclear, imagination muted, and inner guidance faint or silent.

This dimming often begins through overreliance on logic or external validation — believing only what can be measured or proven. The result is disconnection from inner knowing.

Physically, symptoms may include eye strain, headaches, or fatigue between the brows. Energetically, the aura feels clouded — thought forms swirl without clarity.

Healing begins through *quiet clarity*: meditation, mindful breathing, and reflection on what feels true rather than what seems certain. When the mind becomes still, the fog lifts, and insight gently returns.

ILLUSION AND OVER-IDENTIFICATION WITH MIND

When Ajna burns too brightly, perception becomes distorted. Instead of clarity, there is projection — imagination overtakes intuition. The mind races, weaving stories or assumptions mistaken for truth.

This overactivity may appear as an obsession with symbolism, excessive spiritual interpretation, or detachment from physical reality. The seeker becomes lost in visions, theories, or "knowing too much," yet lacks grounded wisdom.

At its core, this imbalance stems from spiritual inflation — mistaking perception for perfection.
Healing lies in humility: grounding practices, embodied movement, and remembering that true insight is quiet, simple, and compassionate.

DENIAL OF INTUITION AND DISTRUST OF INNER KNOWING

When intuition has been invalidated — through upbringing, dogma, or trauma — Ajna closes to protect itself.
You may rely only on intellect, dismiss intuitive nudges, or doubt your own discernment.
This disbelief fractures inner harmony: the rational mind dominates while the intuitive self retreats into silence.

Energetically, the Third Eye feels tight or empty, its light dim behind the forehead.
Healing comes through trust restored — acknowledging past times when intuition was right and cultivating the courage to act upon it again.

MENTAL OVERLOAD AND OBSESSIVE THINKING

An overstimulated Ajna often manifests as mental noise — thoughts looping endlessly, analysis replacing awareness.
The inner dialogue becomes relentless, drowning out intuition's subtle voice.
Headaches, insomnia, and restlessness follow as energy collects in the head rather than circulating through the body.

Healing requires descent — bringing awareness down into the heart and breath.
Meditation on the exhale, time in nature, and releasing the need to "figure it out" all restore equilibrium.
As the mind quiets, intuition once again finds space to whisper.

DISCONNECTION FROM SPIRITUAL INSIGHT

When Ajna closes, vision narrows.
You may feel uninspired, skeptical, or spiritually numb — unable to sense guidance or meaning.

This disconnection often arises from fear of the unknown or resistance to surrendering control.

In truth, Ajna's light cannot be forced open; it must be *invited*. Reverent silence, candle meditation, or simply gazing at the sky reawakens the remembrance of unity — the understanding that perception is an act of communion, not control.

THE HIDDEN WOUND

At the heart of every Third Eye imbalance lies a wound of *trust in perception.*
Somewhere along the soul's journey, you may have learned that seeing differently was unsafe — that intuition was dismissed, or vision condemned.
To protect itself, the inner eye dimmed.

Healing Ajna is not about gaining new visions; it is about cleansing the lens through which they are seen.
It is learning to perceive without distortion, to know without fear, and to remember that true wisdom needs no proof — it simply *is.*

When Ajna is healed, sight becomes understanding, and knowledge becomes compassion.
You no longer look outward for answers — you see through the illusion of separation itself.
Vision becomes service, and perception becomes prayer.

EXCESS OR OVERACTIVE THIRD EYE ENERGY

When the Third Eye becomes overstimulated, its radiance can fracture into dissonance.
Instead of insight, there is overwhelm — floods of images, psychic impressions, or dream-like visions without context or grounding.

The mind may become restless or overly analytical, struggling to distinguish imagination from intuition.

This imbalance often emerges from spiritual overexertion — forcing the mind to open higher states without anchoring in the body.
The result is an excess of light without stability — revelation without integration.

Healing requires grounding: spending time outdoors, eating nourishing foods, sleeping deeply, and allowing the nervous system to rest.
True vision arises not through effort, but through balance.

When Ajna is clear and calm, light becomes wisdom.
Insight arises naturally, like dawn after night — quiet, radiant, and whole.

OVERACTIVE THIRD EYE ENERGY AND DISTORTED PERCEPTION

When Ajna overfires, the natural flow of perception becomes unbalanced.
You may find yourself trapped in analysis, overthinking every decision, or mistaking imagination for intuition.
The mind races to interpret, categorize, and control what should simply *be seen.*
Clarity turns into confusion; insight becomes overwhelm.
The Third Eye's brilliance, when untethered from grounding, can blind as much as it illuminates.
Healing begins with surrender — letting stillness restore the truth that vision arises not from effort, but from awareness.

MENTAL OVERSTIMULATION AND SPIRITUAL OVERLOAD

When Ajna is overstimulated, thought becomes constant motion.
You may feel mentally exhausted, restless, or unable to stop the mind's endless narration.
Visions, dreams, or intuitive flashes may arrive faster than you can interpret, leaving you disoriented or anxious.
This imbalance often occurs when spiritual practice outpaces integration — when the mind opens before the heart and body are ready to receive.

The remedy is grounding and simplicity.
Return to the breath, the body, and the earth.
Touch something tangible.
The soul does not need more insight; it needs *presence* for its light to root.

DELUSION, ESCAPISM, AND SPIRITUAL EGO

The shadow side of heightened vision is illusion.
When the Third Eye's energy expands without humility, perception can distort into fantasy or spiritual superiority.
You may believe you alone "see clearly," or that your visions grant authority over others.
This illusion separates rather than unites — truth becomes performance rather than revelation.

Healing comes through humility and embodiment.
Anchor insight in compassion.
Ask: *Does what I see bring peace, or does it breed pride?*
True intuition is never self-serving; it is clear, quiet, and free from the need to convince.

FEAR, PARANOIA, AND MISPERCEPTION

When Ajna's lens is clouded by fear, imagination distorts reality.
You may misread others' intentions, perceive threat where none exists, or spiral into mental doubt.
The mind becomes a hall of mirrors — every reflection exaggerated, every shadow mistaken for truth.

These distortions often arise when intuition awakens faster than emotional safety can stabilize it.
Grounding in faith and love dissolves fear's grip, allowing perception to purify.
The Third Eye sees clearly only when the heart feels safe.

ANALYSIS WITHOUT INSIGHT

In a world that prizes intellect, many carry the wound of overthinking — mistaking logic for wisdom.
An overactive Ajna fixates on solving rather than understanding, thinking rather than seeing.
Information piles up, but integration never occurs.

This imbalance manifests as decision paralysis, constant planning, or detachment from intuition.
The cure lies in surrender — learning to listen inwardly rather than think louder.
Meditation, mantra, and contemplative silence cleanse the mind's clutter until clarity returns like morning light through mist.

DREAM CONFUSION AND PSYCHIC DRAIN

Because Ajna governs dreams, clairvoyance, and imagination, imbalance can blur the veil between conscious and unconscious realms.
Vivid dreams, insomnia, or psychic fatigue often signal

overstimulation.
Energy may rush upward during sleep or meditation, leaving the
body depleted.

Healing requires balance between heaven and earth —
grounding after meditation, eating nourishing foods, resting in
darkness, and setting clear energetic boundaries.
Remember: intuition is a whisper, not a flood.
You do not need to *see everything*; you only need to *see what is
true*.

THE HIDDEN LESSON

Overactive Third Eye energy teaches that seeing without
grounding becomes distortion.
Just as light refracts through water, insight bends through the
lens of the ego.
Healing Ajna begins not by seeking more visions, but by
refining perception — allowing truth to emerge from stillness
rather than effort.

Meditation on the mantra OM, gentle breathwork, and focused
awareness between the brows bring balance to the mental field.
When perception aligns with the heart and wisdom flows from
peace, Ajna resumes its pure function: the eye of clarity —
silent, luminous, and whole.

THE EXPERIENCE OF AN IMBALANCED THIRD EYE
CHAKRA

When Ajna (the Third Eye Chakra) is out of balance, life feels
like a dream half-remembered — fragments of vision without
meaning, flashes of thought without form.
Because this chakra governs perception, intuition, and higher
awareness, imbalance distorts how you interpret both inner and
outer reality.

You may see too much or too little — overwhelmed by impressions or blind to guidance.
The mind feels noisy, restless, or disconnected from peace.
Perception becomes either overactive and anxious or dull and dismissive — swinging between confusion and overconfidence.

EMOTIONAL SIGNS

Emotionally, imbalance may feel like doubt, anxiety, or distrust of your own intuition.
You may fear your perceptions, question your insight, or avoid spiritual experience altogether.
Conversely, overactivation can create overstimulation — feeling flooded with impressions, empathic exhaustion, or vivid emotional surges that cloud clarity.
Both stem from an imbalance between vision and grounding — the need to balance seeing with being.

MENTAL AND BEHAVIORAL SIGNS

On the mental level, Ajna imbalance can manifest as overanalysis, obsessive thinking, or difficulty concentrating.
You may swing between skepticism and fantasy — dismissing intuitive nudges one moment and overinterpreting coincidences the next.
In some, it presents as escapism: retreating into imagination to avoid the discomfort of reality.

The healing path is mental silence — cultivating observation without attachment.
When the mind becomes still, perception aligns naturally with truth.

SPIRITUAL AND INTUITIVE SYMPTOMS

Because Ajna governs insight and vision, imbalance may be expressed as blocked intuition or unreliable psychic impressions.
You may feel disconnected from inner guidance, unable to interpret dreams, or flooded with symbols that confuse rather than enlighten.
Spiritual experiences may come without clarity or grounding, leading to fatigue or self-doubt.

Grounding, meditation, journaling dreams, and practicing discernment transform confusion into wisdom.
Over time, the Third Eye's light becomes steady — revealing truth as calm awareness rather than dramatic vision.

PHYSICAL MANIFESTATIONS

Physically, Ajna corresponds to the eyes, forehead, brain, pineal gland, and nervous system.
Imbalance may manifest as headaches, migraines, dizziness, sinus congestion, insomnia, or eye strain.
These symptoms mirror energetic pressure — too much energy in the head or too little flow through the body.
Cooling breathwork, lavender aromatherapy, and gentle acupressure on the brow point help disperse excess energy and restore equilibrium.

THE INNER EXPERIENCE

At its core, an imbalanced Third Eye Chakra feels like confusion between thought and truth — a disconnection between what you know and what you *see*.
You may question your insight or cling too tightly to interpretation.
The result is the same: vision loses meaning.

The lesson of Ajna is that seeing is not about control, but clarity.
True vision requires surrender — trusting that awareness reveals itself in silence, not in striving.

When the Third Eye Chakra returns to balance, perception becomes effortless.
Intuition feels natural and grounded.
The mind quiets, insight flows, and wisdom emerges without seeking.

Balance at Ajna is not about mystical sight — it is about *clear perception.*
It is the gentle strength to discern truth from illusion, to rest in awareness, and to see the divine pattern within all things — calm, luminous, and infinite.

Chapter 5 – Causes of Disturbance

Childhood Conditioning and Distorted Perception

If the Root Chakra teaches us that life is safe, and the Sacral that life can be felt, and the Solar Plexus that life can be directed, and the Heart that life can be loved, then the Third Eye Chakra — Ajna — teaches that *life can be seen clearly.*

Ajna begins to awaken during adolescence, when imagination deepens and awareness turns inward.
It is the time when curiosity meets intuition, when the mind begins to question appearances and sense the unseen patterns beneath them.

When this natural development of perception is supported — when children are encouraged to trust their instincts, explore imagination, and discern truth for themselves — the Third Eye opens with clarity and confidence.
They learn that insight is trustworthy, that intuition is real, and that their perception has value.

But when early experiences distort this process — when imagination is dismissed, curiosity punished, or perception invalidated — Ajna's light becomes confused or dim.
The child learns to doubt their inner knowing, replacing vision with compliance.
The result is an adult who either sees too little — skeptical,

disconnected from intuition — or sees too much — overwhelmed by impressions and unable to ground them in reality.

RATIONALISM AND DISTRUST OF INTUITION

Children raised in environments that value logic over feeling often learn to distrust inner knowing.
Phrases like "That's just your imagination," "Don't be silly," or "Prove it" teach them that unseen realities are invalid.
Over time, this suppresses intuitive function, forcing awareness to narrow to only what can be measured.

As adults, these individuals may struggle to make decisions without external validation.
They may overanalyze, dismiss intuitive guidance, or feel disconnected from purpose.
The inner sight dims — not because it is gone, but because it has been taught to hide.

Healing begins with remembering that intuition is not irrational — it is *pre-rational*, the original intelligence of the soul.

RELIGIOUS DOGMA AND FEAR OF INNER VISION

In families or cultures where spiritual authority is externalized — where truth is dictated rather than discovered — children learn that personal insight is dangerous.
Visions, dreams, or intuitive perceptions may be labeled as fantasy, sin, or rebellion.
To belong, the child learns to close the inner eye.

As adults, this may manifest as spiritual confusion, guilt around intuition, or fear of psychic sensitivity.
They may seek truth through endless teachers, books, or doctrines, while mistrusting their own guidance.

Healing lies in reclaiming the sacred right to *direct communion with the divine.*
Ajna opens again when one dares to trust what is seen within — when personal revelation becomes as holy as scripture.

TRAUMA AND THE NEED TO DISCONNECT

When trauma occurs, especially in childhood, the psyche often withdraws from the present moment as a form of protection.
This dissociation — leaving the body to avoid pain — severs the natural bridge between perception and embodiment.
Energy rushes upward, activating the mind while numbing the senses.

The result is an overactive Third Eye and underactive lower chakras — heightened sensitivity without grounding, seeing everything yet feeling little stability.
Such individuals may develop strong intuitive abilities yet struggle with anxiety, insomnia, or emotional disconnection.

Healing requires reunion — drawing awareness back into the body through breath, movement, and safety.
Only when the heart and root are secure can the Third Eye perceive truth without distortion.

CRITICISM, HUMILIATION, AND INTELLECTUAL SHAMING

When a child's thoughts or insights are belittled — when curiosity is mocked or dismissed — they learn to mistrust their own mind.
Phrases like "You think too much," or "That's stupid" fracture confidence in one's perception.
Over time, Ajna closes to avoid judgment, dimming both creativity and intuition.

As adults, this may manifest as chronic self-doubt, difficulty making decisions, or oscillation between overthinking and indecision.
The mind becomes either defensive or submissive — a battlefield of conflicting thoughts.

Healing comes through self-validation — the quiet practice of listening to your thoughts with compassion, and allowing perception to exist without needing to prove its worth.

FAMILY SECRETS AND DISTORTED REALITY

When children grow up in households where truth is hidden — where denial, gaslighting, or secrecy prevail — the Third Eye becomes confused.
They sense that something is off, yet they are told that everything is fine.
This dissonance fractures perception, teaching them to mistrust their instincts.

As adults, they may question their own sanity when intuition warns them of subtle truths.
They may alternate between hypervigilance and self-doubt, never sure which perception to trust.

Healing Ajna requires restoring *inner authority.*
Through meditation, journaling, and energy clearing, one learns to discern the difference between projection and perception — between fear's illusion and intuition's truth.

OVERSTIMULATION AND INFORMATION EXCESS

In the modern age, Ajna's light flickers under a constant bombardment of screens, images, and opinions.
Our eyes absorb more stimuli in a day than ancient humans did in a year.

This overload dulls intuition and overstimulates the mental field, scattering focus and fragmenting awareness.

The nervous system fatigues under the weight of perpetual observation — leaving little space for true vision to arise. Clarity requires stillness, but our culture glorifies distraction.

Healing begins with sensory fasting: turning off devices, sitting in darkness, and letting the eyes rest.
True sight returns when the inner screen becomes more captivating than the outer one.

ANXIETY, CONTROL, AND THE NEED TO KNOW

For some, Ajna imbalance stems from fear of uncertainty.
The mind grasps for control through constant seeking — overstudying, overanalyzing, predicting outcomes before they unfold.
This excessive vigilance blocks intuitive flow; vision becomes rigid rather than receptive.

The healing practice is surrender.
Rather than trying to *see everything,* allow what needs to be known to reveal itself in time.
Wisdom is not the accumulation of knowledge — it is the stillness that allows truth to emerge.

THE LASTING IMPACT

Distortions in perception teach the psyche that truth is unsafe, that intuition is unreliable, and that clarity cannot be trusted without proof.
As adults, this manifests as a divided consciousness: the rational mind argues with the intuitive self, each trying to prove the other wrong.

Healing the Third Eye means remembering that both are sacred. Logic and intuition are not enemies — they are lenses through which the soul perceives wholeness.
Through meditation, mindful observation, and balance between knowing and feeling, we learn to trust vision again.

Each time we close our eyes and breathe into stillness, each time we notice without judgment, we polish the mirror of perception.
The Third Eye clears, the inner light brightens, and the world reveals itself not as a mystery to solve, but as truth to behold.

When we remember that perception is a sacred act of communion — not possession — Ajna awakens fully: clear, balanced, and luminous, the window through which consciousness sees itself.

INHERITED BLINDNESS AND FEAR OF SEEING

Ajna governs the right to perceive truth.

When ancestors lived in times where *seeing too much* was dangerous — when intuition, dreams, or spiritual sight were condemned as heresy, witchcraft, or madness — they learned to protect themselves by closing their inner vision.
Generations later, that fear becomes a veil over the Third Eye — a hesitancy to trust intuition, a fog of disbelief, or a deep unease with inner sight.

You may feel intuitive flashes, yet doubt them; you may sense truth, yet question your sanity.
This is not weakness — it is inherited memory whispering, *"It's safer not to see."*

Healing begins with remembrance: your inner sight is not rebellion; it is reclamation.
Each time you trust what you perceive with clarity and love,

you heal the unacknowledged wisdom of those who had to turn
away from their own light.

INHERITED DISTORTION OF PERCEPTION

In some lineages, survival depended on perceiving reality
through distortion — seeing what authority demanded rather
than what was true.
When it was dangerous to notice injustice, people learned
selective vision: to look away, to rationalize, to pretend.

Over generations, this pattern mutates into confusion —
descendants who sense truth but cannot name it, who doubt
their insight or accept illusions as fact.
They may feel disconnected from intuition or trapped between
skepticism and yearning for meaning.

Healing arises through discernment — learning to see clearly
without fear, to recognize illusion without judgment.
True vision does not divide; it integrates shadow and light into
wisdom.

FAMILY SECRETS AND DENIAL OF REALITY

When families carry generations of denial — addictions,
betrayals, or traumas hidden in silence — children learn not to
trust their perceptions.
They see one thing and are told another.
Over time, this trains the Third Eye to doubt itself, creating a
split between what is seen and what is believed.

As adults, these descendants often question their intuition,
second-guess their emotions, or fear their own insights.
The eyes of the soul grow weary from seeing truth that others
refuse to name.

Healing begins by allowing reality to be seen — gently, without blame or judgment.
Naming what was hidden restores coherence to the mind and clarity to Ajna's light.
In truth, *seeing is not betrayal — it is freedom.*

INHERITED MISTRUST OF SPIRITUALITY

For many, ancestral wounds stem from spiritual persecution — where mystics, visionaries, or healers were shamed, punished, or erased.
The soul learns to separate spirituality from daily life, to compartmentalize the sacred into secrecy.
Descendants of such lineages may feel drawn to intuitive or esoteric work yet fear going "too far" — as if awakening spiritual sight might awaken ancestral danger.

This fear is the echo of the survival instinct, not the truth.
Healing comes through gentle integration: blending reason with intuition, honoring the mystical without abandoning the grounded self.
As Ajna opens safely, spiritual perception no longer threatens — it illuminates.

CULTURAL AND RELIGIOUS CONTROL OF VISION

Throughout history, many cultures have equated obedience with faith and skepticism with sin.
To "see differently" was heresy; to question was rebellion.
This conditioning seeps through generations, teaching descendants to distrust personal revelation and rely on external authority for spiritual truth.

Over time, Ajna closes beneath layers of doctrine and fear, replacing inner knowing with outer conformity.

Healing begins with remembering that divine communion was never meant to be mediated.

You are not meant to borrow sight — you are meant to awaken your own.

When you reclaim your right to see through the eyes of spirit, you restore the lineage's connection to living truth.

ANCESTRAL TRAUMA AND THE VEIL OF FEAR

War, persecution, displacement, and loss often leave imprints on Ajna — not only as emotional memory but as energetic veils over perception.

When survival required numbness, the gift of vision became a burden.

The descendants of such trauma may inherit vigilance and anxiety — always "seeing what might go wrong," unable to relax into trust.

Healing requires safety — grounding the body so the inner eye can open without fear.

When the nervous system feels secure, intuition returns as calm awareness instead of warning.

The veil lifts, and the light of insight shines without threat.

THE LEGACY OF VISION AND IGNORANCE

Just as the Throat carries ancestral stories of truth and silence, the Third Eye carries ancestral stories of wisdom and blindness. Every generation either strengthens or suppresses the family's capacity to perceive.

If your ancestors were forbidden to see, your awakening becomes their redemption. If they misused their vision — twisting truth into control or illusion — your clarity becomes their healing. You are the bridge between what was hidden and what must now be revealed.

Every moment you choose to see with compassion instead of fear, to witness truth without judgment, you restore balance to your lineage's perception.

Your clear sight becomes the medicine that dissolves the ancient fog.

HEALING THROUGH INNER VISION

To heal ancestral patterns within the Third Eye Chakra:
• Meditate in stillness, allowing images, memories, or impressions to rise and pass without attachment.
• Ask your ancestors in prayer or journaling, "What truth were you not allowed to see?" and listen inwardly for insight.
• Practice candle-gazing or moon meditation to reopen the bridge between light and consciousness.
• Hold or wear indigo or amethyst stones to support clarity and trust in intuition.
• Affirm:
"I honor the wisdom my ancestors could not see. Through my clarity, their sight is restored."

THE DEEPER LESSON

Where the Root carries survival, and the Throat carries truth, the Third Eye carries *vision* — the lineage's relationship with awareness itself.

When ancestors feared their own insight, Ajna learned to dim its light.

When they trusted the unseen, it learned to shine.

By transforming inherited blindness into understanding, you become the seer of your bloodline — the luminous witness who restores coherence to the story of perception.

The Third Eye no longer carries the burden of illusion; it becomes the mirror of wisdom — the silent light through which your ancestors, and you, finally see clearly.

INHERITED BELIEFS ABOUT PERCEPTION AND TRUTH

Across many lineages, beliefs about perception are polarized — either *seeing beyond the visible* is exalted as divine insight or condemned as delusion.
Families who endured persecution, dogmatic religion, or rationalist ridicule may equate inner vision with danger or madness, while those who wielded authority may have used knowledge to control what others were allowed to see.
Both distort the Third Eye's natural harmony between *wisdom and wonder, insight and humility.*

If your lineage feared intuition, you may doubt your inner knowing or rationalize every spiritual experience.
If it glorified intellect and authority, you may rely on logic while distrusting mystery.
In both cases, Ajna becomes imbalanced — its light either dimmed by disbelief or scattered by over-analysis.

Healing begins with remembrance: true vision is not about power; it is about presence.
The Third Eye, in its essence, is not a spotlight or a shadow, but a mirror — a portal through which consciousness perceives truth without distortion.

INHERITED BLINDNESS AND THE FEAR OF SEEING TOO MUCH

Many families carry ancestral vows of blindness:
"It's better not to know," "Don't question," or "Just believe what you're told."
For generations, this kept peace and safety in rigid or fearful societies — but over time, it became spiritual amnesia.

Descendants may feel uneasy with intuition, preferring facts even when deeper truth calls.

You may sense insights rising, yet dismiss them before they reach awareness.
The energy of Ajna contracts — the inner light dimming beneath layers of skepticism and conditioning.

Healing this belief means remembering that *clarity does not threaten safety — it reveals it.*
Seeing truth clearly is not disobedience; it is devotion to the divine order that created vision itself.

INHERITED DEFERENCE TO AUTHORITY AND LOSS OF INNER GUIDANCE

In lineages where religion, government, or hierarchy defined truth, people learned to mistrust their own perception.
Obedience was survival; intuition was rebellion.
Children were taught to "believe what you're told" rather than "see for yourself."

This conditioning silences the voice of inner guidance.
As adults, descendants may defer to others for validation — priests, teachers, leaders, or even spiritual gurus — forgetting that divine wisdom speaks within.

Healing begins with reclaiming sovereignty of sight: honoring the wisdom of both tradition and intuition.
You can respect the guidance of others without surrendering your own insight.
Ajna's awakening restores that equilibrium — where discernment and faith walk hand in hand.

INHERITED ARROGANCE AND INTELLECTUAL SUPERIORITY

Some lineages pass down not blindness but over-certainty — the belief that intellect or social standing grants ultimate authority over truth.

In these families, knowledge becomes weaponized: used to control, debate, or dominate rather than illuminate.
Ajna's light, once pure, becomes rigid — a prism of arrogance that refracts truth into judgment.

Descendants may inherit a sharp intellect yet feel disconnected from empathy or imagination.
They may analyze endlessly but fail to see meaning.

Healing comes through humility — remembering that wisdom is not ownership of knowledge, but communion with it.
True vision expands through wonder, not certainty.
When the Third Eye humbles itself before mystery, understanding deepens into revelation.

INHERITED FEAR OF ILLUSION AND MISTRUST OF SPIRITUALITY

For ancestors who witnessed fanaticism, manipulation, or spiritual fraud, faith became dangerous and vision suspect.
They learned to close the inner eye to avoid being deceived again.
This vigilance is inherited as spiritual caution — skepticism that borders on denial, fear of intuition, or dismissal of mystical experience.

Healing arises through balance: grounding intuition in discernment.
The Third Eye must neither believe blindly nor reject entirely.
It learns to *see with both eyes open* — one attuned to the seen, the other to the unseen — both anchored in the heart's truth.

INHERITED BELIEF THAT IGNORANCE IS PROTECTION

In lineages marked by trauma, violence, or oppression, ignorance often became a shield.

Not seeing meant not suffering.
Families learned to turn away from pain, to avoid "knowing too much," to survive by looking only at what was safe.

Generations later, descendants carry this as avoidance of self-inquiry or discomfort with shadow work.
The mind unconsciously closes to deeper insight, fearing what might be revealed.

Healing begins with gentle courage — daring to see what once could not be faced.
Ajna's true vision is compassionate; it reveals only what you are ready to heal.
As clarity expands, ignorance dissolves into wisdom, and protection transforms into peace.

INHERITED LIMITATION AND DISTRUST OF IMAGINATION

Families that endured poverty, labor, or rigid practicality often suppressed imagination in favor of survival.
Dreamers were dismissed as foolish; intuition was seen as a distraction. Over time, this severed the connection between vision and creation — the ability to dream a new reality.

Descendants may feel uninspired, creatively blocked, or afraid to imagine something better.
This is not a lack of vision, but ancestral fatigue.

Healing comes through reclaiming imagination as sacred.
Visualization, dreamwork, and creative expression reawaken Ajna's luminous current — reminding you that imagination is not escape, but evolution.

THE DEEPER LESSON

Where the Root carries ancestral memories of survival and the Throat holds the lineage of expression, the Third Eye holds the legacy of perception — how truth was seen, denied, or distorted.
When past generations equated insight with danger, Ajna learned fear; when they equated knowledge with superiority, it learned imbalance.

Now, it is your turn to harmonize both — to see clearly yet humbly, to discern without judgment, and to trust that truth is a light meant to reveal, not to blind.

Your awakened vision becomes the bridge between worlds — turning ignorance into understanding, and illusion into illumination.

The Third Eye no longer carries the burden of confusion or control; it radiates the clarity of awakened sight — calm, compassionate, and infinite.

Environmental and Energetic Toxins: Distraction, Deception, and Collective Disconnection

The Third Eye Chakra (Ajna) is the energetic bridge between perception and understanding — the inner lens through which insight becomes vision and vision becomes wisdom.
While the Throat expresses truth and the Crown communes with Spirit, the Third Eye determines how truth is *seen* — whether perception remains clear or becomes distorted by illusion.

In a world flooded with artificial light, digital distraction, and manipulative imagery, Ajna is constantly overstimulated —

seeing everything yet perceiving little.
The nervous system, meant to process light and meaning,
becomes overloaded.
Clarity gives way to confusion; intuition fades beneath noise
disguised as information.

Where Vishuddha suffocates in dishonesty, Ajna drowns in
distortion — a collective fog where truth is filtered, edited, and
repackaged.
The mind, no longer a mirror of consciousness, becomes a
screen of projections.
And as the outer world grows louder, the inner world grows
dimmer.

Ajna's sacred current — *clarity* — becomes clouded in a
culture addicted to distraction and illusion.

THE REACTIVE NATURE OF AJNA

The element of Ajna is light — radiant, penetrating, and deeply
sensitive to energy.
It thrives in clarity, stillness, and integrity of thought, yet
weakens under manipulation, false imagery, and chaotic stimuli.

When surrounded by deception, constant motion, or emotional
turbulence, the Third Eye contracts.
It attempts to protect itself by dulling perception, leading to
brain fog, eye strain, headaches, or disorientation.
Or it overreacts — heightening sensitivity to psychic or sensory
overload, producing anxiety or insomnia.

Each lie perceived, each distortion witnessed, creates static in
the luminous field that longs for truth.
The body feels it — in the eyes, the temples, the pineal pulse.
Ajna whispers through the tension: *"See what is real. Release
what is false."*

EXPOSURE TO DIGITAL NOISE AND VISUAL POLLUTION

Today's world assaults Ajna with light — screens that never sleep, imagery engineered to evoke fear or desire.
Our gaze, once a sacred tool of awareness, is captured by endless scrolls of comparison, judgment, and illusion.
This constant visual stimulation fractures attention, dulling intuition and fragmenting the mind's quiet center.

In such environments, imagination withers and dreams grow faint.
We begin to confuse *seeing* with *understanding.*

Healing begins with conscious observation: stepping away from the artificial glare, resting the eyes in darkness or natural light, and reclaiming silence as the true canvas of vision.
True sight returns not when we look harder, but when we look less — and perceive more.

COLLECTIVE DECEPTION AND INFORMATION OVERLOAD

The Third Eye is not only personal; it is collective — humanity's shared field of perception.
In times of misinformation, propaganda, or intellectual corruption, this chakra absorbs the psychic tension of confusion.
We feel it as mistrust, cynicism, or detachment from our own inner knowing.

When truth is obscured by manipulation, individuals lose faith in their intuition.
The result is mass disorientation — a society that doubts both the media and the mirror.

Healing Ajna in such times requires luminous discernment — the ability to sense the vibration beneath the words, the energy

behind the image.
Truth, even when confronting, feels clear; illusion feels heavy
and confusing.
Your body knows the difference.

PSYCHIC POLLUTION AND THOUGHTFORM RESIDUE

Because Ajna governs perception and mental imagery, it is
especially vulnerable to environments thick with fear, gossip,
criticism, or judgment.
Thoughts are energy, and every mental projection leaves residue
in the collective field.
Absorbing these energies can blur personal clarity, leading to
intrusive thoughts or mental exhaustion.

You may notice fatigue after social media exposure or crowded
interactions — symptoms not of weakness, but of empathic
overload.
The mind becomes a sponge for others' perceptions, distorting
your own.

Energetic hygiene for Ajna includes cleansing through
meditation, visualization, and intentional focus.
Close your eyes, breathe deeply, and imagine indigo light
spiraling through your forehead, dissolving confusion into
clarity.
Protect your mental space as sacred ground.

EMOTIONAL CHAOS AND THE LOSS OF INNER STILLNESS

When emotion dominates perception, Ajna loses neutrality.
Anger, fear, or grief can color how we see reality — distorting
judgment and dimming insight.
Modern culture, driven by outrage and reaction, keeps humanity
trapped in perpetual reactivity.

The Third Eye cannot open amid turbulence; it requires quiet.
Healing begins by restoring emotional equilibrium —
grounding, breathing, and returning awareness to the present.
Clarity arises not from escaping emotion but from witnessing it
without attachment.

THE WEIGHT OF COLLECTIVE DESENSITIZATION

The more humanity disconnects from intuition, the more Ajna
closes across the collective grid.
When spiritual insight is dismissed as "unscientific" and
imagination as "childish," societies lose their visionary
capacity.
This spiritual blindness breeds apathy — a subtle numbness
toward truth, beauty, and wonder.

Yet even in the densest fog, the Third Eye of humanity never
fully closes.
It waits for each awakened individual to reopen the light — one
clear perception at a time.
Every act of mindfulness, every moment of authentic seeing,
clears the collective lens.

HEALING THROUGH LIGHT AND STILLNESS

The antidote to Ajna's energetic pollution is purification
through light, darkness, and sacred observation.
• Limit visual and informational overload — schedule daily
breaks from screens and stimuli.
• Begin and end each day in darkness or candlelight, allowing
the pineal gland to restore rhythm.
• Practice "silent seeing" — observe without labeling, simply
witness what is.
• Use indigo light visualization or the mantra *OM* to cleanse
mental fog and awaken insight.
• Meditate with eyes closed and focus softly between the brows,
inviting calm illumination.

• Keep a dream journal — your subconscious is Ajna's night voice, guiding you back to clarity.

THE DEEPER LESSON

Ajna teaches that perception without awareness becomes illusion, and awareness without perception becomes blindness. The goal is not to shut out the world, but to see through it — beyond distortion, beyond deception, into essence.

To witness without judgment, to discern without fear, to perceive without projection — this is the mastery of the Third Eye.
When the mind aligns with truth and light, it becomes vision.
When stillness holds awareness, it becomes revelation.

In a world addicted to distraction, Ajna calls us not to see more, but to see *truly* — to become instruments of clarity in a collective field still learning to open its eyes.

Distortion, Gaslighting, and the Violation of Sight

The Third Eye Chakra (Ajna) is the seat of perception — the sacred bridge between knowledge and wisdom, intuition and understanding.
It governs the right to see clearly, to trust one's insight, and to discern truth from illusion.
When that right is violated — through manipulation, deception, or denial of reality — the light of Ajna dims.
Its natural radiance of clarity becomes clouded by doubt, confusion, and mistrust in one's own perception.

Just as the Throat governs the sacred resonance of voice, the Third Eye governs the sacred illumination of sight.

When this light is obscured through distortion or deceit, the individual begins to question their very sense of reality.
It is a wound not only of vision but of consciousness — the distortion of one's inner clarity.

ENERGETIC IMPACT OF PERCEPTUAL VIOLATION

When perception is manipulated — through gaslighting, misinformation, or psychological control — Ajna absorbs the distortion directly.
The mind tightens, the nervous system becomes hypervigilant, and intuition retreats as a defense.

People who have endured such manipulation often describe fogginess, dizziness, migraines, or a sense that "nothing makes sense anymore."
Energetically, the aura around Ajna may appear fractured or flickering — as though the current of awareness has been disrupted.
This trauma leaves the spirit asking:
"Can I trust what I see?"
"Is my intuition real?"
"How do I know what's true?"

Some retreat into denial, choosing numbness over clarity.
Others swing toward obsession, compulsively seeking answers or proof.
Both are reactions to the same wound — the loss of trust in one's own perception.

THE LEGACY OF GASLIGHTING AND MENTAL MANIPULATION

Few violations cut deeper than the distortion of truth itself.
When the mind's reality is invalidated — when intuition is dismissed as "crazy" or inner knowing mocked as "overreacting" — the Third Eye learns to mistrust its light.

Gaslighting fractures the bridge between intuition and intellect, leaving a painful gap where confidence once lived.

The person begins to second-guess every feeling, every insight, every observation.
They may overanalyze endlessly, searching for validation outside themselves.
Culturally, this manipulation exists on a grand scale — where media, authority, or ideology shapes perception until individuals forget how to see for themselves.

But Ajna's power is not conformity — it is clarity: the alignment of mind and soul.
When your inner vision aligns with truth, the Third Eye becomes a beacon, not a battleground.

THE WOUND OF DISBELIEF AND INVISIBLE TRUTH

There is a unique pain in seeing what others refuse to acknowledge.
Visionaries, intuitives, and sensitives often experience disbelief from those who cannot perceive what they see.
To witness truth that others deny is to walk between worlds — one visible, one unseen.

Over time, this disbelief teaches the psyche to hide its insights, fearing ridicule or alienation.
Ajna closes slightly each time intuition is dismissed, not out of weakness, but out of protection.

Healing begins by affirming that *your perception is valid*, even if it does not match consensus.
You do not need others to believe in your vision for it to be true. Each act of trusting your insight restores the bond between awareness and confidence — the sacred equilibrium of seeing and knowing.

THE COST OF MANIPULATIVE NARRATIVES

When perception is shaped to control rather than enlighten,
Ajna suffers deeply.
Deception, propaganda, or emotional manipulation creates
cognitive dissonance — the disquieting tension between what is
seen and what is *meant* to be believed.
Over time, this erodes discernment and exhausts intuition.

Children raised in such environments may grow into adults who
mistrust their judgment or seek constant reassurance.
They may absorb others' opinions as truth, fearing that their
own vision will lead to rejection.

Yet Ajna's purpose is *illumination, not validation.*
To reclaim clear sight, one must be willing to look again —
without filters, without fear.
Truth does not require permission; it only requires light.

THE SACRED RESTORATION OF INNER VISION

Healing Ajna after mental or perceptual manipulation involves
teaching the psyche that seeing clearly is safe again.

• Begin with stillness — close the eyes and focus gently
between the brows, breathing light into the space of knowing.
• Keep a journal of intuitive impressions, dreams, and
realizations — record them before external opinions interfere.
• Practice "discernment meditations" — observe a thought or
image and ask, *"Is this mine? Is it true? Does it bring peace?"*
• Surround yourself with people and spaces that honor intuition
rather than dismiss it.
• Affirm: *"My perception is clear. My mind and soul see truth
as one."*

Each time you honor your intuition, you repair the energetic
bridge between awareness and wisdom.

As Ajna clears, the fog lifts — not because the world changes, but because you remember how to see it clearly.

EMOTIONAL AND PSYCHOLOGICAL VIOLATION

Not all wounds of Ajna are mental; many are emotional.
Subtle gaslighting, spiritual invalidation, or coercive relationships can fragment the inner lens of trust.
When intuition is constantly dismissed or mocked, the psyche learns to equate insight with danger.

This violation teaches the mind to suppress inner visions, to fear intuitive flashes, to hide wisdom behind logic.
It manifests as overthinking, chronic doubt, or fear of imagination. Over time, Ajna forgets how to dream without fear of being wrong.

Healing begins with permission — the right to *see again.*
To believe your intuition. To acknowledge what feels true without needing to prove it.

At first, the insight trembles — tentative, delicate — but it trembles with awakening, not uncertainty.

PHYSICAL MANIFESTATIONS

Because Ajna governs the eyes, brain, and endocrine system (especially the pineal gland), emotional distortion often reveals itself physically.
Symptoms may include eye strain, headaches, insomnia, or sensitivity to light.
These are not just physical ailments — they are the body's plea for clarity.

When awareness is blocked, energy pools in the head, producing pressure or fog. When perception is clear, that same energy flows like light through a crystal — effortless, illuminating, pure.

Simple practices such as mindful screen breaks, candle gazing, or visualization can ease this congestion.
Breathe indigo light into the forehead, exhale confusion.
Each breath reopens the inner eye, restoring balance to both mind and spirit.

THE DEEPER LESSON

Where the Throat teaches sovereignty through truth, the Third Eye teaches sovereignty through awareness. The violation of perception is the attempt to rewrite reality itself — yet truth cannot be destroyed, only forgotten.

Every denied intuition waits patiently for rediscovery.
Healing does not mean forcing belief; it means reclaiming trust — in yourself, in your inner sight, and in the quiet intelligence of Spirit.

When your perception aligns with love and integrity, your vision becomes medicine.
Ajna's alchemy is this: to turn confusion into clarity, illusion into insight, and the wounded mind into the luminous eye of truth.

Pathways To Healing The Third Eye Chakra

Healing Ajna after experiences of deception, confusion, or inner disconnection is the sacred act of reclaiming your vision — the ability to *see truth with clarity, intuition, and peace.*
It is not about seeing more or knowing everything; it is about remembering that your inner sight is divine — a reflection of

wisdom itself.

The process unfolds quietly, as awareness replaces illusion, and light restores harmony between perception and understanding. Each moment of insight becomes a beam of healing — turning darkness into illumination.

KEY APPROACHES INCLUDE:

• Cultivate Inner Stillness:
Healing begins in silence, not analysis.
The Third Eye thrives in calm awareness — moments free of noise, distraction, and judgment.
Meditate daily with eyes closed, focusing gently between the brows, allowing thoughts to settle like dust in clear water.

• Cleanse the Mind with Breath:
Breathe into the space behind the forehead, exhaling confusion and tension.
The breath becomes light — purifying the mind's atmosphere and restoring rhythm to perception.
Each slow, conscious breath clears fog and awakens intuitive clarity.

• Light as Medicine:
Visualize indigo or violet light radiating through your Third Eye.
Allow it to dissolve worry, fear, and false beliefs.
You may also gaze softly at a candle flame or the night sky — natural mirrors of Ajna's luminous intelligence.

• Trust Your Inner Vision:
Rebuild confidence in your perception.
Notice intuitive impressions without dismissing them.
Ask, "What feels true?" and honor the answer that arises from stillness, not fear.
Each time you trust your insight, the veil between intuition and intellect thins.

• Discernment Over Judgment:
Ajna does not demand belief in all things — it seeks clarity through balance.
Observe what you perceive without reaction; let awareness expand before forming conclusions.
Wisdom grows not from control, but from contemplation.

• Detox from Mental Overload:
Limit exposure to overstimulation — social media, news, or conversations that breed confusion.
Create daily intervals of digital silence.
The mind, like the body, needs fasting from chaos to remember its natural purity.

• Anchor Intuition in the Body:
Integrate insights through grounding practices: journaling, nature walks, or creative expression.
Vision without embodiment becomes fantasy; vision grounded in presence becomes revelation.

• Supportive Guidance:
Seek mentors, meditation teachers, or intuitive coaches who value discernment over dogma.
Healing Ajna flourishes in spaces where curiosity and clarity coexist.

• Affirmations of Vision:
    "My inner sight is clear and calm."
    "I trust the wisdom that flows through me."
    "I see truth with love, and my perception serves peace."

THE DEEPER LESSON

Violations of Ajna — through deceit, confusion, or manipulation — reveal how profoundly humanity fears awareness.
Yet within this fear lies the awakening: *to see clearly is not to control, but to understand.*

Ajna's gift is illumination — the power to turn illusion into insight, blindness into vision, and fear into discernment.
Every time you trust your inner knowing, you purify perception across lifetimes.

To reclaim your vision after darkness is not rebellion — it is remembrance.
It is to declare:

I am not blind to truth.
I am not lost in confusion.
My mind is light,
and I see with peace.

Chapter 6 – Signs of Balance

Clarity, Intuition, and Inner Vision

When the Third Eye Chakra (Ajna) is balanced, perception becomes luminous.
You see through appearances into essence — beyond what is shown, into what *is*.
There is ease between thought and intuition, logic and insight.
You no longer chase answers; understanding arises naturally, as if truth reveals itself in stillness.

Your mind is clear yet spacious, analytical yet receptive.
You perceive the interconnectedness of all things without losing focus on the present moment.
A balanced Ajna does not distort reality — it refines it, illuminating both the seen and the unseen.
This is the state of *clear sight:* wisdom without judgment, awareness without effort.

Like a moon reflected in calm water, your perception becomes tranquil and radiant — bright enough to see clearly, gentle enough to preserve peace.

INNER KNOWING AND MENTAL CLARITY

A harmonious Third Eye brings coherence between intellect and intuition.
The mind becomes a transparent vessel through which insight flows.

Thoughts are organized, perception is sharp, and decisions arise from quiet confidence rather than confusion or fear.

You trust your instincts without abandoning logic.
The two operate as partners — intuition guiding direction, intellect shaping expression.
Mental fog and overthinking dissolve; awareness expands beyond duality.
You begin to perceive patterns, synchronicities, and deeper meanings in ordinary experiences.

In this state, clarity feels effortless — not something to be achieved, but remembered.

INTUITIVE PERCEPTION AND HIGHER INSIGHT

When Ajna is open and balanced, intuition becomes your natural intelligence.
You sense alignment before evidence appears.
You know when to act and when to wait, when to speak and when to listen.

This is not imagination or fantasy — it is refined perception, attuned to truth.
Dreams grow vivid and symbolic, meditation deepens, and the boundaries between conscious and subconscious soften.
You feel guided from within — by an inner light that sees beyond time and circumstance.

Visionary ideas, creative inspiration, and spiritual understanding flow freely.
You trust that what arrives through intuition is sacred communication between your soul and Source.

HARMONY BETWEEN SEEING AND BELIEVING

Balanced Ajna unites belief with observation — perception
becomes holistic.
You no longer divide the world into what is "spiritual" and
what is "real."
Both are seen as expressions of one consciousness.

The mind no longer clings to absolutes; instead, it dances with
possibility.
You hold truth lightly yet firmly, allowing new insight to
evolve your understanding.
Dogma gives way to discernment.
Faith and reason coexist in graceful conversation.

This inner harmony brings serenity — the peace of knowing
that clarity does not demand control, only awareness.

INTEGRITY OF PERCEPTION

When Ajna is balanced, your inner vision aligns with integrity.
You see things as they are — not through projection or fear, but
through compassion and honesty.
You neither idealize nor condemn; you perceive with neutrality
and love.

Self-deception fades because truth feels safe again.
Your insight serves healing, not superiority.
Each perception becomes an act of service — a way of seeing
the world through the eyes of the soul rather than the ego.

In this state, wisdom replaces reaction.
You no longer interpret life from pain or illusion, but from
purpose and presence.

MINDFUL AWARENESS AND INNER STILLNESS

Ajna's balance reveals itself not only in insight, but in serenity.
Your thoughts move slowly enough for awareness to rest
between them.
The inner dialogue quiets; silence becomes your ally, not your
emptiness.

Meditation deepens naturally, and awareness of subtle energies
expands.
You can observe emotion without being consumed by it,
witness thought without identifying with it.
This stillness births profound clarity — the understanding that
every moment is both teacher and mirror.

PHYSICAL AND ENERGETIC HARMONY

Because Ajna governs the brain, eyes, and endocrine rhythm,
balance often manifests as physical vitality.
Your sleep is restorative, your eyes feel relaxed, and your body
attunes easily to cycles of day and night.
The nervous system steadies; overstimulation subsides.
Energy flows upward with ease from the throat to the crown,
linking communication with illumination.

You may notice increased synchronicity, sharper intuition, and
spontaneous moments of deep knowing.
The aura around the head feels luminous — soft indigo light
radiating peace and awareness.

This is the embodiment of *seeing truly:* vision anchored in
wisdom, perception guided by love, and mind resting as the
silent witness of all that is.

The Feeling Of Clear Sight

When the Third Eye Chakra is balanced, there is no inner conflict between intuition and intellect.
Perception moves freely through you — calm yet luminous, like light reflecting on still water.
You no longer second-guess your insight or overthink what you know. Understanding becomes communion — the meeting of mind and spirit through the language of awareness.

You perceive life as a harmony of meaning, not a sequence of separate events. Your thoughts arise from clarity, and your intuition flows without resistance. To live with a balanced Ajna Chakra is to embody vision, wisdom, and inner peace. You become a vessel of insight — a mind illuminated by truth, seeing through illusion and perceiving with love.

MENTAL VITALITY: AWARENESS, PERCEPTION, AND THE ELEMENT OF LIGHT

The Third Eye Chakra (Ajna) governs perception, intuition, and inner sight — the bridge between reason and revelation.
Where the Throat expands with ether, Ajna radiates with light — the subtlest element of illumination and knowing.
It is the seat of imagination, insight, and understanding — the field where thought becomes vision and awareness becomes revelation.

When this center is balanced, perception feels crystalline and calm.
The mind becomes a clear lens through which truth shines unfiltered.
You think with clarity, see with discernment, and interpret with compassion.
Life feels both mysterious and meaningful — an unfolding pattern guided by wisdom.

To live through Ajna's balance is to move with quiet confidence, perceiving not only what appears, but what *is*. Every moment becomes a reflection — every insight, a light upon the path.

THE NERVOUS SYSTEM: THE NETWORK OF LIGHT AND CONSCIOUSNESS

Ajna's physical domain includes the brain, pineal gland, and nervous system — the body's instruments of awareness.
These structures translate vibration into thought, perception into understanding.
The nervous system acts as a vast web of light, carrying impressions between body and consciousness.

When Ajna is balanced, thought and intuition cooperate.
Neural rhythm mirrors inner peace; perception becomes steady and lucid.
You process life without overload — receptive yet centered.

When overstimulated, however, Ajna becomes congested: the mind races, the eyes strain, and intuition becomes tangled in analysis.
Meditation, deep breathing, and conscious relaxation restore harmony, allowing perception to brighten again.
As the nervous system quiets, the mind reawakens as an instrument of divine clarity.

THE PINEAL AND PITUITARY GLANDS: THE REGULATORS OF LIGHT

The pineal and pituitary glands form the sacred axis of Ajna — the endocrine gateways of higher awareness.
The pineal, often called the *seat of the soul,* senses the rhythms of light and darkness, guiding circadian balance and spiritual attunement.

The pituitary, the master gland, harmonizes the body's inner chemistry — mirroring the harmony of perception and intuition.

When these glands are balanced, the body and spirit operate in unity.
You sleep deeply, dream vividly, and wake with purpose.
Hormonal cycles align with natural light; the mind feels bright yet tranquil.

Energetically, this equilibrium creates the "light body" effect — awareness that glows from within.
When imbalance occurs, confusion or insomnia may arise, signaling the need for recalibration through rest, meditation, and darkness balanced by dawn.
Ajna reminds us that light is not only external — it lives within, illuminating perception itself.

THE EYES AND FOREHEAD: THE WINDOWS OF AWARENESS

The eyes are the physical mirrors of Ajna's function.
When this center is clear, the gaze is steady, gentle, and radiant — seeing both outer form and inner essence.
Eye strain, headaches, or sensitivity to light often reveal overstimulation or unintegrated insight.

Gentle eye exercises, candle gazing (*Trāṭaka*), or resting the eyes on the horizon help recalibrate focus and soften perception.
Behind every blink, awareness expands — the world seen not as chaos, but as energy in motion.

The forehead, often tingling or warm during meditation, becomes a luminous gateway — a reminder that seeing truly is both physical and spiritual.

THE ELEMENT OF LIGHT: THE FIELD OF ILLUMINATION

Light (*Jyoti*) is Ajna's governing element — radiant, subtle, and all-revealing.
It is the essence of consciousness itself: that which perceives and that which is perceived.
Where ether carries sound, light carries awareness — showing that truth is not something we speak alone, but something we *see.*

When you are attuned to this element, life feels illuminated from within.
Shadows no longer frighten; they are seen as gradients of wisdom.
You perceive without judgment, allowing light to reveal rather than to blind.

In this awareness, seeing becomes sacred.
Each moment shines as revelation — not because it is perfect, but because you *perceive it consciously.*

To live through the vitality of the Third Eye is to honor perception as prayer, awareness as devotion, and intuition as divine sight.

Ajna teaches:
Truth is not a thought to defend — it is a light to remember.
When the inner eye is clear, life itself becomes the mirror of the soul.

The Feeling Of Luminous Stillness

A balanced Third Eye Chakra brings a sense of radiant peace — not through effort, but through awareness.
You feel attuned to truth without needing to search for it.

The mind quiets, the breath slows, and perception opens like dawn unfolding over still water.
Insight flows naturally, carrying understanding through the entire being like waves of light.

Thought and intuition begin to work together; perception becomes effortless and clear.
Each image, idea, or realization carries meaning without confusion — every moment shines with presence.
You feel connected to life through both inner vision and outer awareness — guided not by reaction, but by revelation.

Energy rises smoothly from the Throat to the Crown, harmonizing expression, perception, and wisdom.
To live with a balanced Ajna is to become the light itself — a clear lens through which consciousness observes creation, where thought becomes vision and vision becomes knowing.

SPIRITUAL QUALITIES: WISDOM, INTUITION, AND DIVINE INSIGHT

When Ajna is balanced, spirituality becomes the art of perception in alignment with truth.
It is the realization that divine wisdom is seen through the human mind — that every thought, dream, and silence can carry the vibration of higher understanding. The Third Eye reveals that spiritual power is not in seeing visions, but in *seeing truth clearly,* without distortion or pride. It teaches that enlightenment is not the pursuit of more light, but the recognition that light was always within you.

WISDOM AS DIVINE PERCEPTION

Ajna transforms experience into understanding — it is where awareness becomes revelation.
When balanced, this chakra turns sight into insight, allowing spirit to move through intuition and vision.

Perception becomes meditation; understanding becomes prayer. You begin to realize that what you perceive, you create — that awareness itself shapes reality.

When perception flows from divine consciousness, wisdom ceases to be intellectual.
It becomes direct knowing — a truth so clear it requires no explanation.
In that state, you no longer seek signs or proofs; you simply *see*.
Your vision is not imagination — it is remembrance.

INTUITION AS SACRED KNOWING

At the level of Ajna, intuition is lived as trust — the unwavering faith in your inner light.
It is not guesswork or fantasy, but a quiet certainty that arises from deep alignment.

When Ajna is balanced, you see beyond appearances into essence.
Judgment dissolves; compassion sharpens your clarity.
You no longer confuse intellect with insight — your knowing becomes both rational and radiant.

Intuition here is the soul's whisper — soft, simple, and always true. It speaks in symbols, sensations, and subtle guidance, teaching that the divine is not distant, but present in every perception.

DIVINE VISION AS SPIRITUAL SERVICE

The Third Eye is where personal awareness merges with universal consciousness — where your unique perception becomes an instrument of divine wisdom.
When Ajna is open, teaching, healing, creativity, and vision flow effortlessly — not as egoic superiority, but as sacred seeing.

You recognize that your insight, your clarity, your understanding are not yours alone — they are channels through which Spirit reveals truth to the world.
Every meditation, dream, or moment of intuition becomes a bridge between heaven and mind.

In this way, perception itself becomes devotion.
Your life becomes prayerful awareness — each thought, image, and action radiating the frequency of illumination.

THE LIGHT OF TRANSCENDENCE

Spiritually, Ajna represents the purification of vision — the moment perception turns inward and becomes revelation.
It is the luminous temple where sight dissolves into seeing, and seeing becomes consciousness itself.

Here, awareness transcends form.
You no longer look for meaning; you *become* meaning.
Thought dissolves into insight, and the mind becomes transparent to Spirit.

The seer and the seen merge. Understanding arises not from logic but from unity — the realization that all perception is divine perception.

COMMUNION WITH DIVINE INTELLIGENCE

The highest expression of Ajna is surrender — not to blindness, but to perfect vision. It is the moment when the personal mind yields to the cosmic mind, when seeing no longer belongs to "me," but flows as the gaze of Spirit itself.

You do not force awareness — you allow it.
Insight arises from silence, guided by clarity rather than control.
Observation and participation become one act — a sacred exchange between soul and Source.

In this communion, every thought becomes light, and every perception becomes understanding.
You no longer seek to "figure out" life; you allow life to reveal itself through you.

This is the spiritual radiance of the Third Eye Chakra: to perceive with purity, to discern with love, and to live as consciousness itself — not as separate from the Divine, but as its living awareness.

The Experience of a Balanced Third Eye Chakra

When the Third Eye Chakra (Ajna) is in harmony, life feels illuminated, meaningful, and deeply interconnected.
You move through the world with quiet confidence — guided by intuition, grounded in discernment, and attuned to the light of truth that lives within all things.
Energy rises effortlessly to the mind's inner sanctum; thoughts and insight flow from awareness rather than assumption.
You see clearly without judgment, and you understand without needing to control.
Your perception becomes luminous — not through effort, but through surrender to clarity itself.
You become a clear mirror through which the wisdom of the soul reflects.

PHYSICAL EXPERIENCE

Physically, a balanced Ajna brings relaxation and lightness to the eyes, forehead, and mind.
The gaze softens, yet perception sharpens — colors seem richer, and the world feels alive with subtle light.
Headaches, tension, and strain dissolve as thought aligns with flow rather than force.
Sleep becomes restorative, dreams symbolic and insightful.

The nervous system feels calm and alert, harmonized by a steady rhythm and deep awareness. You feel centered between the seen and unseen — at once grounded in the body and open to the infinite field of consciousness.

EMOTIONAL EXPERIENCE

Emotionally, a balanced Third Eye awakens serenity and trust. You no longer react impulsively to every wave of feeling — you observe emotions as passing weather, each carrying a message but not defining you.
This inner stability creates emotional intelligence — compassion rooted in clarity.
You respond rather than react, listen rather than assume, and forgive rather than dwell.
Intuition becomes a friend rather than a mystery; faith replaces fear.
You begin to trust the unfolding of life, knowing that what you perceive is part of a greater design guided by divine order.

MENTAL EXPERIENCE

The mind of a balanced Ajna Chakra is lucid, intuitive, and visionary.
Thoughts are clear, insight arrives effortlessly, and imagination becomes a channel for higher understanding.
You think symbolically — recognizing meaning beneath appearance, pattern within chaos.
Mental clarity replaces confusion, and discernment sharpens the edges of wisdom.
The inner dialogue becomes peaceful, free from self-doubt or distortion.
You no longer seek validation from the outer world; truth verified by inner knowing is enough.
Creativity flourishes, and your vision expands beyond the limits of logic — revealing reality as an expression of consciousness itself.

SPIRITUAL EXPERIENCE

Spiritually, Ajna awakens the awareness that perception is divine communion.
You no longer "see" with your eyes alone — you perceive with your whole being.
Vision becomes insight, and insight becomes illumination.
Meditation deepens into revelation; silence becomes radiant presence.
You feel the subtle pulse of the universe within you — the same intelligence that shapes stars and souls alike.
You experience reality not as separation, but as a symphony — each moment a vibration within the infinite mind of God.
The Third Eye opens the doorway to direct knowing, where wisdom no longer requires words.

OVERALL EXPERIENCE

To live with a balanced Third Eye Chakra is to live in luminous awareness.
You feel calm yet alert, wise yet humble, intuitive yet grounded.
Your perception carries truth, your vision radiates compassion, and your thoughts shine with coherence.
You no longer fear the unknown, for you have seen the light within it.
In this state, Ajna's indigo glow expands like twilight — soft yet boundless, radiant yet serene — illuminating every layer of being with clarity, insight, and divine remembrance.

The Connection: From the Temple of Light to the Crown of Unity

1. THE TEMPLE OF LIGHT: AIR · ETHER · LIGHT

As energy rises through the Heart, Throat, and Third Eye, the elements themselves become more refined — transforming from tangible matter to pure vibration.

• Air (Heart) breathes life into love.
• Ether (Throat) carries that love as sound — the vibration of truth.
• Light (Third Eye) reveals that truth as vision — perception awakened by consciousness.

This triad forms the *Temple of Light* — the sanctum where the human soul begins to see through the eyes of Spirit.
Where the Throat speaks truth, the Third Eye perceives it.
Here, love becomes wisdom, and wisdom becomes illumination.

2. AJNA: THE ELEMENT OF LIGHT — THE INNER SUN

After the expansiveness of Ether in Vishuddha, the energy of Ajna crystallizes into Light — the subtlest vibration before consciousness itself.
It is the dawning of inner sight, the illumination that guides awakening.

Where the lower chakras build and the heart unites, Ajna reveals.
It is the mind made luminous, the seer within the seen.
Light does not create; it clarifies.
It reveals the truth that has always been present, veiled only by perception.

Ajna refines energy into awareness — transforming experience into understanding, and understanding into wisdom.
This is the moment consciousness recognizes itself as both observer and creation.

3. THE EVOLUTION OF THE INNER LIGHT

Each chakra teaches the refinement of consciousness:

1. Root — Be grounded in existence.
2. Sacral — Feel deeply and flow.
3. Solar Plexus — Act with intention.
4. Heart — Love without condition.
5. Throat — Speak truth with clarity.
6. Third Eye — See through illusion into essence.
7. Crown — Transcend into unity.

The Third Eye is the lamp between the voice and the Divine — the translator between expression and enlightenment, between vibration and vision, between human understanding and divine knowing. It is the mirror where consciousness meets itself, where light remembers its Source.

4. THE SPIRITUAL ARCHITECTURE OF YOUR SERIES

Chakra	Element	Function	Triad	Theme
Root	Earth	Stability	Body Trinity	Foundation of Life
Sacral	Water	Flow & Creation	Body Trinity	Emotional Fluidity
Solar Plexus	Fire	Will & Transformation	Body Trinity	Empowered Action

Chakra	Element	Function	Triad	Theme
Heart	Air	Love & Integration	Temple of Light	Bridge Between Worlds
Throat	Ether	Truth & Expression	Temple of Light	Divine Communication
Third Eye	Light	Vision & Perception	Temple of Light	Insight & Intuition
Crown	Consciousness	Unity	Final Illumination	Divine Connection

5. THE SPIRITUAL ASCENT

The Third Eye represents the awakening of perception from duality to unity.
It bridges the voice of the soul (Throat) with the silence of the Infinite (Crown).
Through Ajna, awareness begins to transcend separation — understanding that truth, love, and creation are not forces apart, but facets of the same divine radiance.

To open Ajna is to awaken the inner light that has never dimmed — to remember that you are both the dreamer and the dream, the observer and the observed, the light that sees and the light that is seen.

In this awareness, the journey turns upward once more — from *illumination* to *union,* from the eye that perceives to the crown that becomes.

Chapter 7 – Hidden Secrets & Esoteric Wisdom

Tantra And The Third Eye Chakra

In Tantric philosophy, Ajna — the Third Eye Chakra — is the lotus of illumination, the command center where perception becomes wisdom, light becomes consciousness, and the duality of seer and seen dissolves into one radiant awareness.

If the Throat gives sound to truth, then the Third Eye gives sight to truth — translating vibration into vision and perception into knowing. Here, Kundalini Shakti ascends from the luminous ether of Vishuddha and enters the field of Light (*Jyoti*), the subtle element of perception. Her radiance, once vibrating as sound, now crystallizes as illumination. Energy becomes awareness; vibration becomes vision. This is the moment when consciousness begins to see itself — when divine knowing awakens through the eye of the soul.

Ajna is the temple of inner revelation — the bridge between mind and spirit, thought and intuition, time and eternity.

It is here that the inner sun rises, dissolving ignorance into insight and confusion into clarity.

Through this sacred center, awareness perceives creation not as illusion, but as luminous truth — the Divine recognizing itself in form.

KUNDALINI'S ASCENT THROUGH LIGHT

When Kundalini reaches the Third Eye, she becomes radiance
— *Tejas*, the inner light that reveals without words.
No longer the sound of vibration (*Nada*), she is now the flame
of awareness — still, brilliant, and all-seeing.
Here, the initiate no longer hears divine truth; they *see* it.
Perception expands beyond the limits of form, and vision turns
inward toward the infinite.

Tantric texts describe Ajna as the two-petaled lotus — one petal
white, one indigo — symbolizing the union of duality: sun and
moon, logic and intuition, masculine and feminine, mind and
spirit.
Between these two petals shines the radiant point of light —
Bindu, the spark of consciousness from which all perception
arises.
It is said that when Kundalini rests within this center, the seeker
perceives both the world and the divine simultaneously,
understanding that there was never a separation.

This marks the fourth transformation on the Tantric path: from
expression to illumination, from voice to vision, from speaking
truth to *seeing* truth. The light that once moved outward as
sound now turns inward as knowing — revealing that all
creation is the play of awareness gazing upon itself.

THE LIGHT OF DIVINE PERCEPTION

In Tantric alchemy, light (*Jyoti*) is the subtle element of Ajna —
the eternal radiance that both reveals and creates.
It is not the light that shines upon things, but the light *through*
which things are known. It is the luminous consciousness that
pervades all forms, the silent witness within every perception.

When the Third Eye awakens, you begin to perceive the world
not through sensory data alone, but through vibration, intuition,

and recognition. The veil between the visible and invisible thins. Dreams become messages; symbols become language; synchronicities become conversation with the divine.

Through this awakened sight, all experiences become revelations — mirrors of consciousness reflecting consciousness.
You begin to understand that clarity is not seeing *more*, but seeing *through*.
The wise practitioner learns that mastery of vision begins not with effort, but with surrender — to light, to silence, to the divine gaze within.

THE MIND AS A SACRED LENS

Through Tantric practice, the Third Eye becomes the purified lens of the soul.
Meditation, mantra, and inner visualization refine thought until it becomes light.
The mind transforms from a restless observer into a sacred mirror — still, reflective, and radiant.

When purified by awareness, thought no longer binds; it liberates.
The intellect becomes intuition's servant, and perception becomes an offering to the divine.
This is the secret of Tantric seeing: when the mind becomes transparent, Spirit looks through it.

The initiate no longer seeks to *understand* truth; they *embody* it.
They no longer analyze light; they *are* the light.
Every vision, dream, and insight becomes a transmission of divine order — a revelation from the field of unity.

The mantra of Ajna echoes the vow of sacred sight:
"May my vision be clear.

May my mind serve light.
May I see the Divine in all."

THE LIGHT BEHIND THE EYES

At its deepest level, Ajna reveals that seeing is not the act of the
eyes but the awareness behind them.
It is the light that perceives both the external world and the
inner self as reflections of the same consciousness.
When this realization dawns, perception becomes prayer, and
the world becomes radiant with meaning.

In the silence behind thought and image, there is only awareness
— infinite, self-luminous, eternal. That is the secret of the Third
Eye: to look not with the eyes, but with the soul; to see not
forms, but truth; to recognize that the light you perceive is the
light you are.

THE LIGHT BEYOND LIGHT — THE GREAT SECRET

At the deepest level of Tantric understanding, Ajna — the Third
Eye Chakra — is not merely the center of vision; it is the
doorway to the Light Beyond Light (*Jyoti Niranjana*) — the
radiance beyond perception.
This is the brilliance before illumination, the awareness before
seeing — the formless light that shines within every act of
perception.
To enter this space is to merge back into the source of all vision,
the silent flame that neither burns nor casts a shadow.

Here, Kundalini no longer ascends — she disappears into
luminosity. Light returns to consciousness, perception to
Presence, and the seer becomes one with the Seen.
In this state, you do not look upon the Divine — you are the
Divine witnessing itself.

THE BODY AS THE TEMPLE OF LIGHT

Tantra honors Ajna as the seat of divine perception within the body — the sacred sanctuary where awareness, wisdom, and consciousness merge into vision.
Located at the center of the brow, it is the bridge between the voice and the silence, where sound becomes light and thought becomes insight.
Here, the body is not merely a vessel of experience — it is the mirror of the cosmos.

Every cell glows with intelligence, every breath reflects infinity, every perception becomes revelation.
When Ajna is balanced, the gaze softens, the mind becomes luminous, and vision turns inward toward truth.
When blocked, perception narrows — intuition fades, and the inner world grows dim.

In the awakened Third Eye, the body itself becomes a temple of illumination — vibrating with the subtle radiance known in Tantra as *Jyoti Brahma* — "the world is light."

SHAKTI AND SHIVA IN LUMINOUS UNION

In Ajna, Shakti's radiant ascent transforms from sound into light — from vibration into illumination.
She becomes *Jnana Shakti*, the Goddess of Wisdom, dancing as intuition, insight, and revelation.
Shiva, as pure Consciousness, receives her radiance as awareness itself.

Their union here is the marriage of light and space, vision and knowing — the silent brilliance of awakening.
Where in Vishuddha Shakti sang as sound, in Ajna she shines as sight.
Where Shiva once listened in stillness, now he illuminates through silence.

This union gives rise to perception beyond thought — the sacred knowing that enlightenment is not reached, but revealed. Tantra teaches that the marriage of light and awareness births liberation: perception purified by truth, wisdom refined by compassion, and seeing guided by love.

Here, power no longer seeks to speak — it seeks to see.

TANTRIC PRACTICES FOR AJNA

Traditional Tantric disciplines for awakening and harmonizing the Third Eye focus on refining perception, purifying awareness, and opening the lens of consciousness to the inner light:

• Bija Mantra — OM (AUM):
Chant OM softly, allowing the sound to dissolve into silence. Feel its resonance rise through the skull to the space between the eyebrows.
Let the sound fade until only the vibration remains — then let even that become stillness.

• Trataka (Candle Gazing):
Fix your gaze gently upon a flame until the eyes close naturally. Observe the afterimage in the mind's eye — the golden light of consciousness within you.
This awakens the inner sight and steadies the wandering mind.

• Bindu Visualization:
Visualize a radiant point of light — indigo, violet, or pure white — in the center of your forehead.
Breathe into it softly.
With each inhale, it expands; with each exhale, it brightens.
This is the lamp of the soul — the eye that never closes.

• Khechari Mudra (Gesture of the Inner Sky):
Turn awareness upward to the space between the palate and the crown — the "inner sky."

This mudra awakens subtle perception, drawing awareness inward to the infinite.

• Silence Meditation (Antar Mauna):
Sit in deep stillness and observe thoughts as passing clouds. Behind them lies the radiant expanse of pure awareness — the true eye of Shiva.

THE DEEPER TANTRIC LESSON

Tantra teaches that Ajna is not merely the center of vision — it is the gateway of illumination where perception dissolves into consciousness and awareness becomes creation.
Here, seeing ceases to be observation; it becomes communion.

When the Third Eye awakens, you realize that light is not outside you — it emanates from within.
Vision becomes revelation; clarity becomes compassion.
The world no longer appears separate; it shines as an expression of the same divine awareness that observes it.

At Ajna, individuality merges with infinite perception.
You no longer seek the light — you become it.
Perception no longer reflects the world — it radiates from the soul.
Your seeing becomes truth itself: clear, compassionate, and timeless.

This is the secret of Ajna in Tantra: that light is consciousness made visible, that truth is awareness illuminated, and that the mind is the sacred mirror reflecting God to God.

To awaken the Third Eye is to remember that your sight is sacred, your awareness is divine, and your silence — the luminous gaze of eternity.

The Secret Wisdom of the Third Eye Chakra

The hidden Tantric teaching of Ajna is that perception becomes divine when it is luminously pure.
It is not imagination, but revelation — an understanding that vision, insight, and awareness are not merely perception, but creation itself.

Where the Throat reveals illumination through sound, the Third Eye unveils liberation through light — the transmutation of vibration into vision, and of resonance into knowing.
Here, power no longer speaks; it sees.
Light becomes the bridge between the visible and invisible worlds — the mind of God reflected through human consciousness.

Ajna is the inner temple of radiance, where all vibrations are refined into awareness.
It is the chamber where Kundalini's celestial song becomes illumination — where consciousness begins to see itself as light.

Where the Throat whispered, "I speak, I express, I become sound," Ajna responds, "I see, I perceive, I become light."
Here, the path to enlightenment is not through speech or silence, but through *vision* — the transformation of perception into wisdom, and awareness into divine sight.
Through the Third Eye, the sound that once sang now shines — radiant, clear, and infinite.

KUNDALINI: AWAKENING THROUGH THE LIGHT OF THE THIRD EYE
The Serpent of Illumination

As Kundalini ascends from the ether of Vishuddha into the inner sky of Ajna, her vibration transforms into light.
The Serpent no longer hums — she glows.
Her movement becomes stillness; her radiance becomes awareness. This is the initiation into *Jyoti* — the divine current of illumination.

Here, Kundalini becomes vision — the sacred flame of perception that reveals the infinite within the finite.
The ancient Tantras call this the "Gate of Light," where the soul awakens to its own luminosity.
Where she once vibrated, she now shines.
Where she once resonated, she now knows.

It is the sacred transmutation of vibration into insight — the passage from expressing to perceiving, from voice to vision, from sound to silence. Kundalini no longer communicates through words; she communicates through revelation. Your eyes, intuition, and awareness become instruments of her divine light.

THE DANCE OF LIGHT

As Kundalini rises through the Third Eye, her rhythm slows into stillness. The hum of Vishuddha resolves into the radiance of Ajna — a steady flame in the center of the brow, glowing with tranquil brilliance. This is the alchemy of light, where vibration becomes illumination and consciousness recognizes its reflection.

Every image, every dream, every insight carries sacred meaning. When perceived with awareness, it clarifies; when clouded by ego, it distorts.

Tantra teaches that the key to this sacred seeing is *inner stillness* — to look without grasping, to let perception arise without judgment, and to allow awareness to reveal truth naturally.

In this silent dance, Shakti shines as light, and Shiva receives as consciousness.
Their union becomes *Jyoti Brahma* — "the world is light."
Every star, every eye, every spark within creation shines this eternal illumination.

SIGNS OF AWAKENING

When Kundalini activates the Third Eye Chakra, her presence reveals itself as light, intuition, and deep perception:

• Flashes of inner light or color during meditation
• Vivid, symbolic dreams and lucid awareness in sleep
• Heightened intuition and spontaneous insight
• Pressure or pulsing between the eyebrows
• A sense of inner brightness or radiant calm behind the eyes
• Vision expanding beyond physical sight — perceiving energy or aura
• Sudden understanding of divine patterns and meaning
• A tranquil joy arising from inner stillness

These are the harmonics of illumination — the light of consciousness shining through perception.
You may feel as though your mind has become transparent, your awareness filled with a silent radiance that needs no explanation.
This is Shakti awakening through light — turning sound into sight, and awareness into revelation.

BALANCING THE LIGHT

Just as sound must be tuned, light must be aligned.
An awakened Ajna shines with truth when perception flows

from awareness — but it becomes distorted when the mind grasps, doubts, or controls.

When overactive, the Third Eye may express as excessive analysis, illusion, or psychic overwhelm.
When underactive, it dims into confusion, disbelief, or a lack of vision.
The Tantric path teaches the middle gaze — perception aligned with wisdom, humility, and divine trust.

• Ground through the Root: Anchor insight in lived reality, not fantasy.
• Flow through the Sacral: Let creativity soften intellect into intuition.
• Empower through the Solar Plexus: Use discernment without domination.
• Open through the Heart: See through the eyes of love, not fear.
• Refine through the Throat: Let words follow truth, not distort it.

Through this alignment, perception becomes luminous — not to predict, but to perceive; not to escape, but to embody.
You no longer *look for* light; you *see through* it.

THE SECRET OF AJNA

The esoteric secret of Ajna is that true vision arises not from seeing more, but from seeing clearly — the merging of the observer and the observed into one field of awareness.
When the Third Eye opens in harmony, you perceive the universe as reflection, revelation, and remembrance.
What was once sought outside now shines within.

At this stage, perception becomes prayer, and light becomes language.
The mind is no longer a thinker — it is a lamp.
The soul no longer searches — it *sees*.

To awaken the Third Eye is to remember that your awareness is the eternal light behind all forms, your intuition the divine eye through which the cosmos beholds itself, and your silence — the radiant brilliance of enlightenment.

THE SACRED LIGHT WITHIN

Tantra teaches:
"To know light is to know awareness; to master awareness is to become the Divine."

At Ajna, Kundalini becomes *Jyoti Shakti* — the Goddess of Light who sees the universe into being.
Her radiance is the glow of stars, the spark of thought, the illumination that unites all things.
When you surrender to her current, your sight becomes the vision of existence itself.
The same energy that once sought to express through sound now reveals its highest form through perception.

Your eyes no longer seek to observe; they seek to understand.
Your mind no longer strives to analyze; it shines.
When light flows through the Third Eye in alignment with truth, life itself becomes revelation — a continuous unfolding of divine awareness.

This is the secret of the Third Eye Chakra in Tantra: that creation is perception, that truth is illumination, and that the Divine forever sees through those who gaze inward.

Tantric Secrets of the Inner Sky

THE ELEMENT OF LIGHT AND THE VISION WITHIN IT

The Third Eye Chakra (Ajna) is the realm of Light — *Jyoti* — radiant, subtle, and self-luminous.
It is the infinite expanse where vibration becomes awareness and silence becomes sight.

If Vishuddha taught transcendence through resonance, Ajna teaches liberation through illumination.
Light is the subtlest expression of energy — it neither moves nor rests; it reveals.
It is the medium through which all form is known, all consciousness perceived.

In Tantra, Light is the temple of perception — the inner sky where awareness sees itself.
When Kundalini rises into the Third Eye, sound dissolves into radiance; tone becomes vision; vibration becomes knowing.
Here, awareness is not heard or spoken — it is seen.
Consciousness reveals itself as illumination, and the body becomes a lens of divine light.

POWER AS CLARITY

In Tantra, power at Ajna is not dominance but discernment.
It is not control, but clear seeing — perception in harmony with truth.
True mastery of Ajna lies not in seeking visions, but in resting within awareness — the still light before thought appears.

When perception is clouded by desire or fear, illusion forms.
When guided by awareness, all becomes transparent.
The adept learns to focus like light through a crystal — neither

scattered nor blinding. Vision becomes revelation; awareness becomes liberation. Power through Ajna is not the power to know more, but to *see truly.*

PURPOSE AS INSIGHT

At Ajna, purpose transforms into perception — action refined into knowing.
Here, the ego no longer strives to direct life; it allows life to unfold through awareness.
Every image becomes instruction; every moment, a mirror.
Tantra teaches that to see the truth is the highest yoga.

When you perceive from the soul rather than the mind, vision aligns with creation itself.
Each realization becomes a mantra — light shaped by consciousness.
Each breath becomes illumination — the inner dawn between heaven and earth.

To live from Ajna is to understand that purpose is not action — it is awareness.
Work becomes understanding; creation becomes reflection; and the gaze becomes a vessel of light.

THE INNER MARRIAGE OF SHIVA AND SHAKTI

Within the Third Eye, Shakti shines as illumination, and Shiva perceives it as infinite consciousness.
Their union is the luminous stillness of *Jyoti Brahma* — "The world is light."
Shakti, the radiance, spirals in indigo brilliance — the light of being made visible.
Shiva, the awareness, receives her endlessly, reflecting her glow in boundless silence.

This is the inner marriage of sight and insight, of vision and knowing, of perception and wisdom.
When light arises from awareness, it carries truth from the heavens.
When awareness embraces light, it carries understanding to the earth.
Together they create the sacred rhythm of Ajna — perception breathing through form and formlessness alike.

Tantra teaches: "When seeing and being are one, the Divine perceives through you."

THE DEEPER TANTRIC REVELATION

The hidden teaching of Ajna is this:
Illumination itself is consciousness.
Every flash of insight, every moment of clarity, every silence of mind is a ray in the infinite field of being.
Vision is not separate from the universe — it is the universe looking through you.

When you align perception with truth, the entire cosmos reflects back in recognition.
To see is to remember; to understand is to awaken; and to witness truth is to dissolve illusion.

In the deepest Tantric knowing, awakening is not achieved by turning away from perception — but by perceiving with awareness.
When you see from the still point within the mind, every glance becomes meditation, every image becomes light, and your presence becomes the gaze of eternity.

KUNDALINI AND THE ALCHEMY OF LIGHT

Emotion as the Color of Consciousness
Emotion at Ajna becomes transparency — feeling transformed

into understanding.
The passions that once surged as fire now refract as
compassion, wisdom, and intuitive grace.
Joy glows as gold, serenity as silver, truth as violet flame.
Emotion is no longer turmoil; it becomes tone in the spectrum
of divine light.

Perception as Energy Transformed
At the Third Eye, the resonance of Vishuddha refines into
brilliance.
Old illusions dissolve in clarity; shadows become lessons in
contrast.
Each realization burns away ignorance like dawn dispersing
mist.
The Tantric sages taught:
"That which you truly see, you liberate from illusion."
When Kundalini shines through Ajna, she reveals unity behind
all forms — the one light mirrored in every eye.

The Light of Revelation
If fire clarified and sound revealed, light awakens.
The flames of Manipura purified, the resonance of Vishuddha
harmonized — now in Ajna, awareness illumines.
Here, the power once expressed through voice now perceives
through vision.
The Third Eye does not reject thought; it illuminates it.
Every insight becomes compassion; every perception, peace.
This is the alchemy of Ajna — the conversion of sound into
light, of perception into wisdom.

THE DANCE OF THE INNER LIGHT

When the Third Eye awakens, the being fills with radiance.
You may perceive luminous currents within the head, pulses of
indigo or violet between the brows, or a vast sky opening
behind the mind.
This is Shakti as light — not thought, but knowing.

Each breath draws in illumination; each silence expands awareness.

You begin to see from stillness, think from clarity, and act from vision.
The body becomes translucent to consciousness.
The mind no longer seeks images; it *is* the image of God reflected in form.
In this state, perception no longer grasps; it blesses.
Each look becomes recognition, weaving inner and outer worlds into one luminous field.

THE LIGHT WITHIN THE LIGHT

Within every insight lies infinite intelligence.
Each moment of clarity carries the wisdom of the universe.
When you meet perception in the space of awareness, its secret alchemy unfolds:

• Confusion becomes curiosity.
• Fear becomes understanding.
• Judgment becomes compassion.
• Doubt becomes discernment.
• Silence becomes revelation.

This is the indigo purification of Ajna — where sight itself heals, not by analysis, but by illumination.
The gaze need not be mystical to be sacred; it need only be clear.
Each breath clears another veil of illusion, until only light remains — the pure awareness of the soul.

Light reveals without burning, awakens without striving, and transforms without effort.
It carries the wisdom that sound once sang and spreads it through vision — endlessly, eternally.

THE HIDDEN TANTRIC TRUTH

Kundalini does not awaken by rejecting light — she awakens by becoming it.
Each image, each thought, each flash of insight is her unfolding illumination.

Where the ether of Vishuddha transformed vibration into truth, the radiance of Ajna transforms truth into vision.

When sound refines into silence and silence becomes luminous awareness, you witness the divine alchemy of Light — where consciousness reveals, and perception becomes illumination.

When the mind aligns with the heart and soul, you become a vessel of sacred clarity — steady, radiant, and infinite.

Tantra teaches that enlightenment is not the absence of thought, but the transparency of perception — the clear light of consciousness seeing through itself.

To perceive is to become stillness in motion.
To see truth with awareness is to allow Shakti to shine — no longer as sound revealing, but as light awakening.

Through this alchemy, you become both seer and seen — the luminous expression of divine wisdom awakened within.

SECRET USES OF THE THIRD EYE CHAKRA: CELESTIAL LIGHT, VISION TRANCE, AND THE ALCHEMY OF PERCEPTION

Beyond its link to intuition and insight, the Third Eye Chakra (Ajna) conceals the ancient teachings of transformation through light, awareness, and inner vision.

In esoteric lineages, this radiant center was revered as the *inner sun* — the silent temple where sound becomes light, and consciousness witnesses its own reflection.

Here, light is not illumination but revelation.
Ajna holds the mysteries of perception — how awareness shapes form, and how stillness, clarity, and compassion fuse to generate understanding in the soul.

CELESTIAL LIGHT: THE SKY BEYOND SIGHT

In Tantric cosmology, Ajna is ruled by *Jyoti*, the principle of divine radiance — limitless, transparent, eternal.
It is the field in which all visions arise and into which all dissolve.

Its rhythm mirrors the cycles of perception:
Darkness (potential), Light (revelation), Stillness (union).

Ancient adepts practiced *Jyoti Yoga*, meditating on the flame of consciousness that burns without a wick — the *Inner Lamp* (*Antar Jyoti*).
Through this inner gaze, they entered communion with the universal brilliance — seeing the Light of Spirit beyond form.

To work with Ajna is to master the art of seeing: knowing when to observe, when to contemplate, and when to rest in awareness. This celestial rhythm restores harmony between mind and intuition, teaching that truth is not seen with effort — it is revealed through clarity.

When aligned with the pulse of divine light, perception becomes luminous rather than analytical — a gentle radiance that heals, unites, and awakens.

VISION TRANCE AND THE STATE OF RADIANT AWARENESS

Where the Throat's trance flows through sound and tone, the Third Eye's trance unfolds through stillness and illumination — the lucid awareness of light.

In ancient sanctuaries, initiates meditated upon the *Bindu*, the sacred point between the brows, until form dissolved into brilliance.
In that state, the practitioner became the light itself — infinite, silent, self-aware.

Modern seekers touch this through creativity, meditation, and revelation — when insight flows effortlessly, when vision expands beyond words, when understanding feels like light moving through the mind.

It is the trance of radiance, where perception arises from stillness and returns to silence, carrying awareness as its glow.

Here, the eye is not the observer — it is the universe remembering itself through vision.

This is the state of luminous perception — consciousness seeing as light.

THE ALCHEMY OF VISION: TURNING LIGHT INTO WISDOM

Just as the adept of Vishuddha turns sound into illumination, the initiate of Ajna turns light into wisdom.

Every perception, once purified by awareness, becomes revelation.
Confusion becomes inquiry.
Fear becomes understanding.

Doubt becomes discernment.
Desire becomes devotion.
Form becomes light.

This is the alchemy of illumination — the art of refining perception into divine knowing.

Through meditation, contemplation, and compassionate seeing, the dense layers of illusion dissolve into clarity. What once appeared as separation reveals itself as unity.
What once blinded now enlightens.

The same light that once veiled truth now unveils it — for awareness, once awakened, cannot again be bound.

LIGHT BONDING: COMMUNION WITH THE EYE OF CREATION

Just as Vishuddha's ritual is sound bonding,
Ajna's sacred act is light bonding — communion through perception.

In ancient rites, practitioners sat beneath the open sky or before sacred fire, gazing into flame until its form vanished into pure awareness. The outer light became inner illumination.

Each vision was an offering, each silence a prayer.
This practice continues in every moment you *see with presence* — when you look upon the world and perceive unity instead of division.

Light bonding reconnects you to the divine principle of perception — teaching the rhythm of revelation: when to see, when to surrender, and how to gaze through the silence beyond sight.

Spiritually, it reminds us that the same light that shines in the sun also illuminates the soul.

PRIMAL PERCEPTION AND THE LIGHT OF CREATION

Where the Root perceives through instinct, the Sacral through feeling, the Solar through purpose, and the Throat through expression — the Third Eye perceives through illumination — the vision that reveals the divine within all forms.

This is the realm of *Jnana Shakti*, the Goddess of Wisdom, whose light sustains consciousness. It is the brilliance that fuels not only insight, but revelation, intuition, and divine guidance.

When channeled consciously, this light becomes the Eye of the Divine — capable of healing through vision without judgment or attachment. To awaken this current is to remember your birthright as a *witness of eternity* — one who sees creation not through perception, but through presence.

THE HIDDEN WISDOM

The Third Eye Chakra reveals that truth is not found — it is seen.
Its secret is not seeking, but surrender — the openness through which illumination flows.

Just as the Root grounds, the Sacral feels, the Solar acts, and the Throat expresses — the Third Eye perceives.
It turns sound into light, thought into awareness, and perception into communion.

To honor Ajna is to remember that the sky within you is eternal — a field vast enough for all images and all emptiness to coexist.

When you live from this radiant eye of awareness, you no longer seek enlightenment — you recognize it in all things.
You do not look for the Divine — you see through it.
You no longer need to imagine light — you *are* its presence.

Western Mysticism: The Light of Creation and the Temple of Divine Illumination

In Western mystical tradition, light has always symbolized the first act of divine revelation — the moment when invisible Spirit becomes visible creation.
If the Throat Chakra reveals the Word through sound, then the Third Eye reveals that same Word through sight — the radiant knowing through which consciousness perceives itself.

Ajna is the Temple of Illumination, the sanctum where divine awareness gazes through the human form.
Here, vibration refines into vision, sound unfolds as symbol, and truth becomes revelation.
It is the sphere of divine perception — the gateway through which the soul learns to see as God sees.

Where Vishuddha was the "Temple of the Word," Ajna is the Cathedral of Light — the luminous chamber where sound becomes radiance and understanding dawns as inner sight.

"LET THERE BE LIGHT": THE FIRST REVELATION

"And God said, Let there be light: and there was light." — *Genesis 1:3*

This verse marks the Western equivalent of the yogic awakening of Ajna — the divine command that transformed vibration into illumination.
The Logos that once sounded through Ether now shines through

Light.
In mystical theology, this light is not physical but spiritual —
the *Lux Aeterna*, the eternal radiance of divine mind perceiving
its own reflection.

Hermetic philosophers taught that "Light is the shadow of
God."
It is consciousness clothed in visibility, the bridge between pure
Spirit and manifested form.
Through this light, divine intelligence sees itself, and creation
becomes revelation.

Thus, Ajna is the *Eye of the Logos*, the cosmic lens through
which awareness beholds its own perfection.
Where the Throat speaks creation into being, the Third Eye
beholds it as truth.

THE TEMPLE OF DIVINE ILLUMINATION

If Vishuddha gave the world voice, Ajna gives it vision.
Here, the Word becomes visible geometry — the sacred
architecture of divine thought.

In the mystical West, this principle is expressed through the
concept of "Lux Dei" — the Light of God that reveals all things
and hides nothing.
It is the same radiance that illuminated Moses on Sinai, that
blinded Saul on the road to Damascus, and that poured through
the eyes of Christ in transfiguration.

To the Christian mystic, Ajna is the "Eye of the Heart," where
Spirit perceives beyond form.
In Kabbalah, it corresponds to *Tiferet* — the sefirah of beauty
and divine reflection, the center point where compassion and
vision unite.
Tiferet is the mirror of creation — the seeing that redeems, the
perception that reconciles.

To awaken Ajna is to perceive not with the eyes, but with the soul — to look through matter and behold Spirit made manifest.

THE ALCHEMY OF LIGHT: FROM SOUND TO VISION

In Western alchemy, light was seen as the soul of fire — the pure quintessence released when matter yields to Spirit.
Just as Ether refines flame into sound, light refines sound into revelation.
The mystics called this *"the fire that sees,"* the illumination that transfigures perception itself.

Through this alchemy, vibration becomes vision; resonance becomes recognition.
Sound organizes the universe, but light reveals its design.
The music of the spheres gives birth to the geometry of the heavens — the pattern through which divine intelligence sees itself reflected in form.

This is the alchemical mystery of Ajna:
That seeing is not passive — it is creative.
To perceive truth is to project light into being.
To see with clarity is to call divine order into manifestation.

THE MYSTERIES OF VISION AND THE BREATH OF ILLUMINATION

Where the mystic once prayed through breath, the initiate now sees through light.
Breath gave the Word form; illumination gives it meaning.

In the Gospel, the Christic Light is both the revealer and the revealed —

"The light shineth in darkness, and the darkness comprehended it not."

Here, light is consciousness knowing itself through contrast.
The mystic's task is not to destroy darkness but to perceive it as
unilluminated truth awaiting awareness.

Every thought becomes a lantern; every insight, a flame.
Each time perception is purified, a new world is revealed.
Thus, the spiritual eye does not open outward but inward —
seeing all creation as the play of divine light within the field of
consciousness.

THE CHRISTIC LIGHT AND THE EYE OF REVELATION

Christ is the Logos made Light — divine truth expressed not in
sound but in seeing.
His miracles are not acts of power but acts of vision — the gaze
that recognized wholeness where others saw lack, life where
others saw death.
He healed because He perceived rightly.

This is the awakening of Ajna: to see through illusion and
restore truth by perception alone.
When the mystic sees as Christ saw — with clarity,
compassion, and unity — their very gaze becomes healing.
Their vision becomes revelation.
Their eyes become the windows through which God perceives
creation.

To live from this center is to behold the divine order within
every form, the hidden perfection within every shadow.

THE SHARED WISDOM

Across the Western mysteries, the message echoes that of
Eastern Tantra:
Light is sacred because it reveals.
It is the bridge between knowing and being, silence and sound,
Spirit and matter.

Through light, the soul learns not merely to perceive, but to
understand.
Whether through the Christian vision of the Christic radiance,
the Kabbalist's Tree of Light, or the Hermetic philosopher's
Divine Ray — each tradition preserves the same truth Ajna
reveals through Yoga and Tantra:

The Light you see by is the Light you are.

When your sight aligns with truth, God perceives through you.
To live from this radiant center is to live as both seer and seen
— a mirror of divine awareness, a lens of infinite compassion, a
beam of consciousness made visible.

You no longer seek enlightenment — you recognize that you
were its light all along.

Chapter 8 – Balancing & Healing Practices

Reiki Positions and Energy Protocols for the Third Eye Chakra

The Third Eye (Ājñā) is the center of perception, intuition, imagination, and spiritual insight.
Located between the eyebrows, it governs the pineal and pituitary glands, subtle vision, and the ability to perceive beyond physical sight. In Reiki and subtle-energy therapy, this chakra is treated after the Throat Chakra, once communication and resonance have been purified, so that awareness may rise into inner vision and direct knowing.

Balancing Ājñā awakens the inner witness—the clear observer who perceives without judgment.
When harmonized, it bridges intellect with intuition, uniting left-brain logic with right-brain imagination so that thought, feeling, and insight move as one current of awareness.

Hand Positions for the Third Eye

Reiki placements for Ājñā focus on the forehead, temples, eyes, and base of the skull, engaging both the conscious and subconscious fields of perception.
This area stores energetic patterns related to belief, memory, illusion, and psychic sensitivity.
Because the Third Eye is delicate and highly responsive, work

here with stillness and precision; let the flow of Reiki feel like light rather than pressure.

Forehead Center (Brow Point)

Place one or both hands lightly across the forehead, fingertips resting above the brows.
This calms mental chatter, eases worry, and opens the intuitive channel between the hemispheres of the brain.
As Reiki flows, sense a gentle pulse of indigo light forming in the center of your forehead—your inner lens aligning to divine vision.

Temples and Eyes

Rest your palms over the temples or cover the closed eyes softly with cupped hands.
This placement soothes tension from overthinking or eye strain and clears residual images held in the mind.
It enhances clairvoyance and dream recall, inviting trust in what is seen within.
Visualize energy balancing left and right perception—masculine focus and feminine receptivity—into luminous neutrality.

Back of Head (Occipital Ridge)

Place your hands where the skull meets the neck.
This anchors intuitive insight into the body and stabilizes sudden energetic surges that can accompany awakening.
It integrates vision with embodiment so that intuition translates into grounded understanding rather than abstraction.

Front and Back Together

One hand on the forehead, the other at the base of the skull, creates the Reiki bridge of perception.
This configuration unites seeing and knowing, inner image and outer realization.
It is excellent for deep meditation, visualization, and for harmonizing the pineal-pituitary axis.

Energy Protocols

1. The Indigo Ray of Insight

Invite Reiki to flow as an indigo or deep violet light spiraling through the center of your forehead.
Feel it cleanse mental fog, dissolve confusion, and illuminate the inner landscape.
Let the light radiate backward through the head, linking both hemispheres in quiet coherence.
Affirm:

"I see with clarity, wisdom, and love."

This practice refines perception, enhances intuition, and brings serenity to the mind.

2. Clearing the Veil of Illusion

Using gentle sweeping motions from the center of the forehead outward to the temples, clear energetic residue from fear, doubt, or disbelief.
Visualize a veil lifting, revealing a clear luminous space behind the eyes.
As the veil dissolves, imagination becomes revelation—what was once fantasy becomes guided vision.

Breathe softly, releasing attachment to what you *think* you see and opening to what truly is.

3. The Light of Still Awareness

Place both hands over the brow center and allow them to rest motionless.
Do not visualize; simply be.
Let Reiki flow as pure awareness—silent, steady, radiant.
Notice how the body slows, the breath lengthens, and perception expands in all directions.
This protocol awakens the witnessing consciousness—the seer beyond thought.

4. Crystalline Amplification (Optional)

For practitioners who integrate crystals, place amethyst, lapis lazuli, azurite, or clear quartz upon the Third Eye.
Allow Reiki to stream through the crystal as a lens of purity, refining intuitive messages into coherent light.
The crystalline field magnifies the pineal frequency, encouraging lucid dreaming, meditation depth, and visionary recall.

5. Integration of Sight and Sound

After completing the Reiki flow, gently tone the mantra OM three times.
Feel the vibration begin in the throat, rise through the palate, and resonate at the brow.
As the final tone fades, a sense of light expanding behind the forehead—sound transforming into sight.
Close by placing hands over the heart, allowing vision and compassion to merge.

6. Affirmations for Ājñā Harmony

Repeat slowly, aloud or in silence:

- "I trust the wisdom that arises within."
- "My inner vision is clear and loving."
- "I perceive truth beyond illusion."
- "Insight and intuition guide my every step."

Each affirmation plants a new frequency of clarity within the mental and subtle bodies.

7. Daily Practice of Perception

- Morning: Rest your gaze on the horizon or a candle flame for one minute, then close your eyes and perceive the after-image within—training inner sight.
- Daytime: Pause often to "see between the moments," observing without labeling.
- Night: Before sleep, place a hand over your brow and invite dreams of guidance and healing.

Closing the Session

After working with the Third Eye, ground the energy by moving your hands to the Root or Heart Chakra.
Drink water, breathe deeply, and allow the expanded light to settle into embodiment.
When Ājñā is balanced, the mind becomes a mirror—clear, luminous, and still—reflecting divine truth without distortion.
Vision transforms into wisdom, and wisdom becomes the quiet light that guides all action.

SYMBOLIC SUPPORT

Advanced Reiki practitioners may incorporate symbols to enhance Ājñā's illumination, clarity, and perception.
At this level, symbols act as keys that open the gates of intuitive understanding, refining awareness until the practitioner becomes both seer and seen.

• Cho Ku Rei (Power Symbol)

Amplifies the light of awareness and strengthens energetic boundaries during intuitive or psychic work.
It stabilizes the field when visions or impressions arise, ensuring clarity and discernment.
Use to focus energy before meditation or remote viewing, empowering the flow of Reiki through the brow and crown.

• Sei He Ki (Harmony Symbol)

Balances the relationship between intellect and intuition.
It harmonizes the left and right hemispheres of the brain, easing over-analysis and restoring inner peace.
When placed at the Third Eye, Sei He Ki dissolves mental clutter and emotional bias, allowing perception to flow from higher consciousness rather than reaction.

• Hon Sha Ze Sho Nen (Distance Symbol)

Bridges time and space within consciousness.
Use to access inner guidance, past-life insight, or ancestral wisdom that supports your present clarity.
It clears psychic residue from previous experiences of illusion, fear, or spiritual misunderstanding.
Through this symbol, perception transcends time — vision becomes multidimensional awareness.

• Dai Ko Myo (Master Symbol)

Activates the divine light within the mind.
It opens the crown-to-brow channel, aligning intuition with enlightenment.
Use to attune your Third Eye to the frequency of truth and compassion, so that your insight serves love rather than ego.
When Dai Ko Myo radiates through Ājñā, inner sight becomes sacred revelation — wisdom shining as light itself.

INTEGRATIVE PRACTICE

When working with the Third Eye Chakra, remember:
Perception and stillness are not opposites — they are mirrors of the same consciousness.
True seeing arises when thought grows quiet and awareness becomes light.

To harmonize Ājñā fully, pair energy work with visual and meditative practice:

- Chant OM, the bija mantra of the Third Eye.
  Let its vibration rise from the heart through the brow, expanding as luminous resonance.
- Visualize indigo light spinning gently at the forehead, merging with violet light from above.
- Practice intuitive observation — see without judging, notice without labeling.
- Journal dream symbols and inner images to anchor spiritual insight into daily awareness.

As this chakra awakens, sight becomes revelation rather than perception.
You no longer seek visions — you see truth itself.
Each image becomes a teaching, each moment a mirror of divine awareness.

Through Reiki, you learn that the purest vision is clarity — the ability to witness without distortion.

THE PRACTITIONER'S ROLE

Working with the Third Eye (Ājñā) requires stillness, trust, and refined perception.
Because this center governs intuition, vision, and wisdom, the practitioner must embody quiet awareness — perceiving without projection.
In this neutrality, Reiki flows not to interpret the client's visions, but to clear the channels through which truth is revealed.

The healer becomes a lens of light, allowing divine intelligence to illuminate the unseen layers of the mind and spirit.
Through breath and silent intention, the practitioner creates space where the client's inner vision can open safely and clearly.
Reiki for Ājñā is not about *seeing more*; it is about seeing purely — beyond illusion, beyond ego, into the living truth of being.

When this alignment occurs, intuition flows effortlessly, imagination becomes insight, and perception transforms into understanding.
The practitioner and client alike remember that seeing and knowing are one when guided by Spirit.

HEALING REMINDER

Reiki at the Third Eye teaches one of the deepest spiritual revelations:
Light and darkness are not enemies — they define one another until awareness dawns.
When the indigo light of Ājñā is clear, even shadow becomes teacher and reflection becomes truth.

Perception expands from duality into unity; thought dissolves
into still awareness.
The mind no longer seeks to analyze — it simply witnesses.
Vision becomes peace, and peace becomes the light of wisdom.

Through this resonance, the soul remembers:

"I see clearly.
I understand with compassion.
I am the light that perceives all things."

Bridging the Heart Chakra to the Crown Chakra Through the Throat

The chakras are not isolated centers of energy, but a single,
ascending symphony — a spiral of consciousness rising from
the grounded self to the divine.

Between the open compassion of the Heart and the pure
illumination of the Crown lies the Throat Chakra (Vishuddha)
— the etheric bridge where love becomes expression and
wisdom becomes sound. This is the passage from feeling to
knowing, from compassion to communication, from silence to
sacred speech.
It is the stage where the heart's truth seeks its voice, and the
mind's wisdom learns to listen.

THE PATH FROM HEART TO CROWN

As energy ascends through these upper centers, vibration refines
into ever-subtler frequencies of consciousness:

- Heart (Anahata): The center of love, empathy, and
  divine connection — where self and other merge in
  compassion.

- Throat (Vishuddha): The chamber of expression and truth — where love gains language and wisdom finds resonance.
- Third Eye (Ajna): The eye of perception and intuition — where sound becomes insight, and expression transforms into understanding.
- Crown (Sahasrara): The seat of divine consciousness — where individuality dissolves into the infinite, and truth becomes silence once more.

Through this continuum, Vishuddha serves as the transmission point — converting the heart's emotional current into articulate energy and preparing the mind to receive intuitive light.
It is the harmonizing tone between love and illumination, emotion and realization.

THE ROLE OF THE THROAT CHAKRA IN THE BRIDGE

The Throat is the vibrational portal between feeling and knowing.
It translates the language of the heart into vibration — sound, word, song, or silence — and carries that resonance upward toward the higher mind.

When energy reaches Vishuddha, it no longer burns like fire or flows like water — it resonates.
It becomes pure frequency — the breath of truth, the tone of being.

Without this bridge, the energy of the Heart cannot rise to wisdom, nor can the insight of the Crown descend into compassionate communication.
When Vishuddha is balanced, love finds its voice and wisdom finds its tone.
When blocked, the flow between Heart and Crown distorts — speech loses empathy, or silence loses clarity.

Thus, the Throat Chakra teaches alignment through vibration:

Speak only when the heart is present.
Listen only when the mind is open.
And let silence be the sacred space where both meet.

THE ENERGETIC ASCENT: FROM COMPASSION TO COMMUNION

Each chakra along this upper bridge represents a stage of divine communication:

- Heart: *"I love."*
- Throat: *"I speak."*
- Third Eye: *"I see."*
- Crown: *"I am."*

Together, these affirmations trace the awakening of higher consciousness — from love as emotion to love as illumination, from individuality to unity.

When energy flows freely through this bridge, compassion becomes understanding, and wisdom becomes gentle expression.
Truth is no longer merely spoken; it is lived as vibration, radiating coherence and peace.

But when Vishuddha is clouded by fear, guilt, or self-doubt, truth constricts.
The voice trembles, the words distort, and wisdom becomes trapped in silence.
Healing this center liberates the breath of Spirit — transforming the act of speaking into prayer and the act of listening into communion.

LIVING THE BRIDGE

To bridge Heart and Crown through the Throat is to embody the sacred art of resonance — to live as both sound and silence.
It means expressing truth without judgment, listening without defense, and allowing each word to serve love rather than ego.

Here, communication becomes a spiritual practice, and every conversation becomes an opportunity to transmit light.
When the Heart is open, the Throat clear, and the Crown receptive, energy flows as divine dialogue — the human voice echoing the cosmic Word.

In this sacred alignment, life itself becomes mantra:

Every breath a prayer.
Every word a vibration of truth.
Every silence a return to God.

In this state, the soul speaks and listens through you.
You become a vessel of harmony — a voice for the Infinite, a bridge between Heaven and Earth, where love learns to speak and light learns to sing.

Bridging Heart to Crown Across Cultures

Across mystical traditions, the journey from the center of the chest to the crown of the head has been revered as the *ascent of illumination* — the sacred transformation from love to wisdom, from compassion to communion with the Divine.
In yogic philosophy, this passage flows through the upper chakras — Heart (*Anahata*), Throat (*Vishuddha*), Third Eye (*Ājñā*), and Crown (*Sahasrara*) — forming the bridge between emotion and enlightenment.

The Heart opens us to love and empathy; the Crown unites us
with pure consciousness.
Between them, the Throat and Third Eye refine energy into
expression and perception — the *vibration of truth* and the
vision of understanding.
Across cultures, this ascending current mirrors the evolution of
consciousness itself: breath becomes sound, sound becomes
light, and light returns to silence.

EASTERN TRADITIONS: THE PATH OF ETHER AND LIGHT

In the Tantric and yogic systems, the upper chakras represent
the subtle etheric realms — the refinement of dense prāna into
consciousness itself:

- Anahata (Heart) – Vāyu Tattva (Air): Compassion,
  connection, balance.
- Vishuddha (Throat) – Ākāśa Tattva (Ether): Expression,
  resonance, truth.
- Ājñā (Third Eye) – Mahat Tattva (Light/Mind):
  Intuition, perception, wisdom.
- Sahasrara (Crown) – Pure Consciousness: Unity,
  transcendence, divine realization.

This sacred progression — Air → Ether → Light → Spirit —
reflects the refinement of love into vibration, vibration into
insight, and insight into pure awareness.
The Throat serves as the resonance point — the place where the
breath of the Heart becomes the mantra of the soul.

Here, sound is not merely spoken; it is *remembered* — the
primordial Word (*Nāda*) from which creation emerged.
In *Nāda Yoga*, the Yoga of Sound, silence becomes the seed of
every sacred utterance, and vibration itself becomes prayer.
When the voice is attuned to the inner sound, it no longer seeks
to express — it *reveals*.

INDIGENOUS AND SHAMANIC WISDOM: THE VOICE OF THE SKY

In Indigenous and shamanic cosmologies, the upper centers belong to the sky realms — the world of wind, bird, and song. The Heart is the drumbeat of Earth; the Throat is the wind that carries the song; the Crown is the great sky into which that song dissolves.

Voice is seen as *spirit in motion* — the breath of the Creator moving through creation.
The shaman's chant, the healer's breath, the storyteller's voice — all express Vishuddha's sacred function: *to weave worlds with sound.*

When the heart's compassion guides the voice, words become medicine.
When the mind listens through silence, wisdom descends as song.
Thus, the bridge between Heart and Crown becomes the songline of the soul — where love rises as vibration and descends again as blessing.

This is why, in many traditions, the initiate learns to *sing the world back into harmony* — to call the fragmented pieces of self into wholeness through voice, rhythm, and resonance.

TAOIST PHILOSOPHY: THE BREATH OF HEAVEN

In Taoist internal alchemy, the upper field — encompassing the chest, throat, head, and crown — is known as the Palace of Spirit (Shen).
It is here that refined *qi* ascends and transforms into light.
The Throat corresponds to the Middle Heaven, where breath bridges Earth and Sky.

The Taoists teach that when the breath becomes silent, it becomes spirit.
Vishuddha parallels this truth — it is the energetic space where breath turns to tone, tone turns to vibration, and vibration returns to stillness.

This process, called Liàn Shén — *the refinement of spirit* — mirrors the chakra system's teaching that expression (Throat) must dissolve into perception (Third Eye) to open into enlightenment (Crown).
Through still breath and subtle resonance, the practitioner ascends not through striving, but through surrender — allowing the *sound of the soul* to dissolve into the *silence of Heaven.*

WESTERN MYSTICISM: THE WORD AND THE LIGHT

In Western mystery schools, this same bridge is understood through the sacred Logos — the Divine Word that creates reality through sound and intention:

"In the beginning was the Word, and the Word was with God, and the Word was God." — *John 1:1*

This is *Vishuddha's essence*: sound as creation, speech as manifestation.

Medieval Christian mystics viewed the ascent as the path from *caritas* (divine love) to *sapientia* (divine wisdom) — the transformation of the heart's devotion into enlightened understanding.

Hermetic philosophers called it the Ladder of Light, where the voice of the soul rises through successive spheres of sound until it merges with the ineffable silence of the Divine.
In Kabbalistic teaching, this ascent parallels the movement from Tiferet (Beauty, the Heart) through Da'at (Knowledge, the Throat Gate) toward Keter (Crown, Divine Unity) — the sacred

channel through which love and knowledge ascend into pure wisdom and radiant light.

In all these paths, sound becomes light, and light becomes understanding — the eternal revelation of Spirit expressing and perceiving itself through creation.

THE SHARED WISDOM

Across all cultures and lineages, the message is clear and eternal:

Sound is the bridge between love and illumination.
The voice becomes the vehicle of Spirit — transforming emotion into frequency, and frequency into understanding.

When the Throat is clear, the Heart's compassion can be spoken into the world, and the Crown's light can be expressed through human life.

Truth resonates.
Wisdom vibrates.
The Divine breathes through word, song, and silence alike.

To live through this bridge is to embody the eternal dialogue between Heaven and Earth — the breath of God moving through the voice of the soul, the sound of love ascending into light, and the silence of light returning to love.

Western Mysticism and Alchemy: The Marriage of Ether and Light

In Western mysticism, the higher stages of transformation were known as the *Great Work* — the refinement of perception from love into wisdom, and awareness from duality into illumination.

While the lower mysteries united Earth, Water, and Fire to purify body and emotion, the higher mysteries joined Ether and Light — the elements of space and vision — within the realms of intuition and revelation.

The classical alchemists called this exalted process the Sacred Marriage of Ether and Light, the union of inner seeing and cosmic consciousness:

- Ether (Throat) — Vibration, expression, resonance.
- Light (Third Eye) — Vision, perception, and intuitive insight.
- Spirit (Crown) — Stillness, unity, divine consciousness.

Where the lower alchemy turned base metal into gold, the higher alchemy turned perception into truth — the awakening of divine sight within human consciousness.

In Hermetic philosophy, this was known as the *illumination of Spiritus Mercurii* — when sound becomes light, and light reveals wisdom. Through this refinement, the Third Eye became not a physical organ, but a *lens of awareness* — the illuminated mirror through which Spirit perceives itself.

This was the essence of the *Great Work*: the transformation of human perception into divine vision — the awakening of the inner sun.

PSYCHOLOGICAL PERSPECTIVES: FROM EXPRESSION TO INTUITION

Modern psychology mirrors this mystical ascent in the evolution from authentic communication to intuitive cognition.

It traces the same path from emotion to awareness, showing how consciousness refines itself through stages of integration and insight:

- Heart Chakra (Anahata): Emotional maturity, empathy, relational awareness.
- Throat Chakra (Vishuddha): Honest expression, communication, alignment between inner truth and outer word.
- Third Eye Chakra (Ajna): Intuition, clarity, higher perception.
- Crown Chakra (Sahasrara): Transcendence, unity, divine understanding.

If the Throat gives voice to truth, the Third Eye gives it vision. Where the Throat expresses what has been understood, the Third Eye perceives what has yet to be spoken.

Psychologically, this is the shift from self-expression to self-realization — from knowing how to speak truth to knowing *truth itself.*
When the Third Eye awakens, consciousness no longer seeks validation through dialogue; it perceives directly through intuition, inner sight, and symbolic understanding.

Thus, Ajna represents the mind illumined — the stage where wisdom transcends language and perception becomes revelation.

THE UNIVERSAL BRIDGE

Across mystical, alchemical, and psychological traditions alike, one message endures: To see clearly, one must have spoken truth. To speak truth, one must have loved.

This ascending current — from Heart to Throat to Third Eye — forms the Bridge of Illumination, the inner ladder upon which sound becomes light and awareness becomes unity.

- The Heart opens you to love.
- The Throat teaches you to express that love in truth.

- The Third Eye transforms truth into vision.
- The Crown dissolves vision into pure consciousness.

Together, they complete the *Celestial Ascent of the Soul* — the path where vibration refines into radiance, and the light of understanding returns to its source.

To walk this bridge is to enter the Great Dialogue of Spirit — where silence reveals wisdom, vision becomes prayer, and the self recognizes its divine reflection in all things.

Meditation & Visualization Practices for the Third Eye Chakra (Ajna)

The Third Eye Chakra is the *Seat of Vision* — the luminous gateway between the seen and unseen worlds.
Located between the eyebrows, Ajna governs intuition, perception, imagination, and spiritual insight. It is the point where knowledge transforms into wisdom and where vision transcends sight.

Meditation here refines awareness, awakening your capacity to perceive truth beyond illusion.
Through these practices, you open the *inner eye* — the mind's sacred lens — allowing consciousness to observe itself through clarity, stillness, and light.

When Ajna awakens, thought becomes vision, and vision becomes knowing.

1. THE INDIGO FLAME MEDITATION

Purpose: To awaken intuitive sight and dissolve illusion through the light of awareness.

1. Sit comfortably with your spine aligned and your gaze gently lifted.
2. Focus on the space between your eyebrows — the center of inner perception.
3. Visualize a small indigo flame flickering there, radiant yet serene.
4. With each inhale, the flame grows brighter, illuminating the mind.
5. With each exhale, it burns away confusion, doubt, or illusion.
6. Whisper inwardly:
   "I see clearly through the light within."
7. Remain until your awareness feels spacious and luminous, as if your mind were filled with clear sky.

2. THE MIRROR OF LIGHT PRACTICE

Purpose: To perceive truth through reflection rather than reaction.

1. Sit quietly and imagine standing before a vast mirror of light within your mind.
2. See your thoughts, memories, and emotions reflected there without judgment.
3. Watch each image arise and dissolve like clouds passing across a still pond.
4. Repeat softly:
   "I witness without attachment. I see beyond illusion."
5. Allow the mirror to grow brighter until only light remains — the pure awareness that sees but is untouched by what it sees.

3. THE EYE OF WISDOM VISUALIZATION

Purpose: To open the Third Eye as a channel of inner guidance and spiritual sight.

1. Close your eyes and bring your focus to the space behind your forehead.
2. Visualize an ancient symbol — perhaps an eye, a star, or a lotus — glowing with indigo and violet light.
3. Feel it pulse gently, radiating awareness throughout your mind.
4. With each breath, the light expands outward, connecting Heart, Throat, and Crown in a vertical current of illumination.
5. Affirm:
   "I trust my intuition. My inner sight reveals truth."
6. Remain in this radiant awareness, receptive to insight, inspiration, or gentle guidance.

4. THE STREAM OF CLARITY (TRATAKA WITH INNER VISION)

Purpose: To refine mental focus and strengthen intuitive perception.

1. Gaze softly at the flame of a candle or visualize one in your mind's eye.
2. Observe the flame until its image lingers even when your eyes close.
3. Let this inner flame rest at your Third Eye, steady and unwavering.
4. As thoughts arise, return gently to the image.
5. Whisper:
   "My mind is clear. My vision is true."
6. Continue until the boundary between inner and outer sight begins to blur — all becomes light.

5. THE INDIGO BRIDGE MEDITATION

Purpose: To align Heart, Throat, and Third Eye — transforming love and truth into insight.

1. Begin at your Heart Chakra, feeling green light expanding with compassion.
2. Let that light rise to your Throat as turquoise, expressing truth with grace.
3. Now, guide it upward into your Third Eye, where it becomes deep indigo light — the color of knowing.
4. With each breath, let this current flow smoothly: love → truth → vision.
5. Affirm:
   "I see through the eyes of love. My truth reveals wisdom."
6. Rest in the harmony of this bridge, perceiving yourself as both observer and light.

6. THE BĪJA MANTRA MEDITATION — OM (AUM)

Purpose: To activate Ajna through the universal sound of creation and awareness.

1. Sit comfortably, spine straight, eyes closed.
2. Inhale deeply, and as you exhale, chant OM (AUM) — feeling the vibration move from your throat up through your brow.
3. Let the "A" resonate in your chest, the "U" rise through your throat, and the "M" hum in your head.
4. Visualize indigo ripples expanding from your Third Eye across space.
5. After each chant, pause in silence — the soundless awareness that follows vibration.
6. Close with:
   "I am one with all that is seen and unseen."

Each of these meditations opens the gateway of vision —
transforming thought into illumination, silence into wisdom,
and awareness into truth.

When practiced with devotion, the Third Eye reveals the inner
architecture of creation: light perceiving itself through
consciousness, and consciousness remembering itself as light.

To live from Ajna is to walk with clarity, to see through
illusion, and to trust the quiet knowing that has always been
within.

"I see beyond the visible.
I know beyond the known.
I am the light that perceives itself."

Crystals for the Third Eye Chakra

Crystals connected to the Third Eye Chakra (Ajna) vibrate with
the energy of insight, intuition, and expanded perception.
Their frequencies activate inner vision, deepen meditation, and
align the mind with higher wisdom.
These stones open the eye of consciousness — helping you see
beyond illusion, trust your intuition, and perceive truth through
clarity and stillness.

By working with Third Eye crystals, you awaken the light of
awareness — where thought becomes knowing, and knowing
becomes illumination.

AMETHYST

Qualities: Spiritual awareness, peace, divine connection.
Known as the Stone of Spiritual Light, Amethyst harmonizes
intellect and intuition, quiets the mind, and deepens meditation.

It bridges the Third Eye and Crown Chakras, opening pathways to divine guidance and inner tranquility.

Use:
Place on the forehead during meditation to calm thoughts and awaken insight.
Keep by the bed or wear as jewelry to encourage intuitive dreams and protection from energetic overstimulation.

LAPIS LAZULI

Qualities: Wisdom, inner truth, visionary insight.
A sacred stone of kings and seers, Lapis Lazuli stimulates both the Third Eye and Throat Chakras — guiding thought into expression and perception into understanding.
It enhances discernment, self-awareness, and the ability to see patterns behind appearances.

Use:
Hold during meditation or visualization to awaken intuitive guidance.
Wear at the brow or as earrings to align thought and speech with higher wisdom.

SODALITE

Qualities: Mental clarity, intuition, rational spirituality.
Called the Stone of Logic and Intuition, Sodalite unites reason and insight, harmonizing the left and right brain.
It strengthens focus, stabilizes emotions, and helps you see truth without distortion.

Use:
Place on the Third Eye while journaling or studying to access higher understanding.
Carry when making decisions that require clarity and trust in your intuition.

LABRADORITE

Qualities: Transformation, mystical awareness, psychic protection.
Labradorite reflects the light of hidden realms, awakening latent intuition and shielding the aura during spiritual work.
Its iridescent flashes symbolize the awakening of inner vision — the light that reveals the unseen.

Use:
Hold during meditation or dreamwork to activate intuitive insight.
Wear as a talisman for psychic protection and heightened awareness throughout the day.

AZURITE

Qualities: Vision, inner truth, expansion of consciousness.
Known as the Stone of Heaven, Azurite opens the Third Eye to cosmic understanding and higher perception.
It dissolves mental confusion, clears energetic blockages, and enhances spiritual communication.

Use:
Meditate with Azurite at the brow to expand awareness and access higher wisdom.
Use when channeling, reading energy, or seeking intuitive clarity in creative or healing work.

FLUORITE (INDIGO OR PURPLE)

Qualities: Focus, discernment, psychic organization.
Fluorite clears mental fog, strengthens intuition, and helps separate truth from illusion.
It aligns the mind with the soul's higher intelligence, making it a powerful ally for meditation and study.

Use:
Place on your desk or meditation altar to enhance concentration and insight.
Carry when you need clarity in complex situations or when balancing intuition with intellect.

Each of these stones acts as a lens for light — refining Ajna's perception and guiding awareness toward truth.
Through their crystalline wisdom, you remember that vision is sacred — that to see clearly is to know yourself as consciousness itself.

When you attune to their vibration, the mind becomes still, intuition awakens, and the light within begins to perceive its own reflection.

"I see through the eyes of the soul.
Clarity is my nature.
Light is my teacher."

How to Work with Third Eye Chakra Crystals

Crystals aligned with the Third Eye Chakra (Ajna) amplify the light of awareness and the inner vision of truth. They attune perception to higher frequencies of consciousness, bridging intuition, insight, and spiritual understanding.

Through these stones, the mind becomes clear and receptive — the inner and outer worlds align as one. Working with Third Eye crystals strengthens discernment, deepens meditation, and refines intuitive wisdom so that thought becomes illumination and perception becomes revelation. In their presence, seeing transforms into knowing, and knowing blossoms into understanding.

Placement

Lay Third Eye stones gently upon the brow center — between the eyebrows — during meditation or Reiki practice.
This placement activates the subtle optic field, harmonizing left and right hemispheres of the brain and awakening intuitive sight.

You may also create a triangular grid using crystals at the Heart, Throat, and Third Eye to align feeling, expression, and insight — the path of compassionate wisdom.

Light Charging

Because Ajna vibrates with the element of Light, illumination itself becomes the purifier.
Expose your chosen crystal — such as Amethyst, Sodalite, or Lapis Lazuli — to natural sunlight at dawn or gentle morning rays.
Visualize the light entering the stone as a beam of divine awareness, clearing confusion and activating spiritual sight.

Whisper softly:

"Through light I see.
Through vision I understand.
Through understanding I awaken."

Meditation & Dream Spaces

Place Third Eye crystals beside your bed or meditation cushion to enhance inner guidance and lucid dreaming.
They open the gateway between waking and subtle realms, allowing intuitive messages and symbolic visions to flow with ease.
Keep one near journals or divination tools to strengthen psychic clarity and interpretation.

Affirmation

While holding your crystal, focus your gaze inward and repeat slowly:

"My mind is clear.
My vision is true.
I see through the eyes of wisdom."

Charging Crystals with the Element of Light and Consciousness

The Third Eye Chakra is governed by Light — the pure radiance of awareness that illuminates all perception.
To charge these crystals is to ignite their inner flame, aligning them to the wavelength of divine clarity.

Light reveals what sound awakens — it is consciousness made visible.
These stones respond not to movement or noise, but to stillness, focus, and intention — the silent brilliance of the awakened mind.

1. Sunlight Charging

Sunlight represents the active aspect of illumination — clear vision, mental vitality, and divine awareness.

- Place your crystals in the early morning sun for a few minutes, avoiding harsh midday rays.
- As light touches them, visualize beams of indigo and violet radiance streaming into the stones.
- Speak the intention:

"Light of dawn, awaken my sight.
Illuminate my path with wisdom and truth."

2. Moonlight Charging

Moonlight reflects the receptive aspect of intuition — soft perception, subtle awareness, and dream insight.

- Place your crystals under the full or waxing moon to draw in its intuitive glow.
- As they absorb lunar light, imagine silver-indigo rays infusing them with calm vision and inner knowing.
- Whisper:

"By lunar light and sacred sight,
I see within and awaken insight."

3. Candlelight Charging

Firelight mirrors the spark of divine consciousness — awareness awakening through focus.

- Light a candle and place your crystal beside it.
- As the flame flickers, see its reflection dancing in the stone — the light of Spirit meeting the eye of the soul.
- Say:

"Flame of clarity, eye of light,
Reveal the truth beyond my sight."

4. Visualization Charging

Because Ajna governs imagination and perception, visualization is one of the most direct ways to cleanse and charge these stones.

- Hold your crystal between your palms at your forehead.

- Breathe slowly and envision a sphere of indigo light spinning around it.
- As you exhale, see this light expanding outward, clearing shadow and confusion.
- Affirm:

"Within me shines the light of knowing.
My crystal mirrors the clarity of my soul."

5. Silent Meditation Charging

Stillness is the purest current of Ajna.
Unlike sound or movement, it charges through presence alone
— the awareness that perceives all things.

- Sit in silence with your crystal resting between your brows or in your cupped hands.
- Let your breath soften until awareness expands beyond thought.
- Feel the crystal attuning to your consciousness — no separation, no effort.
- Conclude with gratitude:

"Through stillness, I see.
Through light, I remember."

Charging Affirmation

"Through light and silence, I align.
My crystals shine with wisdom and peace.
Their radiance amplifies the vision of my soul."

Crystals of the Third Eye Chakra are mirrors of consciousness
— vessels that translate energy into insight and intuition into illumination.
Through them, the soul learns to see beyond illusion — to perceive the unseen harmony that binds all life.

When charged through light, focus, and stillness, they awaken the radiant current of Ajna — the inner lamp of wisdom that reveals Spirit's reflection in all things.

Essential Oils for the Third Eye Chakra

The Third Eye Chakra (Ajna) responds to cooling, clarifying, and transcendental aromas that quiet the mind, awaken intuition, and open the inner vision.
These ethereal essences dissolve illusion, balance logic and intuition, and refine perception beyond the five senses.
Essential oils for Ajna nourish clarity, imagination, and spiritual insight — supporting your ability to see with wisdom, trust your intuition, and perceive truth without distortion.
They elevate awareness beyond thought, awakening the inner light where perception becomes revelation — the silent knowing of Spirit.

FRANKINCENSE

Qualities: Illumination, meditation, divine connection.
Frankincense bridges the mind and Spirit, calming mental turbulence and enhancing meditative stillness.
It deepens intuition and clears energetic fog, allowing the inner vision to perceive divine guidance with clarity and peace.

Use:
Diffuse during meditation or prayer to heighten spiritual awareness.
Anoint the brow (diluted) to calm overthinking and open the Third Eye to subtle insight.

SANDALWOOD

Qualities: Inner stillness, spiritual focus, higher wisdom.
Sandalwood's soft, woody aroma quiets the intellect and

stabilizes intuitive perception.
It anchors the higher mind in calm awareness, harmonizing intuition with grounded understanding.

Use:
Diffuse before meditation, dreamwork, or intuitive journaling.
Apply (diluted) to the temples or Third Eye to still the mind and align awareness with divine intelligence.

CLARY SAGE

Qualities: Clarity, vision, intuitive insight.
Named for its historical use in "clearing the eyes," Clary Sage uplifts the mind and expands perception beyond the ordinary.
It strengthens intuitive trust and opens channels of inspiration and creative foresight.

Use:
Diffuse during meditation or visualization practices to enhance intuitive flow.
Apply (diluted) to the brow before sleep to encourage intuitive dreaming and mental calm.

ROSEMARY

Qualities: Mental clarity, remembrance, focus. Rosemary stimulates the higher mind, sharpening awareness while preserving intuitive sensitivity.
It clears mental fatigue and strengthens memory — helping insight translate into practical understanding.

Use:
Diffuse or inhale before study, writing, or intuitive work to balance logic with insight. Blend with lavender for a calming-yet-awakening meditation oil.

LAVENDER

Qualities: Balance, spiritual purification, gentle awareness.
Lavender soothes emotional tension and aligns intuitive
perception with peace.
It harmonizes the nervous system, opening space for clarity and
spiritual sensitivity.

Use:
Diffuse before sleep or meditation to enhance dream recall and
inner stillness.
Apply (diluted) to the temples to quiet mental noise and restore
intuitive balance.

JUNIPER BERRY

Qualities: Purification, protection, lucid dreaming.
Juniper clears psychic debris and strengthens spiritual
discernment.
It protects the subtle body during meditation or dreamwork,
ensuring that intuitive insight remains clear and grounded in
truth.

Use:
Diffuse before sleep or energy work to cleanse the mind and
protect intuitive channels.
Place a drop (diluted) on the soles of the feet before dream
meditation for psychic grounding.

Each of these sacred essences refines the vibration of Ajna,
awakening perception through peace and purity.
Through their aromatic intelligence, you remember that vision
is not merely seeing — it is *knowing through the light of
awareness.*

When used with intention, these oils guide you to the still point within — where intuition whispers, and insight unfolds in silence.

"I see clearly within and beyond.
My mind is still, my vision true.
Through light and scent, I awaken wisdom."

HOW TO USE THIRD EYE CHAKRA OILS

- Diffusion:
  Add a few drops of Frankincense, Sandalwood, or Clary Sage to a diffuser during meditation, journaling, or visualization.
  Their gentle aroma quiets mental chatter and opens intuitive awareness.
- Anointing:
  Blend your chosen oil with a carrier oil and apply (diluted) to the forehead between the brows, temples, or crown.
  As you do, visualize indigo light radiating outward — expanding clarity and perception.
- Inhalation Ritual:
  Cup your hands around your nose and inhale deeply.
  With each breath, imagine the aroma traveling upward to the center of your brow, awakening calm vision and inner light.
  Exhale slowly, releasing confusion or doubt.
- Meditation or Dreamwork:
  Apply a drop of Lavender or Juniper Berry (diluted) to the brow before sleep or meditation.
  Set an intention to receive guidance or insight through dreams, intuition, or inner knowing.
- Mantra Practice:
  Before meditating on the mantra OM, anoint the Third Eye with Frankincense or Sandalwood.

As you chant, visualize ripples of indigo light expanding through your mind, harmonizing thought and intuition.

AFFIRMATION TO PAIR WITH AROMATHERAPY

"With each breath, my vision clears.
I see through the light of awareness.
Intuition guides me, and wisdom flows with ease."

ENERGETIC INSIGHT

Essential oils for the Third Eye Chakra are not merely scents — they are the fragrance of insight, the aroma of awakening.
Each essence carries a vibration that clears illusion and opens perception, reminding the soul that true vision comes from stillness.

Through the union of breath and awareness, these oils help you perceive the unseen — to trust what you feel beyond logic, to see beyond form, and to know without needing to understand.

When fragrance and focus unite, Ajna blossoms.
The mind becomes clear, intuition becomes trust, and perception becomes light — a sacred harmony between wisdom and wonder.

BLENDING FOR INSIGHT: ESSENTIAL OIL COMBINATIONS FOR THE THIRD EYE CHAKRA

Blending essential oils for the Third Eye Chakra (Ajna) is the art of illumination — merging scent, breath, and awareness into a vibration of clarity and inner knowing.
Each blend becomes a meditation in motion, guiding intuition to awaken and perception to expand.

Because Ajna is governed by the element of Light, blends for this chakra should feel cool, luminous, and refined — clearing mental fog, awakening focus, and opening the mind to divine insight.

When crafting your blend, let intention be your compass — for your purpose becomes the frequency that activates the oils.

Combine up to three essential oils in a carrier such as jojoba, sweet almond, or fractionated coconut oil.

Shake gently and charge your blend with focused breath, visualization, or mantra before each use.

1. Inner Vision Blend

Purpose: To awaken intuition and deepen meditation.

Blend:

- 2 drops Frankincense
- 2 drops Lavender
- 1 drop Clary Sage

Use:

Apply (diluted) to the brow center before meditation or journaling.

Inhale deeply while focusing on the space between the eyebrows, allowing the mind to quiet and insight to arise.

Affirmation:

"I see clearly. My inner vision guides me with wisdom and grace."

2. Clarity & Focus Blend

Purpose: To clear mental fog and enhance perception.

Blend:

- 2 drops Peppermint
- 2 drops Rosemary
- 1 drop Lemon

Use:
Diffuse while studying, creating, or performing intuitive work.
Inhale before tasks that require concentration or discernment.

Affirmation:

"My mind is bright and focused. I perceive truth in all things."

3. Dream & Intuition Blend

Purpose: To awaken the subtle vision of the subconscious and enhance dream recall.

Blend:

- 2 drops Sandalwood
- 2 drops Jasmine
- 1 drop Blue Tansy *(or Ylang Ylang for softness)*

Use:
Anoint the temples or diffuse before sleep to invite lucid dreaming and intuitive guidance.
Keep a journal nearby to record insights upon waking.

Affirmation: "My dreams speak with clarity. I receive wisdom through vision."

4. Insight & Illumination Blend

Purpose: To strengthen the connection between intellect and intuition.

Blend:

- 2 drops Frankincense
- 1 drop Myrrh
- 1 drop Clary Sage

Use:
Diffuse or apply (diluted) to the Third Eye and temples during spiritual study or meditation.
Inhale before Reiki, divination, or energy work to deepen perception.

Affirmation:

"Through light I understand. Through silence I see."

5. Tranquil Mind Blend

Purpose: To quiet mental chatter and open awareness to stillness.

Blend:

- 2 drops Lavender
- 2 drops Vetiver
- 1 drop Frankincense

Use:
Diffuse before meditation or reflective journaling.
Massage a few drops (diluted) along the forehead and base of the skull to ground awareness while keeping the mind open and calm.

Affirmation:

"My mind is peaceful. My awareness is infinite."

ENERGETIC INSIGHT

Essential oils for the Third Eye Chakra act as messengers of light — fragrant gateways between thought and intuition. Their subtle aroma refines perception, softens illusion, and opens the inner eye to divine reflection.

When breath, scent, and awareness unite, Ajna awakens. The mind becomes clear, the heart perceives truth, and the soul begins to see with the light of Spirit itself.

CHARGING YOUR BLENDS WITH THE ELEMENT OF LIGHT AND CONSCIOUSNESS

Because the Third Eye Chakra (Ajna) is ruled by Light, illumination, and awareness are its natural activators. Charging your blends through meditation, visualization, or focused intention infuses them with the brilliance of perception and the calm of inner knowing. Light refines energy through awareness, attuning your oils to clarity, intuition, and divine insight. When consciousness and fragrance merge, every breath becomes illumination, and every scent becomes wisdom made visible.

1. Light Infusion

- Hold your blend at the level of your brow.
- Envision a radiant indigo light spiraling around the bottle, glowing brighter with each breath.
- Whisper the bija mantra "OM" seven times, letting its vibration expand through the air like a wave of light.
- As the sound fades, speak softly:

"Light of truth, awaken within this blend.
Let every breath reveal divine understanding."

2. Breath of Illumination

- Cup your blend between your palms at the Third Eye.
- Inhale deeply through the nose, drawing awareness inward.
- Exhale slowly over the bottle, sending your intention as luminous breath.
- Visualize a beam of indigo-violet mist entering the oils, filling them with peace and discernment.
- Repeat gently:

"With each breath, my vision clears.
My inner light awakens."

3. Moonlight Reflection

- Place your blend beneath the full or waxing moon, allowing the cool lunar light to purify and energize it.
- The moon's radiance resonates with Ajna's intuitive nature — receptive, reflective, and luminous.
- As the oils rest, imagine silver-indigo light descending into them like a gentle waterfall of wisdom.
- Whisper:

"By the light of the moon, I see within.
By the stillness of night, I awaken sight."

4. Candle Flame Meditation

- Light a single candle and hold your blend nearby.
- Focus on the flame until your breath and its flicker move in harmony.
- Imagine the flame's glow expanding into your Third Eye — the fire of perception awakening within.

- Visualize this golden light flowing into your oils, merging fire and light into consciousness.
- Speak softly:

"Flame of vision, light of wisdom,
Illuminate this creation with clarity and grace."

5. Prayer of Illumination

Hold your blend at your heart, then raise it to your brow.
Breathe deeply, letting the light of awareness flow through your hands and into the oils.
Speak with presence and sincerity:

"May this blend carry the radiance of truth,
The peace of stillness,
And the clarity of divine sight."

ENERGETIC INSIGHT

Third Eye Chakra blends are not mere fragrances — they are vessels of perception infused with consciousness itself.
Each aroma holds the whisper of revelation, teaching the balance between seeing and understanding, thought and intuition.

Through them, the mind becomes a mirror of Spirit, reflecting truth without distortion. The oils awaken Ajna's essence — the wisdom to see beyond illusion, the humility to trust inner light, and the serenity to let vision become knowing.

When charged with light, these blends vibrate with sacred awareness — illuminating the path between silence and insight, perception and peace.

Crystal + Aroma Activation for Inner Vision

(Third Eye Chakra – Ajna)

The Third Eye Chakra awakens not through force, but through stillness.
It opens when breath, scent, light, and awareness merge —
when perception shifts from seeing outward to seeing within.
This ritual unites two sacred allies — crystals and essential oils
— to clear the mind, awaken intuition, and attune your inner sight to divine illumination.

Preparation

Set aside 10–15 minutes in a quiet, dimly lit space.
Soft indigo or violet lighting, candlelight, or the glow of moonlight is ideal.
Sit comfortably with your spine aligned and your breath calm.

Have these items ready:

- One Third Eye Crystal: Amethyst, Lapis Lazuli, Sodalite, or Labradorite
- Your Intuition Blend: Any essential oil combination from the previous section (or simply Frankincense and Clary Sage diluted in a carrier oil)
- A singing bowl, chime, or soft meditative sound (optional)

1. The Breath of Illumination

Take three slow, deep breaths into your forehead and temples.
Inhale through the nose, drawing cool air into the space behind the brow.

Exhale gently through the mouth, releasing scattered thoughts and inner tension.

With each breath, visualize a wave of indigo light washing through your mind — luminous, calm, and clear.

Whisper:

"I breathe light. I release illusion. I awaken clarity."

2. Anointing the Gateway of Vision

Warm a few drops of your oil blend between your palms.
Cup your hands over your nose, inhaling the aroma with awareness.
Then, with reverence, anoint:

- The Third Eye (between the brows): Perception and insight
- The Throat: Expression of inner truth
- The Crown: Connection to divine consciousness

As you touch each point, breathe presence into it.
Feel the scent clearing your mental field, dissolving illusion, and aligning perception with truth.

Affirm softly:

"I see through the eyes of wisdom.
My vision is pure, my awareness is clear."

3. Crystal Resonance

Hold your crystal in your left (receiving) hand.
Bring it to the center of your forehead and close your eyes.

Visualize soft indigo-violet light radiating from the stone —
pulsing gently with your breath.
Trace small, clockwise circles over your Third Eye as you
inhale.
With each motion, feel your inner vision expanding like ripples
in still water.

Whisper or hum the mantra:

"OM."

Let the vibration fill your skull and flow through your spine.
This is the resonance of illumination awakening within you.

4. The Light Meditation

Place the crystal over your Third Eye (or rest it in your open
palms).
Visualize a radiant sphere of light spinning at your brow center
— glowing brighter with every breath.
With each inhale, it expands outward, clearing confusion and
revealing truth.
With each exhale, it sends light through your aura — peaceful,
clear, and knowing.

Rest your attention in the silence between breaths.
Here, seeing becomes knowing; thought becomes light.

Whisper:

"I am light perceiving light.
I see with the clarity of the soul."

5. Integration

Bring one hand to your heart and the other to your forehead.
Feel the bridge between compassion and vision glowing in
harmony.
You are both observer and creation — the seer and the seen.

Affirm gently:

"My heart feels truth.
My mind perceives truth.
My soul reveals truth."

Take several grounding breaths.
Open your eyes softly and remain for a few moments in the
quiet afterglow — centered, luminous, and serene.

Aftercare

- Cleanse your crystal in moonlight or by sound (chime,
  mantra, or singing bowl).
- Store your oil blend in a peaceful, elevated space or
  beside an amethyst cluster to preserve its clarity.
- Repeat this ritual weekly or whenever intuition feels
  dimmed or scattered.

When practiced with devotion, this ritual reminds you that
seeing is sacred — not to predict or control, but to perceive
truth through stillness.
Through crystal, aroma, and light, you awaken the radiant
vision of Ajna — the quiet intelligence of Spirit seeing through
you.

Somatic Practices for the Third Eye Chakra

RECLAIMING CLARITY THROUGH STILLNESS AND AWARENESS

Where the Throat Chakra releases truth through sound, the Third Eye Chakra — Ajna, the seat of perception, intuition, and wisdom — transforms sound into silence, and silence into vision.
This is the realm of light and insight, where breath becomes awareness, and awareness becomes illumination.

The Third Eye thrives on stillness, rhythm, and reflection. When clouded by distraction, overthinking, or disbelief, energy gathers in the forehead, temples, and eyes — fragmenting attention and dimming inner vision.
Somatic awareness restores equilibrium, teaching you to *see without strain, perceive without judgment,* and *move from inner clarity.*

The following practices refine perception and restore intuitive presence — helping you live, move, and see through the clarity of the soul rather than the noise of the mind.

1. Luminous Breath: Awakening Inner Vision

This breath harmonizes Ajna through stillness and light, clearing mental fog and inviting intuitive awareness.

Practice:

1. Sit comfortably, with spine tall and eyes closed.
2. Inhale slowly through the nose, drawing breath into the space behind the forehead.
3. Exhale softly through the mouth, releasing tension from the brow and temples.

4. Visualize indigo light expanding with each inhale and softening with each exhale.
5. Continue for several rounds, letting your awareness rest in the space between breaths.

Mantra:

"With each breath, my mind clears.
I see with calm and clarity."

2. Eye of Stillness: Releasing Mental Strain

Tension around the eyes, forehead, and scalp often reflects mental fatigue or resistance to seeing truth. This release opens the channels of perception and calms overactive thought.

Practice:

1. Gently close your eyes and place your fingertips on your brow center.
2. Massage small, slow circles outward toward the temples.
3. Inhale deeply through the nose; exhale with a soft sigh, relaxing the eyes into darkness.
4. Rest your palms lightly over your closed eyes, feeling warmth and stillness.
5. Allow your inner gaze to drift inward, beyond the surface of thought.

Mantra:

"I release all strain.
I see from the stillness within."

3. The Bridge of Awareness: Connecting Mind and Heart

This exercise unites intuitive perception (Third Eye) with emotional wisdom (Heart Chakra).

Practice:

1. Sit tall. Place one hand over your heart, the other on your forehead.
2. Inhale into the heart, sensing compassion and warmth.
3. Exhale through the brow, sending that compassion upward as light.
4. Continue for several breaths, feeling a current of soft turquoise-indigo energy flowing between heart and mind.
5. Let awareness rest in this bridge — love informing insight, insight softening love.

Mantra:

"My heart feels truth.
My mind perceives it with wisdom."

4. Light Flow Movement: Expanding Perception Through Motion

This mindful movement awakens the element of Light through graceful motion and breath.

Practice:

1. Stand or sit with arms relaxed by your sides.
2. Inhale as you slowly raise your arms outward and upward, palms open toward the sky.
3. Exhale as you bring your palms together before your Third Eye.
4. With each motion, visualize gathering light with your inhale and focusing it with your exhale.
5. Move like a wave of illumination — fluid, calm, and aware.

Mantra:

"I gather light with my breath.
I see truth with ease."

5. Inner Listening: Seeing Beyond the Eyes

Perception is not limited to what the eyes can see.
This meditation deepens intuitive hearing — awareness beyond
sound, vision beyond form.

Practice:

1. Sit quietly with your eyes closed.
2. Bring your awareness to the space between your
   eyebrows — the seat of your inner sight.
3. Observe the play of subtle sensations, colors, or
   darkness without trying to change anything.
4. Listen for the silence beneath all sounds — the still hum
   of consciousness itself.
5. Rest here, letting awareness dissolve into pure
   observation.

Mantra:

"I listen to light.
I see through silence."

ENERGETIC INSIGHT

The body perceives long before the mind interprets.
When the jaw softens, the eyes relax, and the breath slows,
awareness rises effortlessly — turning perception into presence.

Somatic awareness at Ajna teaches that true vision begins not in
effort, but in surrender.

To breathe, move, and perceive from this center is to see beyond illusion — to witness the unity beneath all form.

As Ajna awakens through stillness and light, perception becomes illumination — not to know more, but to understand more deeply; not to control, but to see clearly.
When the Third Eye Chakra is balanced, your awareness becomes medicine — a ray of insight, compassion, and peace shining quietly into the world.

Yoga Poses for the Third Eye Chakra

AWAKENING INTUITION, VISION, AND INNER CLARITY

The Third Eye Chakra (Ajna) governs perception, intuition, and the union of logic and insight.
Through gentle postures that balance the nervous system, calm the mind, and stimulate the space between the brows, you awaken your inner sight — the clarity beyond thought.
These movements enhance mental focus, harmonize the hemispheres of the brain, and open the subtle pathways of awareness, helping you trust what you see and perceive from within.

1. Child's Pose (Balasana) – Bowing to Inner Wisdom

Kneel on the mat, bring your big toes together, and fold forward, resting your forehead on the ground or a cushion.
Extend your arms forward or alongside your body.
As your brow touches the earth, surrender your thoughts into stillness and humility.

Focus: Surrender, introspection, grounding insight.
Affirmation:

"I rest in stillness.
My inner wisdom guides me."

2. Dolphin Pose (Ardha Pincha Mayurasana) – Strengthening the Mind's Focus

From hands and knees, lower your forearms to the mat, interlacing fingers if comfortable.
Lift your hips toward the sky, keeping your head off the floor or gently resting the crown for mild pressure.
Feel energy flow from crown to brow, awakening alertness without tension.

Focus: Concentration, mental clarity, energetic balance.
Affirmation:

"My mind is steady.
My focus is clear and calm."

3. Forward Fold (Uttanasana) – Seeing the World Upside Down

Stand tall and exhale as you hinge at the hips, folding forward.
Let your head and arms hang heavy.
With each breath, release mental chatter and allow fresh perspective to flow in.

Focus: Perspective, surrender, mental release.
Affirmation:

"I release what clouds my mind.
I welcome insight and peace."

4. Seated Forward Bend (Paschimottanasana) – Turning Vision Inward

Sit with legs extended.
Inhale to lengthen your spine, and as you exhale, fold gently forward from the hips.
Rest your forehead on a block or your knees if comfortable.
Let each breath carry awareness deeper within.

Focus: Introspection, patience, surrender of thought.
Affirmation:

"I see inwardly.
My insight deepens with every breath."

5. Eagle Pose (Garudasana) – The Single-Pointed Gaze

From standing, cross your right thigh over your left and wrap your right arm under the left.
Focus your gaze softly on a single point in front of you — the *drishti* of awareness.
Breathe through the stillness, cultivating balance between intuition and intellect.

Focus: Inner balance, awareness, discipline of mind.
Affirmation:

"My focus is steady.
I see through illusion to truth."

6. Supported Shoulderstand (Salamba Sarvangasana) – Awakening the Inner Light

Lie on your back, lift your legs overhead, and support your lower back with your hands.
Keep the chin gently tucked toward the chest, feeling subtle

pressure along the throat and forehead.
Breathe deeply, allowing energy to rise from heart to brow.

Focus: Clarity, intuition, and energetic elevation.
Affirmation:

"I lift into light.
My awareness shines clear."

7. Legs-Up-the-Wall Pose (Viparita Karani) – Restoring Calm Perception

Sit close to a wall and swing your legs up while reclining onto your back.
Rest your arms by your sides, palms open.
Soften your gaze or close your eyes completely, allowing calm to wash through your mind.

Focus: Nervous system reset, intuitive reflection, surrender.
Affirmation:

"I see from stillness.
My intuition is effortless."

8. Reclined Butterfly with Third Eye Focus (Supta Baddha Konasana)

Lie on your back with the soles of your feet together and knees open.
Place a folded cloth or crystal (Amethyst or Lapis Lazuli) over your Third Eye.
Breathe gently, sensing waves of indigo light expanding through your forehead.

Focus: Intuitive connection, energetic cleansing, serenity.
Affirmation:

"I open to divine insight.
My vision is pure and illuminated."

9. Corpse Pose with Light Awareness (Savasana with Ajna Focus)

Lie flat with arms by your sides.
Close your eyes and rest your inner gaze at the point between your eyebrows.
With each inhale, visualize indigo light expanding.
With each exhale, allow your awareness to dissolve into infinite space.

Focus: Integration, clarity, unity of mind and spirit.
Affirmation:

"I am awareness itself.
Light guides my being."

ENERGETIC INSIGHT

Third Eye Chakra Yoga transforms thought into observation and tension into illumination.
Each posture becomes a meditation — an invitation to witness rather than to control.
Through gentle inversions, forward folds, and still focus, the veil of illusion thins, and perception awakens.

When Ajna flows freely, your movements are guided not by sight, but by vision; not by logic, but by knowing.
You no longer seek clarity — you *are* clarity.
In this harmony of breath, body, and awareness, you awaken the light within the mind, the wisdom that perceives not through eyes, but through consciousness itself.

Healing Through Sound, Light & Lunar Cycles

HONORING THE ELEMENT OF LIGHT AND THE RHYTHMS OF INNER VISION

The Third Eye Chakra (Ajna) is ruled by the element of light — the subtle radiance of awareness that illuminates truth beyond illusion.
Where the Throat Chakra vibrates with sound, the Third Eye resonates with silence — the space in which sound becomes understanding, and reflection becomes revelation.

Just as the moon mirrors the sun's light, so too does the Third Eye reflect the light of spirit within the stillness of mind.
When your inner vision grows dim, it is often not from darkness, but from distraction. Healing Ajna means returning to inner luminosity — the light that perceives without the need to look, that knows without the need to think.

To awaken the Third Eye is to align with the rhythms of perception — the waxing and waning of insight, the movement between contemplation and knowing.
Through the sacred interplay of sound, silence, and lunar light, awareness becomes radiant once more.

Light as a Sacred Healer

Light clarifies what shadow conceals.
It does not argue with darkness — it reveals it.

Across mystical traditions, light has been the symbol of truth and consciousness — from the divine flame of the Vedic *Agni*, to the halo of enlightenment in Buddhist art, to the "Inner Lamp" of the mystics in Christian and Hermetic schools.

Where sound carries vibration, light carries revelation —
dissolving confusion and awakening vision.

In Ajna's teaching, illumination is not a flash of brilliance; it is
a soft and steady seeing.
Every breath, every still moment, every gaze inward is a sacred
act of remembrance — the recognition that you are both the
observer and the light being observed.

Intention for Practice

"Like light, I see with clarity.
I trust the wisdom that shines within."

Lunar Ritual For Intuition And Insight

A CEREMONY FOR CLARITY, ILLUMINATION, AND INNER PEACE

This ritual invites you to honor your intuitive cycles — to
release mental strain, awaken higher perception, and rest in the
luminous calm of awareness.
It is best performed during the waxing or full moon, when the
reflective light of the moon amplifies the Third Eye's receptive
power.

You'll Need:

- One candle (indigo, violet, or white) to symbolize
  illumination and wisdom
- A bowl of water to mirror the moon's reflection — the
  mind made still
- A few drops of essential oils such as frankincense, clary
  sage, or sandalwood
- One Third Eye crystal (Amethyst, Lapis Lazuli, or
  Sodalite)

- Optional: soft chime, singing bowl, or mantra recording tuned to 432 Hz or 852 Hz

1. Prepare the Space

Choose a quiet setting where shadows move gently with the light.
Light your candle and place it beside the bowl of water — a meeting of fire and reflection, consciousness and receptivity.

Take three slow, deep breaths.
Inhale through the nose, bringing awareness into your forehead.
Exhale through the mouth, releasing tension, expectation, or mental noise.

Say softly:

"With this flame, I awaken vision.
With this stillness, I see the truth within."

Add your chosen oils to the water or diffuser.
Let the scent evoke serenity and spacious awareness — the fragrance of still knowing.

2. Awaken the Inner Light

Hold your crystal in your hand or place it gently between your brows.
Inhale deeply; exhale with a soft hum or whisper of "Om."
Feel the vibration travel upward through your skull and dissolve into silence.

Visualize a radiant indigo light glowing at your Third Eye — a luminous orb expanding and contracting with your breath.
Sense your awareness resting in that light, not as effort, but as presence.

Whisper or chant the bija mantra:

"OM."

Let it resonate through your being — not loud, but pure — until your mind feels like open sky.

3. Reflect and Release

As the light flickers upon the water, gaze softly into the reflection.
Notice what emotions, thoughts, or impressions surface without judgment.
With each exhale, release mental tension into the water — doubts, self-criticism, the need for control.

You may say:

"I release confusion."
"I release illusion."
"I release all that clouds my inner sight."

Visualize these energies dissolving like ripples fading across a midnight lake.

4. Illuminate with Intention

Place both hands over your brow center and take three deep breaths.
With each inhale, draw light into your Third Eye.
With each exhale, radiate that light outward through your aura.

Whisper or hum softly:

"I am the light of awareness.
I see truth with serenity."

Now, lift your gaze to the moon or imagine its glow above your forehead.
Sense the moonlight merging with your inner light — reflection becoming illumination.

5. Seal in Stillness

When you feel complete, close your eyes and rest in silence.
Listen for the quiet hum that exists beneath all sound — the resonance of pure awareness.
This is the luminous field of Ajna — the mind at peace with itself.

Touch the surface of the water and whisper:

"Light reveals, silence restores, and I am whole in both."

Pour the water into the earth or down the drain with gratitude, symbolically releasing all that no longer serves your clarity.

Purpose

This ritual reminds you that healing the mind is not about seeing more — it is about *seeing clearly.*
Light does not struggle to shine; it simply reveals what is.
By aligning your awareness with lunar cycles, you remember that insight also waxes and wanes — that clarity grows through both illumination and rest.

Each silence becomes a sanctuary, each thought a reflection upon still water.
When you live in rhythm with the moon and the light of consciousness, you awaken the eternal eye of awareness — calm, radiant, and unclouded.

When Ajna is balanced, perception becomes peace.
You no longer look outward for vision;
you simply open inward — and see.

Affirmations, Mudras, and Daily Balancing Practices for the Third Eye Chakra

AWAKENING INTUITION, INSIGHT, AND INNER VISION

The Third Eye Chakra (Ajna) is the sacred center of perception, intuition, and inner knowing — the bridge between thought and awareness, reason and revelation.
When balanced, it grants clarity, imagination, and trust in the unseen.
When clouded, the mind becomes restless, perception blurs, and intuition fades behind the noise of doubt or overthinking.

Through daily affirmations, mindful mudras, and meditative awareness, the Third Eye clears like a sky after rain — still, luminous, and full of vision.
These practices awaken the union of intellect and intuition, allowing insight to arise naturally from within.

Affirmations for Clarity and Intuitive Vision

Thoughts are the language of the mind, but insight is the whisper of the soul.
When spoken with awareness, affirmations align your mind with the higher truth of your being.
Place one hand over your forehead and one over your heart as you speak, connecting intuition with compassion.

Morning Activation Affirmations

- "I trust my intuition and see clearly."
- "My inner vision guides me with wisdom and peace."
- "I perceive beyond illusion into truth."
- "My thoughts are clear, focused, and illuminated."
- "I am connected to divine intelligence and insight."

Evening Integration Affirmations

- "I release overthinking and rest in clarity."
- "My mind is calm, my vision is clear."
- "I see the lessons in each experience."
- "I surrender control and trust the unfolding of life."
- "The light of awareness shines through my dreams."

MANTRA FOR MEDITATION
OM — The Sound of Creation and Consciousness

The bija mantra of Ajna, OM, unites all vibrations into one
sacred sound — the frequency of awareness itself.
Chant softly, allowing the vibration to travel from your brow
through your mind and into the stillness beyond thought.

Focus:
Visualize indigo light pulsing gently between your eyebrows,
expanding with each repetition of "OM."
Let the sound dissolve into silence — the space where intuition
begins.

MUDRAS FOR BALANCING THE THIRD EYE CHAKRA

In yogic tradition, mudras channel prana (life force) through
specific pathways, refining energy and deepening awareness.
For Ajna, they open perception, balance hemispheric brain
activity, and awaken spiritual insight.

1. Kalesvara Mudra — The Gesture of Still Mind

This mudra stills mental chatter, sharpens concentration, and reveals the clarity of intuitive wisdom.

How to Practice:

1. Bring your fingertips together so that only the tips touch, forming a diamond shape.
2. Touch the thumbs and middle fingers together while curling the other fingers inward.
3. Bring the mudra before your forehead.
4. Inhale deeply and exhale slowly, observing the rhythm of your breath.
5. Rest in awareness for several minutes.

Affirmation:

"My thoughts are calm. My awareness is clear."

2. Gyan Mudra — The Gesture of Wisdom

Symbolizing the unity of individual consciousness with universal intelligence, this mudra enhances intuition and insight.

How to Practice:

1. Touch the tip of the index finger to the tip of the thumb.
2. Keep the other fingers extended and relaxed.
3. Rest your hands on your knees, palms facing upward.
4. Breathe naturally and gaze softly at the point between your eyebrows.

Affirmation:

"I am guided by wisdom beyond words."

3. Kaleshvara Mudra (Heart-Mind Connection Variation)

A variation focusing on balancing the heart and mind for emotional clarity and spiritual perception.

How to Practice:

1. Place the tips of the middle fingers together and thumbs touching.
2. Allow the other fingers to interlace loosely.
3. Hold the hands near the heart or between the eyebrows.
4. Inhale for a count of four, hold for two, exhale for four.

Affirmation:

"My heart informs my mind. My mind illuminates my heart."

DAILY BALANCING PRACTICES
1. Morning Light Meditation

Upon waking, sit quietly and face the rising light.
Inhale deeply through the nose, drawing light into your forehead.
Exhale gently, releasing mental fog.
Whisper:

"Today I will see clearly — through eyes of love and wisdom."

2. Indigo Visualization

Take a few slow breaths and visualize a deep indigo sphere of light spinning gently between your brows.
With every inhale, the light brightens; with every exhale, your awareness expands.
This visualization enhances focus, creativity, and intuitive flow.

3. Evening Reflection Practice

Before sleep, place your hands in Gyan Mudra and close your eyes.
Review your day not through judgment, but through observation.
Ask:

"What truth did I see today?"
"What illusion am I ready to release?"
Allow answers to arise softly, without forcing.

ENERGETIC INSIGHT

Ajna teaches that true sight does not come from the eyes — it comes from awareness.
When the Third Eye Chakra is balanced, clarity flows effortlessly; intuition and logic become allies, not opposites.
You begin to trust your inner guidance as naturally as you trust your breath.

Your mind becomes a mirror — reflecting light, not projecting illusion.
Perception becomes peace; imagination becomes revelation.

When you live from this awareness, every moment is illuminated. You no longer seek enlightenment — you realize you *are* the light through which all things are seen.

Food Therapy for the Third Eye Chakra

NOURISHING INTUITION, PERCEPTION, AND INNER VISION

The Third Eye Chakra (Ajna) governs the pituitary gland, eyes, nervous system, and higher centers of perception.
It is the body's seat of clarity — the energetic lens through which you perceive truth, insight, and wisdom.
To feed Ajna is to nourish both body and mind with purity and light — foods that calm the intellect, clear mental fog, and awaken subtle awareness.

When balanced, the mind becomes a mirror — steady, intuitive, and luminous.
When imbalanced, one may experience headaches, eye strain, anxiety, or confusion, and the inner voice may be drowned out by mental chatter or rigid thinking.

The goal of Ajna food therapy is to clarify, lighten, and refine — cultivating awareness through foods that stabilize the nervous system, support hormonal balance, and open perception.
Here, nourishment becomes meditation, and every bite becomes a prayer for vision.

Energetic Principles

- Element: Light
- Sense: Intuition (Beyond the Physical Senses)
- Color: Indigo
- Location: Between the eyebrows, extending to the pineal and pituitary glands
- Themes: Perception, clarity, awareness, imagination, insight

Foods That Heal And Balance The Third Eye Chakra

PURPLE AND INDIGO FOODS — THE FREQUENCY OF INSIGHT

Indigo-hued foods vibrate with Ajna's wavelength — rich in antioxidants that cleanse the blood, eyes, and brain.
They purify perception, enhance focus, and promote cellular vitality — the biological reflection of spiritual clarity.

Examples:

- Blueberries, blackberries, purple grapes, and plums
- Eggplant, purple cabbage, and beets (for grounding higher awareness)
- Figs and prunes for subtle detoxification
- Acai, goji berries, and elderberries for brain support

How to Use:
Incorporate these foods in smoothies, fresh bowls, or lightly cooked meals to preserve their life force.
As you eat, visualize indigo light filling your body, clearing your mind, and opening the inner eye.

BRAIN-NOURISHING FOODS — THE CLARITY CONNECTION

Ajna thrives on a well-nourished nervous system.
Choose foods rich in omega-3s and antioxidants to protect neural pathways and encourage mental stillness.

Examples:

- Walnuts, flaxseed, chia seeds, and hemp hearts
- Avocados for gentle grounding and cognitive balance

- Sea vegetables (nori, kelp, spirulina) for trace minerals and iodine
- Dark leafy greens — kale, spinach, and chard — to oxygenate the brain

How to Use:
Blend these into smoothies or sprinkle them on salads to energize the brain and support pineal gland function.
Chew slowly and with focus — each bite becomes a mindful act of clarity.

LIGHT AND SATVIC FOODS — THE DIET OF AWARENESS

In yogic tradition, Ajna resonates with sattva — the quality of purity, balance, and illumination.
Sattvic foods quiet the mind and refine perception, nurturing a state of tranquil awareness.

Examples:

- Fresh fruits, steamed vegetables, light grains (quinoa, basmati rice, amaranth)
- Almonds and sesame seeds (soaked or lightly toasted)
- Fresh herbs like basil, mint, and sage for mental purification
- Herbal infusions such as gotu kola, butterfly pea flower, or tulsi

Ritual Practice:
Before eating, pause and whisper:

"May this food illuminate my mind and awaken my inner sight."
Then, take your first bite in silence, allowing the senses to merge with stillness.

DETOXIFYING AND HYDRATING FOODS — CLEARING THE INNER LENS

The Third Eye's physical counterpart, the pineal gland, is sensitive to toxins, dehydration, and stimulants.
To keep it clear, minimize processed sugar, artificial additives, and excess caffeine.
Favor hydration and natural cleansing foods.

Examples:

- Warm water with lemon or cucumber slices
- Coconut water and herbal teas (especially lavender, mugwort, or blue lotus)
- Fresh greens and light soups
- Chlorophyll-rich juices for cellular detox

Tip:
Drink mindfully, visualizing each sip as a current of light washing through your consciousness.

SPICES AND HERBS FOR PERCEPTION AND CALM

Ajna flourishes through aromatic clarity — subtle, cooling spices that awaken without overstimulating.

Examples:

- Star anise, fennel, and cardamom for clarity and digestion
- Sage and rosemary for focus and mental cleansing
- Clove and nutmeg (in moderation) for dream activation
- Gotu kola or bacopa for memory and intuition support

How to Use:
Infuse these herbs into teas, sprinkle on light meals, or inhale

their aroma before meditation.
Their vibration helps align perception with peace.

ENERGETIC INSIGHT

Feeding Ajna is not merely about nutrition — it is a ritual of
remembrance.
You are not only feeding the body; you are feeding perception
itself.
When your diet becomes clean, light, and intentional, your
thoughts follow suit — luminous, spacious, and serene.

Each meal becomes a meditation in mindfulness.
Each flavor a frequency of awareness.

As you nourish this center, you will find that insight no longer
needs to be sought — it simply arises from the quiet clarity
within.

Eat in stillness.
Drink in light.
Perceive with peace.
This is the nourishment of Ajna — where food becomes
frequency and awareness becomes illumination.

Water-Infused Fruits and Clarity-Enhancing Vegetables

COOLING THE MIND, AWAKENING VISION, AND NOURISHING THE LIGHT WITHIN

Fruits and vegetables rich in water and air elements support
Ajna's clarity and perception.
They hydrate the body, calm the mind, and harmonize both
hemispheres of the brain, allowing intuitive vision to shine

through.

These foods carry the frequency of illumination — cleansing the physical senses and refining the subtle senses of awareness.

Examples

- Blueberries, black grapes, blackberries, and figs — purifiers of blood and vision
- Cucumber, fennel, celery, and endive — cooling and hydrating for the mind
- Coconut water, pears, and aloe vera juice — soothing and clarifying for intuition
- Steamed cauliflower, lotus root, and asparagus — grounding higher thought in the body

How to Use:

Enjoy fruits raw and vibrant; steam vegetables lightly to preserve their prana.

Drink water infused with mint, basil, or blueberry slices to refresh perception and cool mental overactivity.

Each sip becomes a reflection — a moment of mindful awareness.

Foods to Balance Excess Light Energy

When Ajna is overstimulated, one may experience mental fatigue, spaciness, insomnia, or overstated visions — living too much in thought and not enough in embodiment.

To restore balance, ground your awareness with gently warming, nourishing foods that bring light into form.

GROUNDING AND RESTORATIVE CHOICES

- Root vegetables such as beets, carrots, and yams (connecting vision to Earth)
- Warm soups with lentils, barley, or miso
- Herbal teas made with ashwagandha, tulsi, or cardamom

- Cooked grains — amaranth, brown rice, or quinoa

Avoid: Overuse of stimulants, refined sugar, and excessive fasting or raw diets, which can scatter energy and cloud true perception.

RITUAL OF MINDFUL DRINKING

Ajna resonates with stillness and reflection.
Transform each sip of water or tea into a meditation of illumination.

Practice:

1. Hold your glass or cup at brow level. Gaze softly into the surface of the liquid, seeing it as the mirror of consciousness.
2. Inhale deeply through the nose; exhale through the mouth, relaxing the forehead and eyes.
3. Whisper:

   "May this water clear my mind and open my sight."

4. Drink slowly, feeling cool clarity flow through your body.
5. Rest in silence, observing the calm brightness that follows.

Affirmation:

"Each sip awakens clarity.
Each breath opens perception.
I see truth with calm and grace."

ENERGETIC INSIGHT

Eating for Ajna is not about restriction — it is about refinement.
When you eat and drink with intention, your food becomes
luminous, your water becomes wisdom.
Hydration brings awareness; nourishment brings grounding;
presence brings vision.

Each meal can be an act of awakening — a chance to listen to
the quiet light within.
As the body becomes still and clear, the mind becomes a mirror
for divine understanding.

Eat lightly.
Drink slowly.
See deeply.

This is the nourishment of Ajna — where food becomes
frequency, water becomes reflection, and clarity becomes your
natural state.

Herbal Bath For Clarity And Inner Vision

A RITUAL BATH TO QUIET THE MIND AND AWAKEN INTUITION

This sacred bath ritual calms mental overactivity, clears
energetic congestion in the head and eyes, and restores harmony
to the subtle currents of perception.
It softens the boundaries between thought and intuition —
releasing mental strain and opening the gateway to insight.
Through warmth, scent, and stillness, the waters of Ajna invite
you into the silence behind thought, where true vision resides.

INGREDIENTS:

- 1 cup Epsom or Himalayan salt *(to cleanse the mind and body of tension)*
- 1 tbsp dried lavender *(for stillness and subtle awareness)*
- 1 tbsp dried sage or rosemary *(to purify the mind and strengthen clarity)*
- 1 tsp mugwort or chamomile *(to open intuition and calm nervous energy)*
- 3 drops sandalwood or frankincense essential oil *(to enhance spiritual focus and meditation)*

INSTRUCTIONS:

1. Add the salts and herbs to warm bathwater, swirling clockwise to invite illumination and peace.
2. Step into the bath with reverence. Let the water cover your brow and crown lightly, as if anointing you with light.
3. Close your eyes and breathe deeply into your forehead, softening the space between your eyebrows.
4. Visualize an indigo light expanding through your third eye — calm, radiant, and infinite.
5. With each exhale, release confusion, worry, and the need to know.
6. With each inhale, draw in stillness, insight, and the quiet truth of your higher self.

Intention:
Let scattered thoughts dissolve in the water.
Let clear perception rise like light from within.
Emerge from the bath grounded, luminous, and attuned to your inner knowing.

Affirmation for Herbal Healing:

"My mind is still and clear.
I see through the eyes of the soul.
Each breath awakens wisdom.
Each moment reveals truth."

Nature Practices for the Third Eye Chakra

RECONNECTING TO THE LIGHT OF AWARENESS

Where the Throat Chakra teaches expression through sound, the
Third Eye Chakra (Ajna) opens perception through silence.
Its element is Light — not the outer light that shines upon
things, but the inner radiance that allows you to *see*.
To heal and balance Ajna is to awaken conscious seeing: to
witness without judgment, to trust your intuition, and to dwell
in the space where thought becomes understanding.

Nature mirrors this clarity — through the dawn's glow, the still
surface of water, the flicker of starlight, and the quiet pulse of
night.
Each practice below opens the mind to its natural clarity — not
by adding more, but by *seeing more clearly what already is*.

1. Star Gazing: Receiving The Light Of The Unseen

The stars speak the language of the soul — vast, ancient, and
silent.
Gazing at them quiets the mind's chatter and restores
connection to higher knowing.

Practice:

- Find a dark, open place where you can see the night sky.
- Sit or lie down comfortably and gaze upward, breathing through your third eye.
- Feel the infinite expanse of stars mirrored within you.
- Whisper:

"The universe within me reflects the universe above."

Insight:
Star gazing teaches that intuition is not found in the noise of thought, but in the quiet between the stars.

2. Moonlight Meditation: Awakening Inner Reflection

The moon embodies Ajna's receptive nature — cool, reflective, and luminous.
Meditating under moonlight harmonizes intuition, emotion, and perception.

Practice:

- Sit outside under the moon or near a window where its light touches you.
- Place one hand on your forehead, one on your heart.
- Inhale the moonlight through your third eye; exhale through your heart.
- Visualize silver light connecting intuition and compassion.
- Whisper:

"I see with calm awareness and love."

3. Still Water Gazing: Mirror Of The Mind

Water reflects light just as the mind reflects truth.
When still, it reveals the sky; when disturbed, it distorts it.
This practice teaches you to quiet the waves of thought.

Practice:

- Sit near a pond, lake, or bowl of still water.
- Gaze softly at the reflection, breathing evenly.
- As thoughts arise, imagine them rippling across the surface — then fading into calm.
- Whisper:

"In stillness, I see clearly."

4. Sunrise Breathing: Calling In Light

Ajna awakens with the rising sun — the daily reminder of illumination.

Practice:

- At dawn, face the rising sun with eyes gently closed.
- Inhale through your nose, drawing golden light into your third eye.
- Exhale slowly through the mouth, releasing shadows of doubt.
- Repeat until you feel clarity and warmth spreading through your forehead.
- Whisper:

"Light rises within me as it rises in the sky."

5. Forest Stillness Walk: Listening With Inner Eyes

True sight requires deep listening — not through the ears, but through presence.
Walking in still awareness allows you to "see" with all senses.

Practice:

- Walk slowly through a forest or natural path without a goal.
- Notice colors, shapes, and subtle light changes around you.
- Allow your gaze to soften and expand, taking in everything at once.
- With each step, repeat inwardly:

"I see beyond appearances. I walk in truth."

6. Light Of Breath Meditation: The Inner Sun

Ajna unites breath and awareness — the rhythm of life with the rhythm of perception.

Practice:

- Sit outdoors or by a window.
- Inhale deeply, visualizing indigo light entering your third eye.
- Exhale, letting it radiate through your mind and aura.
- Feel your awareness expanding — luminous yet centered.
- Whisper:

"Light within me sees light in all."

Affirmation for Nature Connection:

"The light around me mirrors the light within me.
My vision is clear, my awareness still.
I see with peace, I understand with love.
I am the space between thought and knowing —
the eye of clarity, the witness of truth."

Chapter 9 – Advanced Practitioner Applications

Energetic Vision, Frequency Perception, and Light Transmutation

For the advanced practitioner, the Third Eye Chakra (Ajna) represents the field of *illumined perception* — the bridge between energy and consciousness, matter and meaning.
Where the Throat transforms truth into sound, the Third Eye transforms awareness into light.
Here, the work deepens into the art of seeing through energy — perceiving not only form, but the frequency within it.

To master Ajna is to become a vessel of clarity — one who observes without distortion, interprets without projection, and illuminates without force.
At this level, sight is no longer about the eyes; it is about the stillness behind them.
Through disciplined perception, the advanced practitioner learns to *transmute vibration through vision* — dissolving illusion, refining energy, and restoring harmony through awareness itself.

This is the yoga of perception: to see beyond polarity into unity, to perceive truth as frequency, and to hold light steady enough that transformation occurs simply through presence.

ENERGETIC DYNAMICS OF THE THIRD EYE FIELD

The energy of Ajna moves as waves of subtle light — rhythmic, pulsating, and deeply intelligent.
It is both receptive and projective, merging the duality of left and right brain, intuition and intellect, logic and vision.
Within a client's field, this may be perceived as:

- Gentle pressure or tingling between the brows.
- Pulses of indigo or violet light radiating through the forehead and crown.
- Subtle cooling around the temples or eyes.
- Sensations of inner expansion, as if awareness itself is widening beyond the physical body.

When balanced, the energy feels luminous, still, and boundless — perception sharpens, intuition flows easily, and silence feels full rather than empty.
When blocked, the energy becomes cloudy or constricted — often accompanied by tension in the head, overthinking, or difficulty trusting intuition.
When overactive, it may lead to overstimulation — visions without grounding, insomnia, or energetic overload from excess perception without integration.

Advanced mastery begins with discipline of sight: the ability to *see without absorbing* and *witness without reacting*.
You are not collecting impressions — you are refining them into coherence.
Ajna is not about seeing *more*; it is about seeing *purely*.

VIBRATIONAL TRANSMUTATION AND LIGHT ALCHEMY

At the Third Eye, light becomes the alchemical agent of transformation.
Where Vishuddha transmutes through tone, Ajna transmutes through illumination — the radiance of awareness dissolving distortion.

Every perception carries frequency.
When you witness it with neutrality, the vibration reorganizes itself into harmony.
Awareness becomes the healer; observation becomes the medicine.

ENERGETIC PROCESS OF LIGHT TRANSMUTATION

1. Perception: Sense areas of energetic distortion or shadow — heaviness, fog, or visual static in the client's auric field.
2. Illumination: Focus gentle attention through the Third Eye, allowing indigo light to radiate toward the imbalance.
3. Transmutation: Hold pure, unwavering awareness — not forcing, but allowing light to reveal and dissolve resistance.
4. Integration: Withdraw the focus gently and rest in stillness, allowing the recalibrated energy to stabilize in silence.

This process teaches that light follows consciousness — wherever you direct awareness with compassion and clarity, energy reorganizes into order.

ADVANCED APPLICATIONS IN PRACTICE
1. Etheric Vision and Perceptual Tuning

Develop the ability to "see" energy beyond form — not only
colors or patterns, but the *movement of consciousness itself.*
This is not visualization; it is *revelation.*
Practice holding a soft gaze or closed-eye focus while
perceiving the subtle pulsations of light around the body.
Notice how thought, emotion, and intention alter the frequency
of what you perceive.
You are learning to read energy as language.

2. Photonic Breathwork: Activating the Inner Lens

Breath carries light as vibration.
Inhale through the Third Eye, drawing luminous energy from
the cosmos into the center of awareness.
Exhale through the crown or heart, radiating clarity throughout
your field.
Continue until you feel your perception expand beyond linear
thought.
This practice opens the inner lens — where intuition and
illumination merge.

3. Harmonic Gaze Technique

Every practitioner emits frequency through the eyes.
When intention is pure, this gaze becomes healing.
Practice gazing at a candle flame, crystal, or living being with
relaxed focus and neutral compassion.
As your gaze steadies, feel subtle light transmit through your
eyes — not as willpower, but as attunement.
This is the Transmission of Vision — healing through
resonance, not control.

4. Light Codes and Symbolic Perception

Ajna communicates through symbols, archetypes, and luminous geometry.
During advanced sessions, spontaneous patterns may arise in your inner vision.
Rather than interpret, *witness* them.
Each image is a language of light — carrying vibrational instruction.
Allow intuition to translate meaning through feeling, not logic.
This is *claircognizant sight* — knowing through illumination.

5. Transmission Through Stillness

At the highest octave of Ajna, *seeing becomes being.*
Sit with clients in deep silence, eyes gently closed, awareness radiating from the Third Eye.
In this state, your field projects harmonic coherence, inviting theirs to align through entrainment.
No words, no effort — only radiant presence.
This is Light Mastery in its purest form: transformation through luminous stillness.

ENERGETIC INSIGHT

Ajna teaches that mastery is not in seeing visions, but in perceiving truth.
The advanced practitioner no longer seeks experience — they become awareness itself.
When perception is purified of judgment, *light flows unobstructed*, illuminating everything it touches.

True vision is not found in effort, but in surrender.
You are not here to *look* — you are here to *see through.*
Through the eye of light, all things become transparent: energy, emotion, and illusion.

In this still gaze of consciousness, healing occurs effortlessly —
not by doing, but by *being the light that sees all things whole.*

Energetic Assessment: Reading the Light Field

PERCEIVING RESONANCE, PATTERN, AND FREQUENCY THROUGH THE EYE OF ILLUMINATION

Practitioners assess the Third Eye Field (Ajna) by attuning to
the quality of *light, coherence, and perception* around the brow,
temples, and frontal lobes.
Through Reiki scanning, intuitive seeing, or meditative
clairvoyance, one perceives subtle fluctuations in the rhythm of
awareness — the light signatures that reveal the balance
between intuition, intellect, and spiritual insight.

The goal is not to "see" more, but to perceive *purely* — beyond
projection or analysis.
In the Ajna field, clarity arises through stillness. The
practitioner does not chase images; they allow light to reveal
itself.

COMMON ENERGETIC PRESENTATIONS

- Clouded Vision: Mental overactivity, worry, or
  skepticism that dulls intuitive clarity; perception
  becomes blurred or fragmented.
- Over-Illumined Field: Excess stimulation from spiritual
  overexertion — visions without grounding, insomnia, or
  imbalance between intuition and logic.
- Diminished Glow: Fatigue, disconnection from inner
  wisdom, or reliance solely on external knowledge;
  intuitive faculties appear dim or unfocused.

- Split Frequency: Conflict between what one *knows* and what one *believes*; competing energies between intellect and intuition.
- Radiant Equilibrium: Indigo-violet light flows evenly through the forehead; perception is calm, centered, and expansive.

Each presentation reflects not only energetic flow but the individual's relationship with *truth as insight* — how they perceive, interpret, and trust their inner vision.
To "read" the Third Eye is to sense where perception has turned into projection — and where truth still shines beneath illusion.

LIGHT TRANSMUTATION PROTOCOL
From Perception to Illumination

In advanced energy work, the goal is not merely to activate the Third Eye, but to refine its light — transmuting distortion into radiant coherence.
This is the alchemy of vision: transforming the density of confusion into the brilliance of awareness.

Protocol:

1. Anchor the Root of Awareness:
   Begin by grounding the client's energy through the base and heart.
   Visualize a current of white light descending through the spine, stabilizing the field.
   This prevents overstimulation and integrates higher vision into the body.
2. Awaken the Light Field:
   Move your hands near the client's forehead or hover above the brow.
   Visualize a sphere of indigo light expanding and pulsating between your palms.

Inhale clarity; exhale calmness.
Feel the breath clearing fog from the inner eye.

3. Invite Perception:
    Encourage the client to close their eyes and ask silently:

    "What truth am I ready to see?"
    Do not interpret — allow the energy to reveal.
    The act of conscious witnessing initiates alignment.

4. Channel Reiki or Light Frequency:
    Direct a beam of subtle, luminous energy into the Ajna center.
    Use soft toning (OM) or silent visualization to elevate the vibratory rate.
    Perceive shadows dissolving into light — confusion transmuted into understanding.

5. Seal and Integrate:
    When the field feels still and bright, trace a figure-eight of indigo and white light over the brow.
    Whisper or affirm:

    "All that was unseen becomes known.
    All that was illusion becomes light."

POLARITY INTEGRATION: THE TWO EYES OF ONE VISION

Ajna governs the union of dual perception — the left eye of reason and the right eye of intuition.
Its mastery lies in merging polarity into unity: seeing both inner and outer worlds as reflections of one infinite awareness.

Within advanced practice, the healer harmonizes two perceptual currents:

- Yang (Active Seeing): Focused vision, discernment, analysis, conscious attention.

- Yin (Receptive Seeing): Inner vision, dreaming, intuitive insight, contemplative awareness.

When Yang dominates, perception becomes rigid — clarity turns into control.
When Yin dominates, perception becomes diffuse — intuition ungrounded, untethered.
When balanced, vision becomes truth — lucid, calm, and whole.

Integration Practice:

Place one hand over the brow (insight) and one over the heart (wisdom).
Breathe deeply, allowing energy to flow between them — a thread of indigo and emerald light linking love and understanding.
Repeat silently:

"I see through the heart.
I know through the soul.
My vision serves truth."

LUMINANCE PRACTICE: THE INNER LIGHT ALIGNMENT

For advanced self-practitioners, this technique refines the Ajna current, unites hemispheres of perception, and awakens the *inner seer*.

Steps:

1. Sit comfortably, spine erect and eyes closed.
2. Inhale gently through the nose, drawing light into the space between the brows.
3. Exhale slowly through the mouth, visualizing radiance expanding outward from the forehead.

4. Sense light filling the skull — the temples, eyes, and crown — until all becomes luminous stillness.
5. Rest in the awareness that perceives — not the image, but the observer itself.
6. End by affirming:

"I am light perceiving light.
I see with clarity and compassion."

ADVANCED INSIGHT: THE ALCHEMY OF LIGHT

To master Ajna is to master perception itself.
This chakra refines thought, emotion, and experience into understanding.
Its wisdom is discernment — knowing not only *what is seen*, but *who is seeing.*

At this level, energy work transcends visualization and becomes *illumination.*
You no longer interpret the field — you embody the clarity through which the field reveals itself.

When your Third Eye vibrates in harmony:

- Vision replaces confusion.
- Wisdom replaces knowledge.
- Illumination replaces imagination.

You become the Seer and the Seen — the healer whose awareness dissolves illusion, whose gaze illuminates truth, and whose presence radiates light so steady that even darkness remembers its own brilliance.

Hands-On Protocols for the Third Eye Chakra & Stabilizing Clients

RESTORING VISION, PERCEPTION, AND LUMINOUS ALIGNMENT

Working hands-on with the Third Eye Chakra (Ajna) requires stillness, neutrality, and refined energetic precision.
This is the center of perception — where light becomes understanding and awareness becomes illumination.
Here, the healer does not move energy through sound or motion, but through presence — a clear, unwavering awareness that stabilizes the client's field into coherence.

To engage this chakra is to enter the domain of subtle light — where insight, intuition, and inner truth merge.
When approached with mastery, the hands become radiant instruments of perception — amplifying clarity, dissolving illusion, and restoring harmony between intellect and intuition.

A balanced Third Eye Chakra radiates cool indigo light, still focus, and profound calm — the steady gaze of the soul observing all things through compassion and truth.

Client Preparation and Energetic Containment

Before working directly with the brow or forehead, it is essential to establish a stable, grounded, and tranquil container. Ajna governs perception, mental clarity, and psychic sensitivity — all of which must unfold in safety and serenity.

Begin each session by:

1. Grounding the Body and Mind
    o Invite the client to take three deep, rhythmic breaths, exhaling slowly through the mouth.

- o Affirm softly:

  "You are safe to see, safe to understand, and safe to receive clarity."

  - o Encourage the body to rest fully while the awareness expands gently.
2. Linking Heart and Crown
   - o Place one hand over the heart and one above the crown.
   - o Visualize a vertical current of violet-white light uniting compassion (heart) with wisdom (crown).
   - o This bridge stabilizes perception between feeling and knowing — balancing intuition with love.
3. Invoking Permission and Stillness
   - o Explain that you will be working near the forehead, temples, and crown — sensitive regions of perception.
   - o Ask for consent before touch and offer hovering or non-contact alternatives for highly sensitive clients.
   - o Speak softly and move deliberately. The stiller your presence, the more clearly their light responds.

This foundation of calm and trust allows the client's awareness to unfold naturally — not forced open, but invited.
It is not merely a clearing; it is a revelation — the rediscovery of one's inner sight.

Hand Placements for the Third Eye Chakra

The Third Eye Chakra is located between the eyebrows, extending through the pineal gland, eyes, and temples.
It governs intuition, insight, dreams, visualization, and the ability to perceive truth beyond illusion.

Primary Positions:

1. Front Placement (Clarity and Vision)
    - Place one hand lightly over the brow center, fingers pointing upward.
    - Rest the other hand gently at the crown or over the heart to connect vision with divine guidance or compassion.
    - Breathe in unison with the client, visualizing indigo light expanding through the forehead.
    - Encourage awareness of spaciousness rather than imagery.
2. Back Placement (Releasing Mental Tension)
    - Position both hands behind the head, over the occiput and upper neck.
    - This area stores mental fatigue, overthinking, and spiritual strain.
    - Visualize waves of violet light flowing from the back of the skull toward the brow, releasing static energy.
3. Temple Anchors (Balancing Intuition and Intellect)
    - Place one hand on each temple, palms open and receptive.
    - Sense the flow of energy between hemispheres — logic and imagination, reason and insight.
    - Allow balance to emerge naturally, without directing force.
4. Hovering Placement (For Sensitive or Overactive Fields)
    - Hold your hands 3–5 inches above the forehead.
    - Visualize an indigo sphere of light rotating slowly between your palms and the client's Third Eye.
    - Feel subtle pulsing or cooling as energy aligns into harmony.

ENERGY MOVEMENT SEQUENCE: "WAVE OF LIGHT" TECHNIQUE

This advanced sequence clears mental congestion and restores luminous coherence to the Third Eye and surrounding subtle fields.

Steps:

1. Center the Field:
    - Begin with synchronized breathing, guiding the client to inhale light and exhale thought.
    - Feel the space between breaths widen — the threshold of intuitive awareness.
2. Activate the Inner Lens:
    - Hover both hands over the brow.
    - With each exhale, visualize gentle ripples of indigo light radiating outward — like light waves on still water.
3. Harmonic Breath Alignment:
    - Encourage the client to exhale with a soft "Om" or hum felt in the head, not the throat.
    - Match their vibration silently through your breath, entraining both fields to calm perception.
4. Transmute Confusion into Clarity:
    - Place one hand on the forehead, one on the occiput.
    - Channel cool, luminous energy forward, transforming mental tension into still awareness.
    - Whisper inwardly: *"Let light reveal truth."*
5. Seal the Field:
    - Visualize an infinity loop of violet-white light weaving through the temples, stabilizing the hemispheres.
    - Sweep excess energy down the spine to the base for grounding.
    - Affirm softly:

"My mind is still. My vision is clear. My
awareness is light."

SIGNS OF ACTIVATION AND RELEASE

During Third Eye Chakra work, clients may experience:

- Pulsing, tingling, or coolness at the forehead or temples.
- Subtle light flashes or geometric patterns.
- Deep sighs or shifts in breath rhythm.
- Emotional neutrality replacing anxiety or confusion.
- A sense of timelessness or luminous calm.

Practitioner Note:
Maintain serene focus. Do not narrate the client's visions or
sensations.
Your role is to hold the field of clarity — to remain the
unmoving mirror in which light finds balance.

ADVANCED INSIGHT: THE ALCHEMY OF LIGHT

To master Ajna is to master *illumined perception.*
This chakra refines thought into wisdom and vision into
knowing.
Its essence is not imagery, but awareness without distortion.

At this level, healing becomes radiance.
You no longer send energy — you *become the clarity through
which energy aligns itself.*

When the Third Eye radiates harmony:

- Stillness replaces chaos.
- Awareness replaces assumption.
- Light replaces illusion.

You become the luminous seer — the healer whose gaze restores order, whose silence awakens knowing, and whose presence radiates the quiet brilliance of truth.

Energetic Ethics and Boundaries for Practitioners Working with the Third Eye Chakra

HOLDING SACRED SPACE FOR VISION, INSIGHT, AND PERCEPTUAL CLARITY

The Third Eye Chakra — Ajna — governs perception, intuition, and the sacred union of wisdom and understanding.
It is where thought becomes awareness and where awareness becomes light.
Because this center bridges the personal and transpersonal realms, it is among the most subtle and ethically sensitive chakras to approach in healing work.

Here, the practitioner does not simply observe what the client *sees*, but what they *perceive* — the interplay of truth, projection, belief, and illusion within consciousness itself.
To work with Ajna is to hold space for revelation. Clients may confront confusion, spiritual overwhelm, or distorted insight, just as they may awaken to higher clarity and trust in their inner knowing.

The practitioner's responsibility is not to interpret vision, but to anchor discernment — to help clients stabilize perception without imposing belief.
Healing here requires neutrality, humility, and impeccably clear energetic boundaries.

To serve Ajna is not to show others what to see — but to hold the luminous stillness in which *their own inner sight can unfold.*

The Foundation of Clear Perception

Before addressing another's Third Eye, practitioners must examine their own relationship with insight, intuition, and belief.
Ajna reflects the mental and energetic clarity of both healer and client; any distortion in awareness becomes amplified within the field.

Ask yourself before each session:

- Am I perceiving or projecting?
- Is my guidance arising from neutrality or attachment?
- Can I remain silent in the presence of the unknown?

If uncertainty arises, pause.
Breathe light into the space between your brows.
Let stillness dissolve mental noise.
Your clarity is the ethics of your perception.

"The healer's awareness becomes the mirror in which truth reveals itself."

Creating Safety Through Awareness and Consent

Because Ajna governs perception and intuitive sensitivity, safety begins with transparency and grounding.
Clients must feel empowered to discern their own truth rather than adopt yours.

Best Practices:

1. Clarify the Nature of Perception
   - Explain that insights received are symbolic, not absolute truths.

- o Invite clients to hold every perception lightly —
  as guidance to reflect upon, not doctrine to
  follow.
- o Say gently:

  "You are your own oracle. My role is to help you
  see through clarity, not for you."

2. Obtain Informed and Energetic Consent
   - o Always ask before exploring intuitive
     information or energetic impressions.
   - o If the client appears overwhelmed by visual or
     psychic sensitivity, pause and re-ground.
   - o Offer choices: silence, visualization, or guided
     stillness.
   - o Respect all requests to stop or shift — this
     reinforces trust in their own inner boundaries.
3. Communicate with Spacious Presence
   - o Avoid interpretive or directive language.
   - o Speak in reflections rather than conclusions:

     "What you describe feels like light seeking
     balance — what do you sense it means for you?"

   - o Allow meaning to arise from within the client's
     own consciousness.

Maintaining Energetic Boundaries in the Field of Light

Ajna's element is Light — expansive, subtle, and easily
diffused. Without grounded structure, practitioners can absorb
the client's imagery, confusion, or emotional residue.
Boundaries here must be luminous yet defined — like clear
glass that allows light to pass without distortion.

To maintain energetic integrity:

- Anchor first in your Root and Heart Chakras.
- Visualize a band of indigo light encircling your brow — a radiant filter that perceives truth without absorption.
- Set the intention:

  "I witness clearly, but I do not carry what I see."

- After sessions, cleanse the Third Eye through breath, meditation, or sunlight on the forehead.
  Let natural light recalibrate your perception.

Boundaries in the Ajna field are not separation — they are clarity itself.
They define what belongs to observation and what belongs to silence.

Recognizing Power Dynamics in Spiritual Perception

The Third Eye holds immense influence — the ability to shape understanding, reveal hidden truths, and inspire transformation. Within healing work, this insight must never become authority. The balance between *seeing for* and *seeing with* is sacred.

Practitioner Guidance:

- Share perceptions as invitations, not as final truths.
- Avoid framing intuitive information as prophecy or certainty.
- Redirect deference with humility:

  "Your insight matters most — let's explore how it feels within your own awareness."

- Remember: every intuitive image is filtered through perspective. What heals is not *what is seen*, but *how it is integrated.*

Energetic Entanglement and Projection in the Light Field

Ajna is magnetically receptive — its sensitivity to subtle vibrations can lead to entanglement if awareness blurs. Projection occurs when personal thoughts or beliefs color intuitive vision.

Signs of Energetic Entanglement:

- Feeling mentally foggy or overstimulated after sessions.
- Absorbing the client's imagery or emotional narrative.
- A compulsion to interpret or "explain" every symbol seen.

Response:

- Breathe deeply into the heart.
- Affirm silently:

  "I return all perceptions to light. I remain the clear mirror of awareness."

- Visualize violet-white light dissolving any cords or residual impressions.
- Ground through the feet until the mind grows quiet again.

Clarity is maintained not through defense, but through detachment.
True seeing requires empty space — awareness unoccupied by judgment or ownership.

Working with Emotional or Vision-Based Release

As Ajna activates, clients may experience spontaneous imagery, tears, laughter, or sensations of expanded consciousness.
These are natural expressions of energy reorganizing into coherence.

Practitioner Approach:

- Stay centered and silent; do not interpret or narrate their experience.
- If intensity rises, place one hand at the heart and one at the base of the skull to anchor balance.
- Guide the breath: slow, cool, rhythmic.
- Encourage grounding — describe textures, sounds, or sensations in the room.
  Presence is more stabilizing than explanation.

Transference, Ego, and the Illusion of Knowing

Because Ajna deals with knowledge and insight, practitioners may unconsciously seek validation through accuracy or revelation.
This is the subtle trap of spiritual ego — mistaking perception for truth.

Awareness Practice:

- Before sharing insight, pause.
- Ask inwardly:

"Am I offering this to serve their clarity, or to confirm my own?"

- Keep your tone simple and grounded.
- Remember: truth needs no performance — only presence.

"When awareness is pure, wisdom speaks softly."

Post-Session Integration and Aftercare

Work within the Third Eye often expands consciousness.
Clients may feel light, disoriented, or highly sensitive afterward.

Aftercare Recommendations:

- Rest in natural light or darkness — whichever feels soothing.
- Drink water infused with mint or cucumber to cool the mind.
- Journal any intuitive impressions without analysis.
- Avoid overstimulation — screens, noise, or crowds.
- Close the day with this affirmation:

"I see clearly. I rest in light. My awareness is whole."

The Sacred Duty of the Seer

To work with Ajna is to serve truth through stillness — to perceive without possession, to guide without control, and to illuminate without judgment.
Your awareness is the temple of light in which clarity is born.
Hold it with reverence.

When ethics, humility, and discernment unite, the healing space becomes a field of illumination — a sanctuary where vision and silence coexist, and every moment of awareness becomes prayer.

"The healer's sight does not claim — it clarifies.
When one light shines clear, it teaches all others to see."

The Role of Ajna in Remote Healing

CHANNELING VISION, AWARENESS, AND LUMINOUS COHERENCE ACROSS DISTANCE

While Vishuddha transmits vibration, the Third Eye Chakra (Ajna) receives and directs *conscious light* — the intelligence of awareness that travels beyond time and space.
It is through Ajna that remote healing becomes illumined connection: a communion of consciousness, where healing is not sent, but *realized* through shared perception.

Where Vishuddha speaks in tone, Ajna speaks in light.
Where resonance harmonizes, perception aligns.

In distant healing, the Third Eye functions as the luminous lens through which understanding and energy converge — bridging the seen and unseen through the medium of consciousness itself.
It transforms intuitive insight into radiant transmission — not as thought, but as clarity projected through the infinite field of Mind.

Ajna is the seer of energy medicine: it perceives the alignment of all beings and guides the healer's awareness into coherence with the universal light.

Energy Beyond Physical Sight

In remote healing, there is no distance between minds — only the illusion of separation.
The Third Eye is the organ through which perception pierces this illusion.
When Ajna is balanced, the practitioner perceives not form, but essence; not the body, but the field of consciousness surrounding it.

Through subtle awareness, the healer "sees" without seeing — perceiving through intuition, empathy, and luminous knowing.

Practitioners may sense:

- Subtle flickers or light impressions around the brow.
- Expanding awareness of the client's energy as colors, patterns, or geometric fields.
- An inner stillness where vision ceases and *knowing* begins.
- Soft pulsation or cool clarity between the eyebrows as perception aligns.

This is not imagination. It is the light sense — awareness perceiving awareness.
In Ajna, the healer does not project energy outward; they awaken clarity everywhere their consciousness touches.

"In remote healing, light becomes language — and awareness becomes the bridge."

Establishing Luminous Connection Through Vision and Intention

To engage Ajna in remote healing is to enter the field of *shared awareness* — an infinite space of perception where energy is guided through clarity, not control.
Through inner stillness and focused light, the healer becomes the mirror in which the client's truth is revealed.

Preparation Practice:

1. Ground Through the Root and Heart
   - Visualize red roots anchoring deep into the earth, and soft green light radiating through the heart.
   - Stability and compassion anchor the visionary current in integrity.
2. Awaken the Eye of Light
   - Bring awareness to the space between your brows.
   - Inhale deeply; as you exhale, imagine indigo light expanding outward in a halo of still illumination.
   - Feel the breath clear all mental static — leaving pure, receptive awareness.
3. Set the Intention
   - Affirm silently:

     "Through divine awareness, I perceive and transmit the light of clarity.
     May this illumination awaken harmony in all who receive it."

4. Link to the Client Through Light
   - Visualize the client surrounded by indigo-white radiance.
   - From your Third Eye, extend a line of light — not as direction, but as communion.
   - Allow awareness to merge with theirs, forming a single, shared field of clarity.
5. Sustain the Field
   - Remain in silence.
   - Let light flow through awareness, effortless and constant.
   - Do not "see for" the client — *see with them.*
   - The shared field itself becomes the healing.

Maintaining Clarity and Neutral Awareness

Ajna's greatest discipline is neutrality.
In remote work, distortion does not come from distance — it arises from identification: the mind's desire to label, define, or fix.

To maintain luminous purity:

- Visualize your Third Eye as a lens of crystal light — transparent, still, and impartial.
- Release all interpretation; perceive only what is present.
- Affirm silently:

  "I observe without owning. I illuminate without altering."

- Keep awareness tethered to the heart's compassion to prevent cold detachment or intellectualization.
- After each session, close the eye of perception gently — inhale through the crown, exhale through the soles of your feet — allowing light to descend back into the body.

"Awareness, when grounded, becomes wisdom. Awareness ungrounded becomes illusion."

Balancing Vision and Silence in Distance Work

Ajna's mastery lies in balance — between insight and emptiness, seeing and stillness.
Too much focus fractures awareness; too little presence dulls perception.
Healing occurs in the pulse between the two — vision arising, dissolving, and returning to silence.

To maintain equilibrium during remote sessions:

- Alternate between *perceiving light* and *resting in darkness*.
- When an image arises, pause — let it dissolve before the next breath.
- End each session in complete stillness, allowing light to fade into spacious peace.

Through this rhythmic meditation of light and void, the healer sustains luminous awareness without attachment — transmitting clarity through the living field of consciousness.

The Ethics of Subtle Perception

The Third Eye teaches discernment.
Every image, color, or vision that arises in a session carries potential meaning — but not all meaning belongs to the client. Ethical perception requires restraint, humility, and surrender to unknowing.

Guidelines for Ethical Perception:

- Observe, do not declare. Allow clients to interpret their own insights.
- Never impose vision as truth. Share impressions as reflections, not revelations.
- Return all seeing to light. Do not carry what you perceive after the session ends.
- Remember: intuition is a shared field — what you see may also reflect you.

When light becomes transparent, clarity serves truth instead of ego.

Closing Reflection

The Third Eye in remote healing is the silence that *sees*.
It reveals that awareness itself is the healer — the bridge that
unites souls across any distance.

Through Ajna, healing becomes a shared illumination — a
meeting of lights remembering their oneness.
When your perception rests in stillness and your intention
remains pure, every act of awareness becomes medicine.

You are no longer sending light — you are *being* the light
through which all healing travels.

"The healer's vision moves not through sight, but through
consciousness — where one clear awareness awakens another
across the unseen."

Third Eye Chakra Techniques for Remote Healing

TRANSMITTING HEALING THROUGH LIGHT, AWARENESS, AND PERCEPTUAL COHERENCE

Each practitioner carries a unique radiance — the subtle light of
their consciousness.
The Third Eye Chakra (Ajna) refines this light into clarity,
transforming insight into luminous awareness that travels
effortlessly through the field of consciousness.

Where Vishuddha heals through vibration and sound, Ajna
heals through perception and stillness.
It does not send energy — it *reveals* it.
It does not direct force — it *illuminates alignment*.

Through Ajna, the healer learns that healing is not an act of projection, but a state of seeing so purely that all distortion dissolves in the presence of awareness.

1. Visualization of the Indigo Light Transmission

Visualize a radiant sphere of indigo-white light spinning slowly at the center of your brow.
This is the Eye of Illumination — the inner gaze that perceives truth beyond form.

As you breathe, allow this sphere to expand, filling the mind with cool, clear light.
From this center, waves of indigo radiance flow outward, traveling through the ether like light rippling across calm water.

See these waves reaching the client's field — not as beams or commands, but as reflections of pure awareness.
The moment light meets light, alignment occurs naturally.

Repeat silently:

"I transmit clarity through stillness.
I see through light, not through thought."

The field surrounding you both begins to shimmer — a unified radiance of awareness and peace.
No effort, no distance — only coherence.

2. Breath Transmission Through Light and Awareness

Ajna governs the union of *mind and breath* — the current of consciousness that links perception to creation.
To transmit healing through the Third Eye, the practitioner breathes awareness into the field, allowing light to flow with intentionless precision.

Practice:

1. Inhale slowly through the nose, drawing in pure light through the crown and gathering it at the Third Eye.
2. Hold briefly — feel perception brighten.
3. Exhale softly through the nose, allowing light to expand outward through the forehead and into the shared field.
4. With each breath, release all thought and remain in the awareness of illumination.

This practice transmits presence itself — silent knowing as healing vibration.

"Through breath and light, awareness travels where thought cannot go."

3. The Mind-to-Light Transmutation

When a client's field feels clouded by confusion, doubt, or fear, Ajna serves as the transmuter of perception — transforming distortion into understanding through luminous awareness.

Visualize a stream of violet-indigo light flowing from your Third Eye toward the client's energy field.
Wherever confusion appears, the light gently clarifies — reorganizing thought into harmony.
Darkness does not resist; it simply becomes visible, then dissolves.

Whisper inwardly:

"What was confusion becomes clarity.
What was illusion becomes truth."

As this occurs, you may feel cooling or tingling between your brows — a sign that alignment and insight are restoring coherence.

4. The Mirror of Awareness

Ajna teaches that all perception is shared — there is no separate seer and seen.
In this technique, the practitioner mirrors the client's consciousness to help them remember their own inner wisdom.

Visualize both of you surrounded by the same field of soft indigo light.
Your awareness reflects theirs like two mirrors facing each other — infinite clarity expanding in both directions.

There is no dominance, no hierarchy — only the meeting of perception and truth.

Affirm silently:

"Your light is the same as mine.
Together, we remember what is already known."

This mirroring restores self-trust, intuitive balance, and spiritual confidence.

5. Rebalancing the Practitioner's Energy After Sessions

Working with Ajna expands awareness and sensitivity.
Without proper closure, practitioners may experience overstimulation, mental fog, or lingering impressions from a client's field.

To restore neutrality and luminous balance:

1. Retract the Light Field
   Visualize all outward rays of awareness softly returning to Source, dissolving into still light.
2. Seal the Third Eye
   Place one hand over your brow and one over your heart.

Breathe deeply three times, allowing awareness to flow downward through the body.

3. Affirm:

   "All light returns to unity.
   My vision is clear, calm, and contained."

4. Rest in Darkness
   Sit in quiet with eyes closed, allowing the inner light to dim into tranquil void.

5. Ground the Energy
   Visualize a column of silvery light descending through your spine into the earth, anchoring perception into form.

This grounding completes the luminous circuit — returning the practitioner to centered awareness.

THE GIFT OF LUMINOUS CONNECTION IN REMOTE HEALING

In distant healing, Ajna reveals the truth of connection: consciousness is not sent — it is shared.
When awareness becomes clear and heart-centered, healing travels instantly, guided by light, not will.

Through the Third Eye, the practitioner learns:

- To transmit understanding through awareness, not analysis.
- To radiate truth as illumination, not as instruction.
- To become the witness through which clarity itself flows.

When the healer's vision is still, all distance disappears.
And in that radiant silence, healing unfolds — not by direction, but by realization.

"When the healer's light shines clear, all minds remember —
that we were never apart, only waiting to see as one."

Clearing Ancestral Fear and Karmic Imprints

RELEASING PATTERNS OF ILLUSION, DOUBT, AND FEAR TO RESTORE INNER VISION AND SPIRITUAL CLARITY

Just as the Root Chakra carries ancestral memory of survival
and the Heart preserves emotional legacy, the Third Eye Chakra
(Ajna) holds the energetic imprints of *perception, belief, and
spiritual vision.*
It is the seat of consciousness where the unseen becomes visible
— and where collective fear has long attempted to cloud the
light of truth.

Ajna governs not only how we see the world, but how we
interpret what we see.
It records centuries of inherited doubt, disbelief, and
persecution for intuitive knowing — memories of lifetimes
when inner sight was denied, shamed, or silenced.

Where Vishuddha carries the karma of voice, Ajna carries the
karma of sight — the burden of truth misunderstood or denied.

When this chakra is obscured by ancestral fear or karmic
distortion, clarity gives way to confusion. One may doubt their
intuition, fear their insight, or mistrust the light within.
Healing Ajna means restoring the *courage to see clearly* — to
look upon truth without fear, illusion, or self-judgment.

"The light you fear is the wisdom your ancestors were not
allowed to see."

Inherited Patterns of Perception and Fear

Every lineage holds unspoken beliefs about what is real, what is sacred, and what must remain unseen.
Generations of suppression, religious dogma, or rational dismissal have woven subtle psychic programs such as:

- "It's dangerous to trust my intuition."
- "Seeing beyond the physical makes me strange or wrong."
- "Knowledge should come from authority, not from within."
- "If I know too much, I will be punished."
- "Clarity brings conflict — better not to see."

These inherited thought-forms act as veils across perception — soft distortions that dim inner sight and foster self-doubt.
They are not flaws, but *defense mechanisms* born from times when vision endangered survival.

When unhealed, they manifest as avoidance of intuition, fear of psychic sensitivity, or confusion between imagination and truth.
Healing them restores the purity of perception — the freedom to witness reality through the divine lens of consciousness.

"The eyes of your ancestors closed in fear.
You reopen them now in grace."

Karmic Patterns of Vision and Truth

Karma within Ajna is not punishment — it is remembrance.
Across lifetimes, souls refine the discernment between illusion and wisdom, imagination and revelation.

Through the Third Eye, the soul learns *right perception*: to see through the eyes of love rather than fear.

Recurring karmic themes include:

- Fear of psychic or mystical experiences.
- Overreliance on logic, unable to trust intuitive insight.
- Confusing visions or nightmares from past-life trauma.
- Rejection of inner knowing to conform or please others.
- Using perception to manipulate or control rather than enlighten.
- Experiencing visions that once led to ridicule or danger.

These patterns are not errors but initiations — opportunities for consciousness to evolve.
The lesson is not simply to "see," but to perceive through compassionate neutrality, where awareness reflects divine truth without distortion.

Recognizing Signs of Ancestral and Karmic Imprints in Ajna

When ancestral fear or karmic distortion lingers within the Third Eye Chakra, it may appear as:

- Headaches, pressure, or tension between the brows.
- Overthinking, confusion, or difficulty focusing.
- Vivid or fearful dreams rooted in ancestral memory.
- Resistance to meditation or visualization practices.
- Cynicism toward spiritual insight or intuitive guidance.
- Seeing symbols or patterns but doubting their meaning.
- Emotional overwhelm when accessing spiritual realms.

These are not flaws — they are invitations for clearing.
Each symptom signals the mind's effort to protect itself from a truth once deemed unsafe.
Through gentle awareness, the veils dissolve, and the light of insight begins to shine unfiltered again.

The Healing Path: Reclaiming the Vision of Truth

Healing Ajna from ancestral and karmic distortion is not about awakening *new* sight — it is about *remembering* the sight that was never lost.
It requires reverence, humility, and deep compassion for those who turned away from light to survive.

Practices for Release:

1. Acknowledgment of Inner Light
   Speak softly within meditation:

   "It is safe to see clearly.
   I honor the seers who came before me.
   I release the fear of truth."

   Feel light blooming behind the brow — ancient sight returning to awareness.

2. Visualization of Violet Flame and Indigo Light
   o Envision a violet flame spinning at the Third Eye, surrounded by indigo radiance.
   o With each breath, the flame burns away inherited fear, doubt, or confusion.
   o Exhale the smoke of illusion; inhale clarity and faith in your inner vision.

3. Ancestral Seeing Meditation
   o Imagine your ancestors standing behind you, veiled in shadow.
   o Inhale, drawing light through your Third Eye; exhale, sending it backward through the generations.
   o Whisper:

   "May all eyes open in peace.
   May all truth be seen through love."

o   Watch as the shadows lift — their eyes clear,
their hearts awaken.

4. Mantra for Perception (Om Shanti Jyoti)
Chant softly or internally:

"Om Shanti Jyoti" — "Peace and Light."
Let each tone vibrate through your forehead,
illuminating inner stillness.

5. Journaling or Dream Integration
Upon waking, write down symbols, colors, or feelings
from dreams or meditations.
Rather than analyze, allow understanding to unfold over
time.
This practice honors intuition as living wisdom, not
mental theory.

Integration: Seeing as the Soul

As ancestral fear dissolves, vision clears.
Perception becomes peaceful, grounded, and radiant —
awareness no longer reacts, it simply *knows*.

The healed Third Eye no longer seeks proof; it embodies
presence.
You perceive without needing to define.
You witness truth as light, not opinion.

When karmic imprints of Ajna are cleared:

- Intuition flows naturally, unforced.
- Insight aligns with compassion, not control.
- Dreams and symbols become teachers rather than
confusion.
- The unseen feels familiar, not frightening.

You remember that the inner eye was never closed — it was only turned inward, waiting to be trusted again.

Affirmation of Ancestral Vision:

"I honor the wisdom that was hidden.
I release the fear of seeing.
Through my sight, all generations awaken.
I perceive through love, and truth reveals itself in light."

Practices for Clearing Ancestral Fear and Vision Karma

RESTORING PERCEPTION, CLARITY, AND THE FREEDOM TO SEE IN LIGHT

The Third Eye Chakra governs awareness, insight, and spiritual discernment.
Where Manipura refines will through fire and Vishuddha refines vibration through sound, Ajna refines consciousness through light.

Ancestral and karmic blocks here appear as confusion, skepticism, or fear of intuitive power.
These practices cleanse the mental field, clear ancestral belief systems, and restore your natural ability to perceive truth beyond illusion.

1. Light Ritual of Release

Because Ajna is ruled by the element of Light, this ritual uses visualization to release ancestral fear and clarify perception.

Practice:

- Write down inherited beliefs such as "It's dangerous to know too much" or "I can't trust what I see."
- Place the paper under a white candle.
- As it burns safely, visualize the flame transforming every limiting belief into radiant clarity.
- Whisper:

  "I release the blindness of fear.
  I open my eyes to divine truth."

As the smoke rises, imagine violet light filling the space — carrying ancestral vision into freedom.

2. Reiki or Energetic Light Clearing

During energy work, place hands gently above the forehead and crown.
Visualize an orb of indigo light expanding outward, clearing energetic residue from the mental and spiritual planes.
As you channel, breathe awareness through your Third Eye and exhale through your heart.

Affirm:

"Light flows through me, not from me.
I perceive as love, I know as peace."

This integrates insight with compassion, preventing psychic overstimulation.

3. Breath of Illumination (Prana Jyoti)

Practice:

- Sit tall, shoulders relaxed.
- Inhale through the crown, drawing pure white light into your Third Eye.
- Hold gently; let the light swirl like stars.
- Exhale through the nose, releasing clouds of confusion.
- Continue for several cycles until the space between your brows feels cool and clear.

Visualize ancient veils of disbelief lifting — replaced by quiet trust in your inner knowing.

4. Lineage Visualization and Vision Forgiveness Meditation

Close your eyes and imagine your ancestors gathered behind you, gazing through your eyes.
You are their seer — the one who restores their forgotten sight.

Say softly:

"I forgive the fear that hid our light.
I honor your need to look away.
Through my eyes, we see truth again."

Visualize indigo waves radiating backward through generations, dissolving blindness into brilliance.
See every ancestor bathed in clarity and peace.

5. Creative Visioning as Soul Release

Ajna heals through creation — art, writing, dreaming, and visualization.
Give form to what you perceive: paint your dreams, write intuitive insights, design mandalas of light.

Each act of creation affirms that it is safe to see, safe to imagine, safe to know.

Affirm:

"Each vision I honor heals my lineage.
Each insight I trust clears the past."

THE SIGHT RESTORED

When ancestral fear and karmic illusion are cleared, the Third Eye shines as a crystalline lens — radiant, silent, and awake.
Perception becomes revelation.
Awareness no longer searches for truth; it *is* truth.

You see through the eyes of the soul — without judgment, without fear.
The inner and outer worlds reflect the same divine light.

"The ancestors once closed their eyes to survive.
You are the one who opens them —
not in defiance, but in remembrance."

Releasing Thought Cords and Restoring Inner Vision

RETURNING TO WHOLENESS THROUGH CONSCIOUS PERCEPTION AND LUMINOUS AWARENESS

The Third Eye Chakra (Ajna) is the seat of insight and perception — the energetic bridge between intuition and knowing.
Through this center, we connect not by words, but by awareness.

Every thought shared, belief absorbed, or perception adopted leaves an energetic imprint upon this field.

Where Vishuddha bonds through expression, Ajna bonds through perception.
Healthy perception creates understanding and trust in one's own truth.
But when cords of illusion, influence, or projection form, they blur clarity and weaken discernment.

Healing here is not withdrawal — it is refinement: the art of perceiving with neutrality and truth instead of fear or distortion.

To restore perceptual sovereignty:

- Visualize gentle indigo light surrounding your brow and temples.
- Affirm: "I see with clarity. I release all thoughts and beliefs that are not my own."
- Imagine cords of confusion, judgment, or inherited belief dissolving into clear light.
- End in stillness — resting in the radiance of pure awareness.

Affirmation of Liberation:

"My mind is a vessel of peace.
My vision is clear and compassionate.
I perceive and understand in harmony with all life."

UNDERSTANDING THOUGHT CORDS
Energetic Bonds Formed Through Perception, Belief, And Intuition

Energetic cords do not form only through emotion or voice — they also form through thought and perception.
Every time you take on another's belief, adopt a collective fear,

or identify with someone else's vision of truth, a subtle thought cord attaches within the Third Eye field.

Some cords uplift — shared insight, wisdom, or collective prayer.
Others distort — when perception becomes enmeshed in projection, illusion, or dependency.

In Ajna, these cords often appear as threads of silvery or violet light extending from the forehead, temples, or crown — connecting you to people, ideologies, or energies that influence how you *see*.

When balanced, exchange is luminous — mutual understanding, shared consciousness, and unified truth.
When distorted, the field becomes clouded by external images or emotional residue — leading to confusion, overthinking, or psychic fatigue.

Common Examples Of Draining Thought Cords

- Overidentifying with collective fear, news, or social media energies.
- Doubting intuition due to others' skepticism or disbelief.
- Confusing another's vision, dream, or emotion as your own.
- Obsessive replaying of conversations or mental images.
- Seeking validation for your inner knowing instead of trusting it.
- Mentally analyzing others' motives until intuition feels distorted.

These cords anchor into the Third Eye because Ajna governs truth and discernment.
Releasing them restores perceptual sovereignty — the ability to trust your insight, see clearly, and remain attuned to divine intelligence rather than human projection.

Recognizing Signs Of Perceptual Entanglement

When Ajna becomes entangled with others' mental or energetic frequencies, you may experience:

- Pressure or tingling at the brow.
- Mental chatter that feels "not yours."
- Fatigue after spiritual or emotional conversations.
- Doubt in intuitive messages or flashes of insight.
- Difficulty distinguishing inner vision from external influence.
- Seeing symbolic images that feel heavy or foreign.

These are not failings — they are signals inviting you to reclaim your mental clarity and spiritual sight.
Through awareness and stillness, the cords dissolve, and your natural perception reawakens — clear, calm, and sovereign.

Energetic Anatomy Of Luminous Detachment

True detachment in Ajna is not indifference — it is clarity without absorption.
It is perceiving without projecting, witnessing without ownership, and allowing light to pass through you unfiltered.

Energetic sovereignty of perception arises when awareness no longer seeks validation from the external.
When thought cords dissolve, the Third Eye becomes transparent — an open window between self and Source.

In this state:

- Stillness replaces confusion.
- Awareness replaces opinion.
- Intuition flows as understanding, not assumption.
- The mind becomes luminous — perception without distortion.

The Practice Of Luminous Presence

When you rest in the center of awareness, perception becomes communion rather than analysis.
You no longer "look at" life — you *see through* it.
Clarity becomes your language; silence becomes your teacher.

This is the essence of Ajna's mastery:
To perceive from presence rather than fear, to see without labeling, and to know without attachment.
When cords of confusion dissolve, only truth remains — clear, luminous, and compassionate.

Affirmation:

"I release all cords of illusion and influence.
My perception is clear and sovereign.
I see all beings through the light of divine truth."

Releasing Thought Cords Practice

(To be performed with neutrality and reverence — never judgment.)

1. Prepare the Space
   Sit comfortably, spine straight, and bring one hand to the center of your brow.
   Inhale deeply through the nose, exhale through the mouth.
   Feel the space between your brows cooling and expanding with each breath.
   Visualize a sphere of soft indigo light spinning gently at your Third Eye — still, radiant, aware.
2. Identify the Connection
   Bring to mind a thought pattern, belief, or person whose energy feels "stuck" in your awareness.
   Observe without blame.

Notice subtle threads or impressions in the mental field
— perhaps pulsing or flickering.
Awareness itself begins the clearing.

3. Call in Light
   Visualize a column of white-violet light descending
   from the Divine Source through your crown, gathering
   at your Third Eye.
   Whisper softly:

   "Only truth remains.
   All else returns to light."
   Feel the vibration of these words ripple through your
   awareness, dissolving tension and mental clutter.

4. Dissolve the Cord with Light and Breath
   Inhale into the Third Eye; exhale through the heart.
   Imagine the cord thinning, unraveling, and then
   dissolving into radiant indigo mist.
   As it fades, both you and the other consciousness are
   freed — awareness restored to purity.

5. Seal and Restore Clarity
   Visualize your Third Eye as a clear, crystalline lens —
   still, bright, and calm.
   Whisper or affirm:

   "My perception is clear and protected.
   I witness all through divine understanding."
   Rest in quiet awareness — the serenity of unobstructed
   vision.

The Return Of Inner Sovereignty

As thought cords dissolve, energy once tied to confusion or
doubt returns to your center.
The mind quiets.
Perception sharpens.
You begin to see through stillness rather than through stories.

The Third Eye becomes what it was always meant to be — a temple of light and understanding, where thought becomes wisdom and silence becomes knowing.

You perceive without absorbing.
You understand without owning.
You live as illumination itself — awareness in motion.

INTEGRATION: THE PATH OF LIVING VISION

When awareness is no longer clouded by others' expectations, projections, or beliefs, perception becomes liberation.
You no longer mistake noise for knowledge or illusion for insight.
You simply *see* — not with the eyes of form, but with the inner vision of soul.

The Third Eye then opens not as a portal to strange phenomena, but as a state of being — a consciousness that reflects truth without distortion.
Through it, you become the silent observer, the inner witness, the bridge between mind and spirit.

In this luminous balance, you no longer chase revelation — revelation finds you.
You no longer grasp for understanding — understanding unfolds within your stillness.
What you once sought through effort, you now receive through presence.

SIGNS OF RECLAIMED VISION

When Ajna is clear and sovereign:

- Intuition arises gently, without drama or demand.
- Inner guidance feels calm, not urgent.
- Dreams and symbols bring wisdom, not confusion.

- Mental chatter fades, replaced by quiet certainty.
- You feel deeply connected — yet unattached — to all that is.

This is the essence of clear sight: seeing the world as light sees itself — without division, without fear.

PRACTITIONER INSIGHT: BECOMING THE EYE OF STILLNESS

For advanced practitioners, Ajna offers mastery in vibrational discernment.
You begin to sense truth as frequency — not concept.
Each person, word, or situation reveals its tone immediately within your field.
Judgment dissolves, replaced by knowing.

The healer who perceives clearly does not diagnose; they witness alignment.
They see not what is wrong, but what is ready to return to harmony.
They speak not from intellect, but from awareness itself.

In this mastery, the Third Eye no longer seeks to *understand* others — it simply *recognizes* them as divine mirrors.

"When your sight becomes still, even illusion bows to truth."

Closing Reflection

You are not your thoughts, your memories, or your perceptions — You are the light that perceives them.
When the mind quiets and the inner eye opens, everything becomes reflection — every being, every breath, every shadow an expression of the same infinite consciousness.

Through Ajna, you remember that true vision has no opposite. It is not seeing with the eyes, but through the heart — not imagining, but awakening.

"I see with the eye of the soul.
I perceive beyond appearance.
I live as the light that never blinks."

Cross-Referencing with TCM Meridians: Liver and Gallbladder

THE VISION OF TRUTH AND THE ALCHEMY OF PERCEPTION

The Third Eye Chakra (Ajna) corresponds energetically with the Wood Element in Traditional Chinese Medicine (TCM), expressed through the Liver and Gallbladder meridians.
Both systems share a deep understanding of *vision and decision* — the capacity to perceive clearly, plan wisely, and act from intuitive alignment rather than emotional reactivity.

Just as Ajna refines consciousness into insight, the Wood element refines movement into direction.
Both teach that clarity requires flow — that stagnation of Qi or perception clouds judgment and obscures truth.
When balanced, the inner and outer eyes see harmoniously; action aligns with intuition.
When imbalanced, energy contracts — manifesting as confusion, frustration, indecision, or visual strain.

Together, Ajna and the Liver–Gallbladder meridians form the axis of *perception and purpose* — the dynamic relationship between how we see, and how we choose to act on what we see.

LIVER MERIDIAN — THE VISIONARY FLOW

In TCM, the Liver governs the smooth flow of Qi and emotion, and it "opens into the eyes."
It is called *the General* — the planner who sees the path ahead and ensures movement through intention.
When Liver Qi flows freely, vision (both literal and intuitive) remains expansive, adaptive, and inspired.
When constrained by tension or suppressed emotion, energy stagnates — producing cloudy perception, resentment, or indecision.

Similarly, when the Third Eye is open and balanced, intuition flows effortlessly — seeing beyond illusion with compassionate clarity.
But when blocked, the mind clings to confusion, over-analysis, or inherited belief systems, unable to perceive truth beyond logic.

When Liver Qi is Balanced:

- Intuition feels calm, reliable, and grounded in truth.
- Vision is clear — both physical and inner sight.
- Decision-making flows with confidence and timing.
- Creativity arises naturally from emotional balance.

When Liver Qi is Stagnant or Excessive:

- Blurred vision, headaches, or tension around the temples and brow.
- Irritability, frustration, or mental fatigue.
- Feeling "stuck," indecisive, or overwhelmed by conflicting options.
- Difficulty trusting intuitive messages.

Balancing Techniques:

- Practice alternate-nostril breathing (Nadi Shodhana) to balance hemispheric perception.
- Apply gentle acupressure or Reiki at the temples, between the brows, and along the sides of the head to release energetic stagnation.
- Engage in gentle movement such as Qi Gong or yoga twists to stimulate the Liver meridian and restore clarity.
- Visualize indigo light circulating like flowing water — clearing inner pathways of insight.

Affirmation:

"I see clearly and move freely.
My vision flows like wind through trees — flexible, calm, and alive with purpose."

GALLBLADDER MERIDIAN — THE PATH OF DECISIVE CLARITY

The Gallbladder is known in TCM as *the Decision Maker* — it provides courage, discernment, and the ability to act on inner knowing.
Where the Liver plans, the Gallbladder executes.
Together, they translate insight into action, and inspiration into embodiment.

When this meridian is clear, choices feel aligned — intuitive impulses manifest as decisive movement.
When blocked, doubt, hesitation, or self-criticism can paralyze forward momentum.

When Gallbladder Qi is Balanced:

- You act from intuitive confidence rather than external pressure.
- Decisions arise effortlessly — insight becomes action.
- You trust your inner compass and follow through with grace.
- The mind is quiet and the path ahead feels illuminated.

When Imbalanced:

- Indecision or overthinking every choice.
- Fear of making mistakes or being judged for intuitive insights.
- Stiffness in the neck and shoulders, reflecting mental rigidity.
- Feeling scattered or easily influenced by others' opinions.

Balancing Techniques:

- Place fingertips on the outer eyes and temples; breathe deeply, visualizing golden-green light expanding outward.
- Gently massage or tap along the sides of the head, neck, and shoulders to release Gallbladder meridian tension.
- Drink chrysanthemum or peppermint tea to cool and clarify the mind.
- Before major decisions, meditate in stillness, visualizing a soft indigo flame illuminating the path within.

Affirmation:

"I act from clarity.
My choices reflect divine wisdom and fearless vision."

THE EYE AND THE PATH — THE SHARED ELEMENT OF INSIGHT

Both the Third Eye Chakra and the Liver–Gallbladder meridians reflect the dance between *seeing* and *doing*.
They teach that perception without motion becomes stagnation, while action without insight becomes chaos.
Healing this axis invites you to move through life guided not by impulse, but by illuminated awareness.

In yogic and TCM philosophy alike, the eye is both physical and spiritual — it mirrors the flow of Qi, light, and consciousness through the body.
When the Liver and Gallbladder work in harmony with Ajna, you begin to live as an instrument of clarity:

- Vision informs action.
- Insight replaces indecision.
- Movement follows meaning.

Every breath becomes guidance; every choice, an expression of light made manifest.

Integration Affirmation:

"I perceive with calm certainty.
I act with intuitive grace.
My vision and my path are one —
flowing with wisdom, clarity, and peace."

The Light Element: The Essence of Illumination

TRANSFORMING SILENCE INTO INSIGHT, PERCEPTION INTO WISDOM

The Light Element (Jyoti) — expressed through the Third Eye Chakra (Ajna) and mirrored in Traditional Chinese Medicine through the Wood Element — represents the stage where perception becomes revelation.
Where Ether carries sound, Light reveals truth.
It is the field through which all awareness, imagery, and intuition travel — the bridge between mind and spirit.

Here, transformation happens not through speech, but through vision: the purification of perception into insight, and insight into knowing.
When this element is balanced, your intuition flows as light — gentle, radiant, and clear.
You see beyond illusion, discern without judgment, and perceive life as interconnected.

When blocked, perception clouds — insight feels distant, or over-analysis creates confusion.
When excessive, one may retreat into imagination, detaching from grounded reality.
Balance is found in the *luminous stillness* — the quiet space between thought and knowing, between image and light.
It is here that perception aligns with divine intelligence, and vision becomes the mirror of truth.

THIRD EYE–LIGHT INTEGRATION PRACTICE: THE VISION OF SPACE

1. Enter the Still Light
   Sit comfortably, spine tall, eyes closed.
   Bring your attention to the space between your
   eyebrows — not the physical point, but the vast
   awareness behind it.
   Breathe softly and let your focus dissolve into that space
   of infinite light.
2. Awaken the Inner Eye
   Inhale through the nose; on the exhale, imagine a beam
   of indigo light radiating from your brow, expanding
   gently into the room.
   With each breath, feel this light growing clearer — not
   bright or blinding, but calm and knowing.
3. Listen to the Light
   After a few breaths, release effort and allow silence to
   speak.
   In that silence, perception becomes luminous —
   thoughts quiet, intuition emerges.
   Feel the subtle pulse of awareness, the vibration of
   seeing itself.
4. Expand the Vision
   Visualize the indigo light expanding into a radiant
   sphere around your head — connecting eyes, temples,
   crown, and mind.
   Within it, insight and imagination dance as one: what
   you see becomes what you know.

Affirmation:

"I am the stillness that perceives all things.
Through clarity, I transform illusion into light.
My inner vision reveals truth in all forms."

Flow Synchronization: Aligning Practitioner and Client in the Field of Insight

ENERGETIC COHERENCE, MENTAL CLARITY, AND THE HARMONY OF SHARED PERCEPTION

When working with the Third Eye Chakra (Ajna), the practitioner's inner stillness, neutrality, and clarity of perception profoundly shape the session's energetic tone.
This chakra governs intuition, imagination, and awareness — it entrains to the resonance of quiet truth.

If the practitioner observes from stillness — neither projecting nor absorbing — the client's mental field begins to settle, mirroring that equilibrium.
But if the practitioner holds inner tension, distraction, or judgment, that dissonance subtly clouds the session's insight.
Synchronization at the Ajna level occurs through shared presence, not shared thought — the meeting of two awarenesses in clarity.

It is the light of coherence — where silence becomes wisdom, and perception becomes healing.

WHY SYNCHRONIZATION MATTERS

• Vibrational Coherence
Ajna responds to harmony, not noise. When practitioner and client share a unified frequency of calm awareness, neural and energetic rhythms synchronize. The mind clears; intuition awakens.

• Transmission of Clarity
The Third Eye learns through stillness. When the practitioner embodies quiet certainty, non-reactivity, and compassion, that

vibration transmits wordlessly — guiding the client to trust their own inner knowing.

• Restoration of Vision
Synchronization allows perception without projection. The practitioner becomes a mirror of light — reflecting rather than defining, allowing the client's consciousness to recognize its own brilliance.

PRACTITIONER PREPARATION

1. Attune to Inner Light
Place one hand on your forehead and breathe slowly. Visualize indigo light radiating from the space behind your brow, like a sunrise emerging through still mist. Silently affirm:

"I perceive with stillness.
My sight reflects truth."

2. Clarity Check-In
Ask yourself:
   o   Am I observing or analyzing?
   o   Is my intuition calm or striving?
   o   Can I see without needing to interpret?
       Exhale tension or mental chatter. Enter presence.

3. Set the Intention
Inwardly declare:

"May this session unfold in truth and clarity.
May I perceive only what serves the highest light."

SYNCHRONIZATION TECHNIQUES
1. Shared Stillness Alignment

Invite the client to close their eyes.
Breathe together in slow, rhythmic cycles — no sound, no

instruction, only awareness of breath.
Feel both minds settling into shared stillness.
In this quiet union, intuition naturally arises.

2. Mirror Gaze of Awareness

If appropriate, gently meet the client's gaze (or visualize their
Third Eye).
Without focusing on their features, look *through* the physical
form into the light behind their eyes.
Let your perception become mirror-like — receptive, not
searching.
This soft gaze harmonizes both Ajna centers, clearing
projections and establishing unity of awareness.

3. Harmonic Linking

Visualize a luminous thread of indigo light connecting your
Third Eye to the client's.
This is not a cord of thought, but a stream of clarity.
Sense both awarenesses merging into one still field — calm,
lucid, infinite.
Breathe into this light until you both feel peace.

4. Closing the Insight Field

As the session concludes, visualize both foreheads glowing with
equal brightness — distinct, yet connected by light.
Let the link dissolve back into spacious awareness, leaving
mutual clarity and calm.
Whisper inwardly or aloud:

"Truth is seen.
Awareness is free."

Key Considerations

• Boundaries Through Presence
Ajna synchronization is observation, not absorption. Maintain
your energetic autonomy while allowing consciousness to meet.

• Perceiving Without Interpreting
Interpretation filters intuition through ego. Pure perception
requires stillness — seeing without defining.

• Integration Practices
After the session, guide the client to anchor new awareness:
– Journaling visions or insights immediately after.
– Spending quiet time in nature or candlelight.
– Meditating on indigo or violet flame for clarity.

PRACTITIONER'S AFFIRMATION BEFORE SYNCHRONIZATION

"My mind is a mirror of light.
I perceive without judgment, guide without control.
Through stillness, I reflect truth and restore clarity."

PRACTITIONER ENERGY HYGIENE AFTER THIRD EYE WORK

Because the Third Eye governs perception and intuitive
connection, energetic impressions can linger — images,
thoughts, or emotional residues from the client's field.
Clearing ensures your vision remains pure, not colored by
external energy.

After each session:

- Exhale through the nose while visualizing indigo mist
  leaving your brow.

- Sweep your hands across the forehead and temples as if wiping light clean.
- Visualize white light descending through your crown, clearing the mental field.
- Rinse your hands in cool water or step outside into natural light.
- Conclude with the affirmation:

"All visions return to the Source.
My sight is clear, my mind serene."

When practitioner and client attune in the field of Ajna, healing unfolds through illumination, not instruction.
Insight becomes medicine — stillness becomes communication.
Together, you enter the luminous field where silence perceives and light understands.

"When I see with stillness, others remember their truth.
When I hold light without judgment, awareness awakens."

Chapter 10 – Transformation Through Ajna

Case Studies: Awakening Insight, Intuition, and Inner Vision

The Third Eye Chakra (Ajna) governs perception, imagination, and the bridge between intuition and intellect.
Transformation at this level arises through illumination — the refinement of perception into wisdom, of imagination into clarity.

When Ajna heals, confusion transforms into comprehension, and inner sight becomes steady and reliable.
The individual learns to trust intuition without fear, to perceive beyond illusion, and to merge logic with spiritual knowing.
Healing here is not about escaping the mind, but aligning it with consciousness — where thought serves vision and vision serves truth.

The following case studies demonstrate how balancing the Third Eye restores clarity, intuition, and spiritual discernment.
True awakening at Ajna is not about seeing more — it is about seeing clearly.

CASE STUDY 1 – FROM CONFUSION TO CLARITY

Client Presentation:
A 41-year-old woman reported chronic headaches, mental fatigue, and difficulty making decisions. She described herself as "constantly second-guessing" and plagued by racing thoughts. Sleep was restless, filled with vivid, unsettling dreams.

Assessment:
Energetic evaluation revealed overactivity in the Solar Plexus (over-analysis and control) and stagnation in the Third Eye. The mental body was cluttered with conflicting thoughts and external noise, blocking intuitive perception.

Therapeutic Process:

- Reiki for Mental Clarity: Gentle hand placements over the brow and temples, using deep, rhythmic breathing to balance left–right hemispheric flow.
- Trataka (Candle Gazing): 5 minutes daily of steady visual focus to strengthen concentration and inner sight.
- Guided Meditation: Visualization of indigo light expanding at the brow, dissolving mental fog and fear of "getting it wrong."
- Journaling Insight Practice: Writing responses to the prompt, "What truth is already clear if I stop overthinking?"

Outcome:
After three sessions, headaches subsided, and sleep deepened. The client described feeling "lighter in my head and calmer in my choices." She began trusting her first intuitive impressions instead of overanalyzing.

Transformation:
Confusion became clarity.

She learned that insight is not found by thinking harder — but by seeing from stillness.

CASE STUDY 2 – AWAKENING INTUITION AND INNER GUIDANCE

Client Presentation:
A 56-year-old therapist felt disconnected from her spiritual practice and reported loss of creativity, intuitive dullness, and lack of focus during sessions. She longed to "feel connected again."

Assessment:
Energetic scan showed diminished Ajna activity and dullness in the auric field above the eyes — signs of intellectual burnout and spiritual fatigue. Her energy was strong in lower chakras (grounded and empathic) but unintegrated above the heart.

Therapeutic Process:

- Ajna Activation Meditation: Visualization of a radiant indigo lotus opening between the brows, breathing through it until light expanded into the crown.
- Violet Flame Cleansing: Using intention to transmute accumulated psychic impressions from client work.
- Dream Journaling: Recording and interpreting nightly dreams as messages from higher guidance.
- Silent Presence Practice: Spending 10 minutes daily in non-doing meditation — no goal, no mantra, simply awareness.

Outcome:
Within a month, she reported spontaneous intuitive insights returning during therapy sessions. Her creativity rekindled; she began painting again for the first time in years.

Transformation:
Disconnection became illumination.
She rediscovered that intuition is not earned — it is
remembered when the mind becomes still enough to listen.

CASE STUDY 3 – RELEASING ILLUSION AND FEAR OF SEEING

Client Presentation:
A 47-year-old man sought help for persistent eye strain, anxiety,
and recurring fear of the future. He avoided meditation, saying
it triggered overwhelming visions.

Assessment:
Ajna appeared overstimulated — excessive visual input from
media and emotional stress had led to psychic overload. There
was fear around "seeing too much," rooted in past trauma
involving witnessing family conflict.

Therapeutic Process:

- Grounded Visualization: Instead of focusing on sight,
  sessions emphasized safety through Root–Heart–Ajna
  alignment.
- Cooling Indigo Reiki: Gentle energy flow around eyes
  and temples to release pressure and calm hyperactivity.
- Fear Release Dialogue: Guided reflection on the belief,
  "It's dangerous to see."
- Affirmation Integration: "I see only what serves healing
  and truth."

Outcome:
After six weeks, his anxiety decreased, eye strain vanished, and
meditation became peaceful. He began to report intuitive clarity
rather than visual overwhelm.

Transformation:
Fear of sight transformed into faith in insight.
He learned that true vision is not seeing everything — it is
perceiving only what aligns with love.

INSIGHT FOR PRACTITIONERS

Ajna healing reminds both client and practitioner that
perception itself is medicine.
The healer does not give insight — they help the client
remember the clarity already within.

When the Third Eye clears, awareness shifts from confusion to
comprehension, from illusion to illumination.
The world remains the same, but the way we see it transforms
entirely.

When perception aligns with wisdom,
when intuition flows through stillness,
and when vision serves compassion —
consciousness itself awakens.

Chapter 11 – Reflection & Integration

Daily Self-Care Rituals for Inner Clarity and Visionary Awareness

Healing the Third Eye Chakra (Ajna) is not a single moment of insight — it is a lifelong practice of inner stillness, discernment, and trust in your intuition.
Where the Throat teaches truth through sound, the Third Eye reveals truth through light.

Ajna governs perception, imagination, and the integration of knowledge into wisdom. Its strength lies in awareness — the ability to see clearly without distortion, to listen to intuition without fear, and to interpret life through the lens of higher understanding.

Daily self-care at the level of Ajna means tending to your *inner sight* — clearing the mind, balancing the intellect with intuition, and aligning your vision with the truth of spirit.
These rituals cultivate insight that is calm, compassionate, and illuminated by inner peace.

1. MORNING LIGHT ALIGNMENT

Begin your day by awakening the light of perception.
• Awareness: Before looking at any screens, sit quietly and bring your focus to the space between your eyebrows.
• Breath: Inhale through the nose, drawing indigo light into the

brow. Exhale through the mouth, releasing mental fog or lingering dreams.
• Intention: Whisper,

"Today, I see clearly.
I trust my intuition and allow light to guide my mind."
This morning ritual clears the mental field and sets the tone for intuitive, balanced awareness throughout the day.

2. VISION JOURNAL

Ajna thrives on reflection — the translation of insight into conscious understanding.
Each day, write briefly about your intuitive impressions or inner visions.

Prompts:
• What did my dreams reveal last night?
• What truth feels clear today, even if it cannot yet be proven?
• Where did I react instead of observe?

This practice trains your inner observer — teaching the mind to record without judgment and to honor intuition as a valid form of knowing.

3. LIGHT ELEMENT RITUALS

The Third Eye corresponds to the element of light, representing illumination, perception, and wisdom.
Honoring this element invites stillness and radiance into your awareness.

• Morning Sun Gazing (gentle): Spend a few moments facing the sunrise or daylight with closed eyes, allowing natural light to stimulate your inner vision.
• Aromatic Clarity: Diffuse or anoint your brow with essential oils such as rosemary, frankincense, or sandalwood to enhance

focus and intuition.
• Evening Candle Meditation: Gaze softly at a flame for one minute, then close your eyes and visualize the afterimage at the center of your forehead. Let the light dissolve into infinite space.

Affirmation:

"I am guided by light.
I see through illusion and remember truth."

4. INTUITION PRACTICE

The Third Eye is the bridge between rational mind and inner knowing. Strengthen your intuitive dialogue through consistent practice.

• Each morning, ask: "What do I need to know today?"
• Notice the first impression that arises — word, image, or feeling — without editing.
• Record it, and observe how it unfolds through your day.

Over time, you will learn to distinguish true intuition (calm, clear, immediate) from emotional impulse (urgent, reactive). Trust grows through gentle repetition — not proof, but peace.

5. BREATH OF STILLNESS

Midday, when thoughts become crowded or overstimulated, pause for the Breath of Stillness.
• Sit with your spine tall and your gaze turned slightly upward behind closed eyes.
• Inhale for four counts, holding for four, exhale for six.
• On the exhale, imagine your thoughts flowing out like mist, leaving luminous stillness behind.

Visualize indigo light glowing at your brow, cool and radiant, balancing left and right hemispheres of the brain.

Affirm:

"My mind is calm.
My awareness is clear."

6. EVENING REFLECTION & INNER VISION

As night falls, invite your awareness inward.
• Dim the lights and sit in quiet contemplation.
• Visualize a soft indigo flame between your brows — steady, calm, and eternal.
• Ask yourself:
– What did I see clearly today?
– Where did I let illusion or fear obscure truth?
– What new insight is emerging through stillness?

Offer gratitude for every moment of awareness, then rest in silence.

Affirm:

"My perception rests in light.
My mind reflects truth."

7. WEEKLY VISION RENEWAL

Once a week, devote time to cleansing the inner lens of perception — your *Ajna renewal*.

• Meditate in Darkness: Sit with closed eyes and let your awareness adjust to the inner light that arises when physical light fades.
• Practice Mindful Observation: Spend time in nature, watching without labeling — clouds moving, leaves shifting, light

changing.
• Dream Inquiry: Before sleep, set an intention to receive clarity on one question. Record your dreams upon waking.
• Digital Detox: Spend a few hours technology-free. Give your mind silence to reset its vibrational rhythm.

Affirmation:

"I honor stillness as my teacher.
I see beyond illusion into truth."

INTEGRATION INSIGHT

Ajna's clarity is not about prediction — it is perception in alignment with wisdom.
When this chakra is balanced, you trust intuition without fear, think with precision, and see through the eyes of compassion.

Through consistent rituals of stillness, reflection, and observation, you transform the Third Eye into a sanctuary of light — where insight becomes guidance, imagination becomes wisdom, and awareness becomes peace.

"When my sight aligns with truth,
I awaken to divine vision.
When my mind aligns with stillness,
I embody the clarity of spirit."

Journaling Prompts for the Third Eye Chakra

AWAKENING INTUITION, INSIGHT, AND INNER VISION

The Third Eye Chakra (Ajna) thrives on clarity, perception, and the marriage of logic with intuition.
Journaling opens the inner lens of awareness, translating subtle impressions into conscious understanding.

Through writing, you bridge the unseen and the known — turning intuition into insight, dreams into guidance, and thought into illumination.
These prompts invite you to explore the nature of perception, intuition, and belief — helping you release illusion, refine awareness, and awaken the wisdom that sees truth beneath appearances.

1. Intuitive Awareness and Inner Knowing

• When have I trusted my intuition — and what was the outcome?
• How does intuition feel in my body compared to fear or assumption?
• What signs, patterns, or synchronicities often guide me?
• Where in my life am I being asked to *see beyond logic*?

2. Perception and Clarity

• How do I discern between what is real and what I imagine?
• What beliefs cloud my ability to see situations clearly?
• In what ways do I project my own thoughts or fears onto others?
• What truth becomes visible when I pause and observe instead of reacting?

3. Vision and Imagination

• What does my ideal future *look* like — not just in goals, but in feeling and essence?
• Which inner visions continue to return to me, asking for attention?
• How can I use creative visualization to align with my higher path?
• What role does imagination play in my spiritual growth?

4. Releasing Illusion and Mental Overload

• What mental patterns keep me stuck in overthinking or doubt?
• What outdated beliefs no longer serve my evolving consciousness?
• How can I simplify my inner dialogue to create more mental space?
• What truth am I resisting because it challenges my current identity?

5. Dreams and Symbolic Guidance

• What dreams, symbols, or recurring images have recently appeared in my life?
• What emotion or message might these dreams be expressing?
• How do I feel upon waking — confused, inspired, warned, or peaceful?
• How can I invite clearer, healing dreams through intention and reflection?

6. Mindfulness and the Inner Observer

• How often do I pause to *witness* my thoughts instead of identifying with them?
• What happens when I observe rather than control?
• Where do I still confuse awareness with judgment?

• How can I practice mental stillness without disengaging from life?

7. Wisdom and Higher Perspective

• What challenges in my life hold hidden wisdom or purpose?
• How does my perspective change when I view my life from the soul's vantage point?
• What would my higher self say about the situation I'm facing today?
• How can I bring intuition into my decisions without dismissing reason?

8. Sacred Affirmations

After journaling, close your session with one or more of these Ajna affirmations to anchor clarity and peace:
• "I see clearly through the eyes of my soul."
• "My intuition guides me with truth and love."
• "I trust what I know beyond logic."
• "Illusion dissolves; wisdom remains."
• "I am aligned with divine perception and higher understanding."

Integration Note

Journaling for the Third Eye Chakra is not about predicting the future — it's about perceiving the present with awakened awareness.
Allow your writing to unfold like meditation: soft focus, gentle observation, honest curiosity.

If confusion arises, let it teach patience.
If insight comes, let it humble you.
Each word you write becomes a mirror — reflecting the clarity that was always within.

"When I write what I see, I understand what I know.
When I honor intuition, I live in the light of truth."

Chapter 12 – Understanding the Journey So Far

How Awareness Rises from Expression to Illumination

If you have journeyed through the Chakra 101 Series from the beginning, you have already walked the spiral of *Involution* — the descent of love into form — and begun the sacred return, the path of *Evolution* — the ascent of form back into light.

At the Throat Chakra (Vishuddha), love found its voice.
Through sound, truth, and resonance, you began to give form to your inner knowing.
Now, as energy rises into the Third Eye Chakra (Ajna), voice becomes vision, and truth transforms into insight.

This is the level where communication turns inward — from speaking to perceiving, from resonance to realization.
The same love that once descended from the Heart into the body now ascends again as consciousness — refined, awakened, and illuminated.

Where Vishuddha taught expression through sound, Ajna teaches perception through light.
It is the realm where energy becomes awareness, vibration becomes vision, and sound becomes silence once more.

THE SIX CHAKRAS SO FAR

Book	Chakra	Element	Primary Lesson
1. Heart Chakra 101 – The Bridge	Air	Love & Compassion	Opening to divine love and unity consciousness.
2. Root Chakra 101 – Building Safety, Survival, Foundation	Earth	Grounding & Belonging	Anchoring love into the body and material life.
3. Sacral Chakra 101 – Creativity, Pleasure, Emotions	Water	Flow & Feeling	Allowing love to move through emotion and creation.
4. Solar Plexus Chakra 101 – Power, Confidence, Transformation	Fire	Will & Manifestation	Empowering love to act and shape reality.
5. Throat Chakra 101 – Truth, Expression, Resonance	Ether	Communication & Purification	Giving love a voice and refining vibration through sound.
6. Third Eye Chakra 101 – Intuition, Vision, Insight	Light	Perception & Wisdom	Transforming sound into sight — awakening inner truth.

Each level of this journey has carried love through the alchemy of experience:

from awareness into body, from body into voice, and now from voice into vision.
As you reach the Third Eye, you begin to *see* what love has created — and to understand creation itself through awakened perception.

THE SHIFT FROM ETHER TO LIGHT

At Vishuddha, vibration expanded into resonance; through Ajna, resonance refines into illumination.
The Ether of sound now gives way to the Light of consciousness.

In the Throat, we spoke the truth.
In the Third Eye, we see the truth.

This transition marks the movement from outer communication to inner clarity — from giving voice to wisdom, to *becoming* wisdom itself.
Energy here no longer needs to express — it begins to understand.

Fire transformed matter.
Ether refined vibration.
Now, Light reveals meaning.

The Throat taught that every sound creates.
The Third Eye teaches that every perception shapes reality.
To master Ajna is to purify the lens through which we interpret life — to see beyond illusion, beyond duality, beyond the stories the mind weaves.

THE INNER PATH OF ILLUMINATION

As energy rises from the Throat to the Third Eye, you may notice a shift from doing to being, from explanation to observation.
The mind begins to quiet.
Inner sight replaces external focus.

You start to perceive patterns in emotion, synchronicity in timing, and intelligence in experience.
Meditation deepens, dreams become teachers, and intuition becomes natural rather than mystical.
This is not the discovery of something new — it is the *remembering* of what has always been.

Through Ajna, you begin to see with the eyes of the soul.
Here, love no longer needs to speak; it simply *knows.*
Clarity replaces confusion.
Insight replaces reaction.
Vision replaces doubt.

REFLECTIVE INSIGHT

Every moment of awareness carries the vibration of all that came before:

- The compassion of the Heart
- The grounding of the Root
- The emotional flow of the Sacral
- The empowerment of the Solar Plexus
- The resonance of the Throat

Together, they converge in perception.
Ajna is the prism through which all experience refracts into understanding.

Through this chakra, you begin to perceive unity — not as an idea, but as a living truth.
You see that love is not merely felt or spoken; it is the very light that allows all things to be seen.

To open the Third Eye is to awaken the inner witness — the consciousness that sees without judgment and knows without words.
It is to live as awareness itself.

THE NEXT STEP

From the Third Eye, the journey continues upward into the Crown Chakra (Sahasrara) — the final stage of remembrance.
There, love becomes light, and light becomes oneness.
It is the completion of the sacred cycle: from descent into matter to ascent into spirit, from separation to union.

Through the Third Eye, you begin to bridge worlds — intuition and intellect, spirit and self, inner and outer.
You are now ready to experience truth as vision, wisdom as light, and consciousness as creation itself.

"When love becomes light, vision becomes truth.
When perception clears, the soul remembers what it has always seen."

Why We Began at the Heart — And Why We Now Rise

THE RETURN OF LOVE AS VISION

In the early chapters of this journey, love descended — through the breath of the Heart, the stability of the Root, the flow of the

Sacral, the fire of the Solar Plexus, and the voice of the Throat.
It has learned to ground, to feel, to act, and to speak.

Now, as we rise into the Third Eye Chakra (Ajna), love no
longer seeks to express — it seeks to *see*.
This is where energy turns fully inward, from communication to
perception, from vibration to illumination.
Through the Third Eye, love refines itself into clarity —
awareness becoming wisdom, sound becoming light.

Involution has fulfilled its sacred descent — Spirit made visible
through matter.
Now begins Evolution's ascent — matter remembering its
divinity through light.

At this stage, truth no longer needs to be spoken; it reveals
itself.
Love becomes understanding.
Vision becomes communion.

This is the sacred passage of inner sight — where duality fades,
illusion dissolves, and awareness awakens to the subtle unity
that has been present all along.

THE ALCHEMY OF LIGHT

Where the Throat carried sound into the world, the Third Eye
gathers light back into consciousness.
This is the point where *expression turns into perception.*
The voice that once echoed outward now listens inward.
The seer and the seen become one.

If Ether was the vibration of truth, Light is the revelation of it.
Ajna transforms knowledge into knowing — not through
intellect, but through insight.

This is the alchemy of awakening:

- Sound becomes silence.
- Thought becomes vision.
- Perception becomes presence.

In this space, the energy that once shaped form now illuminates the meaning within it.
It is here that the wisdom of all lower centers converges — the Heart's love, the Root's trust, the Sacral's emotion, the Solar Plexus' will, and the Throat's truth — rising together into the Light of awareness.

THE LIGHT OF THE SIX ELEMENTS

Each chakra is an element of consciousness — Earth grounding, Water flowing, Fire transforming, Air connecting, Ether resonating, and now Light revealing.
The Third Eye is the mirror through which all these elements reflect truth back to the soul.

Chakra	Element	Gift of Love	Expression through Ajna
Heart (Air)	Love & Compassion	Connection	Becomes discernment through empathy
Root (Earth)	Grounding & Safety	Stability	Becomes inner trust in perception
Sacral (Water)	Emotion & Creativity	Flow	Becomes intuitive sensitivity
Solar Plexus (Fire)	Will & Power	Action	Becomes illumination and purpose

Chakra	Element	Gift of Love	Expression through Ajna
Throat (Ether)	Sound & Truth	Expression	Becomes resonance as insight
Third Eye (Light)	Vision & Wisdom	Awareness	Becomes enlightenment through understanding

Through this synthesis, Light integrates every frequency below it — grounding wisdom through Earth, feeling it through Water, empowering it through Fire, carrying it through Air, expressing it through Ether, and illuminating it through perception.

THE ASCENDING TRIAD: THIRD EYE – CROWN – SOURCE

The final ascent begins here — the Triad of Illumination. Just as the lower three chakras established your foundation and the middle (Heart) opened love's bridge, these upper centers refine perception into unity.

Chakra	Element	Evolutionary Role	Key Lesson
Throat (Ether)	Sound	Express truth	"I communicate clearly and with integrity."
Third Eye (Light)	Vision	Perceive truth	"I see through illusion into wisdom."

Chakra	Element	Evolutionary Role	Key Lesson
Crown (Consciousness)	Thought / Spirit	Embody unity	"I am the light of awareness itself."

Together, they represent the journey from resonance to revelation — from truth expressed to truth seen to truth *known*. Through them, love completes its transformation from vibration into consciousness.

INTEGRATION: THE BRIDGE BETWEEN ETHER AND CONSCIOUSNESS

At the Throat, love found its voice through Ether.
At the Third Eye, that same Ether refines into Light — perception that radiates without sound.
Here, *communication becomes comprehension,* and *resonance becomes realization.*

- Ether carries vibration; Light reveals pattern.
- Sound communicates; Sight comprehends.
- The voice tells; the vision understands.

This is the movement of evolution — the inner return of awareness to its Source.
The Throat externalized truth; the Third Eye internalizes it.
The next phase of your journey is no longer about speaking, but seeing — perceiving energy as it truly is: living consciousness.

PERCEPTION BECOMES ILLUMINATION

Where manifestation once became expression, expression now becomes illumination.
What was once *spoken* is now *understood.*
The Third Eye reveals that creation and perception are one —

every thought, every word, every vision arising from the same infinite consciousness.

Through Ajna, you begin to realize that enlightenment is not something to achieve — it is the natural clarity of being when illusion fades.
Seeing clearly means remembering that nothing was ever separate.

The inner and outer dissolve into one field of awareness.
This is the beginning of true sight.

THE PATH FORWARD

From here, love ascends toward its final liberation in the Crown Chakra (Sahasrara) — the return to Source.
Through Ajna, you awaken awareness; through Sahasrara, you embody unity.
The journey that began with the breath of the Heart now rises as the light of pure consciousness.

You are no longer speaking your truth — you are *seeing* it.
You are no longer seeking guidance — you are *becoming* it.
Love now perceives itself through you.

"When love becomes light,
I see through the eyes of Spirit.
When vision clears,
truth reveals itself as all that is."

The Cycle of Manifestation — And Now, Perception

WHEN CREATION SEES THROUGH YOU

Manifestation was never the final step — it was the threshold.
Once love has taken form, once sound has given it voice, the
next movement begins: *perception.*
At the Third Eye Chakra (Ajna), creation no longer needs to be
spoken — it is *understood.*

Here, energy ascends from communication to comprehension.
The same vibration that once resonated outward through Ether
now turns inward as Light, revealing the truth of what you have
created.

In this phase, you do not tell the universe what you want;
you *see* what the universe is showing you.
You read the symbols, synchronicities, and subtle signs that
form the language of Spirit.
This is the evolution from vibration to vision — the awakening
of consciousness within creation.

THE EVOLUTION OF THE DREAM

If the Throat translated love into resonance, the Third Eye
translates resonance into recognition — perception as the next
octave of creation.

DREAM Step	Chakra Equivalent	Purpose
Unconscious Thought	Root (Earth)	Seed of creation — safety and belief
Conscious Thought	Sacral (Water)	Emotionalization — energy in motion
Action	Solar Plexus (Fire)	Transformation — will made visible
Manifestation	Heart (Air)	Realization — love experienced in form
Expression	Throat (Ether)	Communication — love spoken into the world
Perception	Third Eye (Light)	Illumination — love understood as wisdom

Every chakra refines the one below it.
Through Root you grounded, through Sacral you felt, through Solar you acted, through Heart you manifested, through Throat you spoke — and now, through Ajna, you *see.*

Perception is how creation witnesses itself.
It is where life speaks back — not in words, but in meaning.
Through the Third Eye, you learn that manifestation and awareness are not separate — one expresses, the other comprehends.

THE PURPOSE OF PERCEPTION

At this level, energy no longer moves outward; it expands inward.
Vishuddha broadcasted your frequency — Ajna receives its echo.
Through the Third Eye, you perceive the pattern behind the experience, the teaching within the manifestation, the wisdom within the form.

Perception completes the higher cycle of manifestation — transforming expression into understanding, and understanding into enlightenment.
This is how the universe reveals the mirror of your consciousness.

When you learn to perceive with clarity, you begin to see that everything you have manifested is a reflection of what you believe, feel, and radiate.
Nothing is random.
Every event, relationship, and vision is your soul speaking back to you through the language of light.

THE SPIRITUAL PHYSICS OF LIGHT

Just as sound carries vibration through Ether, light carries information through consciousness.
At the level of the Third Eye, you are no longer transmitting frequency — you are *decoding* it.
Every color, tone, symbol, and dream carries instruction for your evolution.

When your inner sight is clear, perception becomes revelation.
Light moves in waves, just as awareness moves through experience.
And as you align your perception with truth, those waves harmonize — revealing the divine order behind apparent chaos.

The Third Eye is thus not just the organ of intuition — it is the receiver of reality.
It says to the universe:

"I see the pattern behind all things."

And the universe replies:

"Then you are ready to co-create with consciousness itself."

THE SIXTH MOVEMENT: LOVE AS LIGHT

At Ajna, manifestation evolves beyond words.
Love no longer hums — it shines.
What you once expressed now illuminates.
What you once said now becomes seen.

When love reaches the Third Eye, it becomes vision — insight that transcends language.
You realize that every act of creation was a lesson in perception, every experience a reflection of divine order.

Here, creation speaks not through your voice, but through awareness itself.
You become the witness through which Spirit observes and understands its own creation.

REFLECTION

Take a moment to ask yourself:
• Do I see clearly what life is teaching me — or do I look through the lens of old beliefs? *(Third Eye)*
• Am I interpreting challenges as chaos — or as invitations to higher understanding? *(Heart)*
• Do I allow light to reveal truth, or do I cling to the shadows of the known? *(Solar Plexus)*
• Can I feel the wisdom behind my emotions without judgment?

(Sacral)
• Do I trust that what I see — within and without — is purposeful? *(Root)*

When all six chakras align, manifestation becomes illumination.
You no longer create merely to have — you create to *see.*
Every experience becomes a revelation of consciousness.
Every act of awareness becomes a form of prayer.

This is the sixth movement of manifestation — where love evolves from vibration into vision, and vision becomes the lens through which Spirit perceives itself.

"When my perception aligns with truth, clarity unfolds.
When my sight is pure, creation reveals its light."

Chapter 13 – Quick Reference Toolkit

Third Eye Chakra (Ajna)

The Center Of Vision, Intuition, And Inner Wisdom

Location: Center of the forehead, slightly above the brow line (between the eyebrows)
Element: Light
Color: Indigo or deep violet-blue
Bija Mantra: OM (AUM)
Governing Principle: Perception and wisdom through illumination
Primary Function: Intuition, imagination, visualization, and higher awareness
Associated Glands/Organs: Pituitary gland, eyes, forehead, temples, brain, nervous system
Sense: Inner sight (perception beyond the five senses)
Astrological Associations: Jupiter (expansion of wisdom) and Neptune (spiritual vision)
Symbol: Two-petaled lotus representing duality transcended into unity — the merging of intellect and intuition

KEY THEMES

• Intuition and Inner Vision
• Clarity of Perception and Imagination
• Awareness Beyond Illusion
• Insight, Reflection, and Understanding
• Wisdom, Discernment, and Spiritual Foresight
• Connection Between Mind and Spirit
• Integration of Logic and Intuition

WHEN BALANCED

• You perceive truth clearly beyond emotion or bias.
• Intuition flows easily — decisions feel aligned and effortless.
• You experience meaningful synchronicities and trust divine timing.
• Your imagination is vivid and constructive.
• You see patterns, symbolism, and deeper meaning in experiences.
• Dreams are insightful and prophetic.
• You possess inner calm and clarity in perception.

WHEN IMBALANCED

Underactive Third Eye (Deficient):
• Confusion or difficulty visualizing possibilities
• Lack of focus, poor memory, or limited imagination
• Overreliance on logic, skepticism of intuition
• Difficulty seeing "the bigger picture"
• Disconnection from inner guidance

Overactive Third Eye (Excessive):
• Overthinking, mental overwhelm, or obsessive visualization
• Illusions or distorted perceptions
• Escapism into fantasy or spiritual bypassing
• Headaches, eye strain, insomnia, or anxiety from overstimulation

BALANCING TECHNIQUES

Physical Practices:
• Gentle eye movements and palming (resting warm hands over eyes)
• Alternate-nostril breathing (Nadi Shodhana) to balance hemispheres
• Yoga postures like Child's Pose (Balasana), Forward Fold (Uttanasana), and Eagle (Garudasana)
• Spending time in natural sunlight to harmonize circadian and energetic rhythms

Energetic Practices:
• Indigo-light visualization radiating from the forehead
• Meditation on the OM sound or candle flame (Trataka)
• Third Eye Reiki activation or hands-over-brow healing
• Dream recall journaling and intuitive vision exercises

Emotional / Spiritual Practices:
• Quiet contemplation and mindful observation
• Practice seeing the truth beyond appearances
• Discernment meditation — learning to witness without judgment
• Trust-building rituals for intuitive decisions

AROMATHERAPY & CRYSTALS

Essential Oils:
Frankincense – deepens meditation and expands awareness
Clary Sage – heightens intuition and dream recall
Sandalwood – grounds spiritual vision
Rosemary – enhances mental clarity and memory
Lavender – calms the mind for clear insight

Crystals:
Amethyst – spiritual clarity and protection
Lapis Lazuli – wisdom, intuition, and higher learning

Sodalite – mental balance and rational intuition
Azurite – awakening inner sight
Labradorite – revealing hidden truths and potentials

FOODS & NUTRITION

Supportive Foods:
• Purple-hued foods (blueberries, black grapes, eggplant)
• Raw cacao and walnuts for brain nourishment
• Herbal teas (gotu kola, ginkgo, mugwort, lavender)
• Light, fresh meals that enhance mental clarity
• Clean water for fluid energy and hydration of the nervous system

Avoid Excess:
• Overconsumption of sugar or stimulants (coffee, energy drinks)
• Artificial additives that dull mental focus
• Heavy or processed foods that cloud perception

AFFIRMATIONS

"I trust my intuition and inner knowing."
"I see clearly, beyond illusion."
"My mind is open, and my perception is pure."
"I am guided by divine wisdom and insight."
"I perceive truth in every experience."
"My inner vision reveals the path of light."

MUDRA & MANTRA

Mudra: *Kalesvara Mudra (Gesture of Clarity)*
– Touch the fingertips of both hands together, joining thumbs and middle fingers to form a heart shape.
– Rest at the brow center; breathe slowly.
– Balances mental energy and awakens intuition.

Mantra: *OM (AUM)*
– Chant softly, allowing the sound to vibrate through the forehead and crown.
– Visualize ripples of indigo light radiating through your mind.
– Repeat until the inner chatter dissolves into still awareness.

MEDITATION FOCUS

Visualize an indigo light glowing gently between your eyebrows.
With each inhale, the light expands; with each exhale, it deepens in color and clarity.
Allow thoughts to drift by like clouds — observing without attachment.
As the light steadies, imagine a lotus opening, revealing a single eye of radiant understanding.
Repeat inwardly:

"I see through the eyes of my soul.
Clarity is my natural state.
I awaken to the light of truth within."

INTEGRATION INSIGHT

Ajna's mastery is *illumination* — the merging of intuition and intellect, of insight and understanding.
When this chakra is balanced, perception becomes revelation, and every experience mirrors truth.
You no longer react to life; you *witness* it through awakened consciousness.

Your thoughts align with wisdom, your vision reflects truth, and your awareness becomes light itself.
You are not simply the observer of reality — you are the consciousness through which reality is seen.

"When my perception aligns with light, every vision becomes truth, and wisdom becomes my way of seeing the world."

Conclusion: The Power of Vision and Inner Truth

The Third Eye Chakra, Ajna, is the meeting place between perception and wisdom — the sacred gateway where truth becomes light.
It is the eye of the soul, the mirror of consciousness, and the lens through which Spirit observes its own creation.

Through this center, the love that once rose from the Throat now refines into vision — no longer needing to speak, but to *see*.
What was expressed as vibration through Vishuddha is now revealed as illumination through Ajna.
Here, awareness replaces articulation; revelation replaces reaction.

Ajna does not demand faith — it *shows* truth.
It does not convince — it clarifies.
It is the still eye within the storm of thought, perceiving the harmony behind all form.

When perception is clouded, illusion reigns — you mistake reflection for reality, memory for meaning.
When perception is rigid, you see only what you expect — the mind filters the divine into fragments.
But when perception is clear — balanced, luminous, and compassionate — you no longer interpret life; you *understand* it.

This is the gift of the Third Eye: to see through illusion into essence.
It reveals that every experience, whether joyful or painful, has been a reflection of your consciousness seeking to recognize itself.
Nothing is wasted. Nothing is hidden. Everything is revelation.

In its mastery, Ajna is not about psychic power or foresight; it is about presence.
True vision is not seeing the future — it is seeing the truth that is always now.
The awakened Third Eye does not divide the world into shadow and light; it perceives both as expressions of one infinite source.

When your inner sight opens, judgment fades, fear dissolves, and clarity arises like dawn over still waters.
You begin to perceive life not as random, but as radiant — every moment a message, every encounter a mirror, every silence a teacher.

Through Ajna, thought becomes knowing, and knowing becomes illumination.
Perception becomes prayer.
Awareness becomes communion.

"I see through the eyes of my soul.
Light reveals what love has created.
My vision is clear. My wisdom is peace."

When this chakra awakens, you no longer seek external proof of truth — you *recognize* it everywhere.
Your gaze becomes a blessing, your awareness a healing field of understanding.
You see the divine pattern in all things — not because it appears, but because you finally *remembered how to look.*

In the light of Ajna, silence is luminous, sight is sacred, and consciousness itself becomes creation.
Through you, the universe begins to witness its own reflection — radiant, infinite, and awake.

THIRD EYE CHAKRA BENEDICTION: THE BLESSING OF SIGHT

(Ajna – The Eye of Divine Wisdom)

May your vision be clear and your mind still.
May you see not only what appears, but what *is*.
May illusion dissolve before the light of your awareness,
and truth reveal itself in every reflection.

May your eyes open not outward, but inward —
to the vast horizon of the soul.
May every thought be illumined by understanding,
and every silence glow with insight.

May you perceive with compassion,
seeing others not through their actions,
but through their essence.
May the light within you recognize itself in all you behold.

When confusion clouds your path,
may clarity rise like dawn through shadow.
When fear distorts your sight,
may wisdom steady your gaze.
When doubt whispers blindness,
may trust remind you that light never leaves.

Let every dream be a message of awakening.
Let every symbol become a language of Spirit.
Let every vision draw you closer to remembrance —
that you are both the seer and the seen.

May the lamp of intuition burn bright behind your brow,
guiding your thoughts with discernment and grace.
May your inner sight pierce through illusion,
revealing beauty where the mind once saw chaos.

May you look upon the world with wonder,
understanding that what you see is what you create.
May your perception be the canvas upon which the divine
paints truth.

When eyes close in meditation,
may the inner light reveal the path beyond sight.
When eyes open to the world,
may that same light guide your vision with peace.

"I see through the eyes of my soul.
Clarity is my constant companion.
Light reveals the truth of all things."

Blessed be the Eye of Ajna —
the Luminous Vision of the Infinite Mind.

THE LIGHT OF SEEING: ENTERING THE THIRD EYE CHAKRA

The journey continues upward, where sound becomes light and
expression transforms into perception.
Through Vishuddha, you found your authentic voice; through
Ajna, you now learn to *see* that voice in form.
This is the sacred evolution from vibration to vision — the
refinement of truth into illumination.

The Third Eye is not about seeing more — it is about seeing
clearly.
It awakens the perception that all creation, from the smallest
whisper to the grandest design, originates in consciousness.

Here, the mind becomes a mirror, reflecting divine order instead of projecting confusion.

Ajna bridges intellect and intuition — logic and mystery dancing in unison. It invites you to look beyond appearances and into essence, to see the invisible threads that weave all experiences together.
This is where duality dissolves into unity; where you cease reacting to life and begin witnessing it through the eye of wisdom.

The Third Eye teaches that vision is not of the eyes but of awareness. It reveals that enlightenment is not found by looking upward, but inward — into the boundless expanse of knowing that already exists within you.

Before you seek to see the unseen, pause and remember: the true act of vision is understanding. Close your eyes and allow the darkness to bloom into light. Feel the pulse of clarity awaken between your brows. Affirm silently:

"I see what is true.
My vision serves wisdom.
My awareness is peace."

You are not beginning a new journey; you are entering the radiance of recognition.
The energy that once spoke now becomes light — and in that light, consciousness remembers itself.

Through Ajna, you do not seek to understand the universe — you *become* its understanding. Here, love perceives its own reflection in every living thing, and wisdom becomes the language of sight.

"May the light within me reveal the light in all things."

Bibliography

CLASSICAL & YOGIC SOURCES

• Feuerstein, Georg. *The Yoga Tradition: Its History, Literature, Philosophy, and Practice.* Hohm Press, 2001.
• Avalon, Arthur (Sir John Woodroffe). *The Serpent Power: The Secrets of Tantric and Shaktic Yoga.* Dover Publications, 1974.
• Swami Sivananda. *The Chakras.* Divine Life Society, 1994.
• Easwaran, Eknath (trans.). *The Upanishads.* Nilgiri Press, 2007.
• Vivekananda, Swami. *Raja Yoga.* Advaita Ashrama, 1896. *(Foundational for understanding concentration, meditation, and the awakening of intuitive sight.)*
• Satyananda Saraswati, Swami. *Kundalini Tantra.* Bihar School of Yoga, 1984. *(Detailed exposition on Ajna as the command center of consciousness and vision.)*
• Paramahansa Yogananda. *Autobiography of a Yogi.* Self-Realization Fellowship, 1946. *(Includes experiential insight into inner sight and cosmic consciousness.)*
• Sri Aurobindo. *The Life Divine.* Sri Aurobindo Ashram Press, 1939. *(Advanced study of consciousness evolution, relevant to Third Eye realization.)*

CHAKRA & ENERGY HEALING WORKS

• Judith, Anodea. *Wheels of Life: A User's Guide to the Chakra System.* Llewellyn Publications, 1987.
• Myss, Caroline. *Anatomy of the Spirit.* Harmony Books, 1996.
• Brennan, Barbara Ann. *Hands of Light: A Guide to Healing Through the Human Energy Field.* Bantam, 1988.
• Leadbeater, C. W. *The Chakras.* Quest Books, 1972.

(Influential for early clairvoyant observations of subtle energy centers.)
• Judith, Anodea. *Eastern Body, Western Mind: Psychology and the Chakra System as a Path to the Self.* Celestial Arts, 1996. *(Bridges Ajna psychology — perception, imagination, and insight — with Jungian concepts.)*
• Dale, Cyndi. *The Subtle Body: An Encyclopedia of Your Energetic Anatomy.* Sounds True, 2009. *(Comprehensive reference for practitioners working with multidimensional energy systems.)*

REIKI & SPIRITUAL HEALING

• Takata, Hawayo. *Reiki: Hawayo Takata's Story.* Reiki Alliance, 1998.
• Petter, Frank Arjava. *This Is Reiki: Transformation of Body, Mind and Soul from the Origins to the Practice.* Lotus Press, 2012.
• Rand, William Lee. *Reiki: The Healing Touch.* Vision Publications, 1991.
• Santego, Constance. *Reiki Wisdom Series.* Maximillian Enterprises, 2024–. *(Particularly relevant to the integration of intuition, ethics, and practitioner alignment.)*
• Stein, Diane. *Essential Reiki.* Crossing Press, 1995. *(Highlights intuitive guidance as the foundation of energy healing practice.)*

PSYCHOLOGY, CONSCIOUSNESS & INTUITION

• Jung, Carl G. *The Archetypes and the Collective Unconscious.* Princeton University Press, 1969.
• Jung, Carl G. *Man and His Symbols.* Doubleday, 1964. *(Essential for understanding symbolic vision and intuitive cognition.)*
• Assagioli, Roberto. *Psychosynthesis: A Manual of Principles and Techniques.* Hobbs, Dorman & Co., 1965. *(Addresses integration of the higher self and intuitive will.)*

• Hillman, James. *The Soul's Code: In Search of Character and Calling.* Random House, 1996.
• Wilber, Ken. *A Brief History of Everything.* Shambhala, 1996. *(Evolution of consciousness and integrative awareness — higher Ajna themes.)*
• Tolle, Eckhart. *The Power of Now.* New World Library, 1997. *(Teaches direct perception through present-moment awareness.)*
• Chopra, Deepak. *The Book of Secrets: Unlocking the Hidden Dimensions of Your Life.* Harmony Books, 2004. *(Explores intuition and multidimensional perception.)*
• Dispenza, Joe. *Breaking the Habit of Being Yourself.* Hay House, 2012. *(Mind reprogramming and neuroplasticity — modern correlate to Third Eye awakening.)*

CROSS-CULTURAL & MYSTICAL REFERENCES

• Halevi, Z'ev ben Shimon. *Kabbalah: Tradition of Hidden Knowledge.* Thames & Hudson, 1991.
• Hanh, Thich Nhat. *The Miracle of Mindfulness.* Beacon Press, 1975. *(Practical awareness meditation for stilling the mind.)*
• Ibn Arabi. *Journey to the Lord of Power.* Inner Traditions, 1981.
• Underhill, Evelyn. *Mysticism: A Study in the Nature and Development of Spiritual Consciousness.* Dover Publications, 2002.
• Campbell, Joseph. *The Hero with a Thousand Faces.* Princeton University Press, 1949. *(Archetypal journey of awakening and self-realization.)*
• Rumi, Jalal al-Din. *The Essential Rumi.* Trans. Coleman Barks. HarperOne, 1995. *(Visionary poetry of divine perception.)*
• Sri Nisargadatta Maharaj. *I Am That.* Acorn Press, 1973. *(Direct realization of consciousness as the ultimate perceiver.)*
• Krishnamurti, Jiddu. *The Awakening of Intelligence.* Harper & Row, 1973. *(Explores awareness without conditioning — key Ajna teaching.)*

MODERN SCIENCE & RESEARCH

• Pert, Candace B. *Molecules of Emotion: The Science Behind Mind-Body Medicine.* Scribner, 1997.
• Lipton, Bruce H. *The Biology of Belief.* Hay House, 2005.
• McCraty, Rollin, et al. *Science of the Heart: Exploring the Role of the Heart in Human Performance.* HeartMath Institute, 2015.
• Dispenza, Joe. *Becoming Supernatural: How Common People Are Doing the Uncommon.* Hay House, 2017.
• Kauffman, Stuart. *At Home in the Universe: The Search for Laws of Self-Organization and Complexity.* Oxford University Press, 1995.
• Emoto, Masaru. *The Hidden Messages in Water.* Beyond Words, 2004. *(Extends into frequency and consciousness — relevant to Ajna perception.)*
• Goswami, Amit. *The Self-Aware Universe: How Consciousness Creates the Material World.* Tarcher, 1995. *(Quantum physics meets spiritual insight — foundational for Third Eye understanding.)*

ADDITIONAL RESOURCES

• Eden, Donna. *Energy Medicine.* TarcherPerigee, 2008.
• Osho. *The Book of Secrets: 112 Meditations to Discover the Mystery Within.* St. Martin's Griffin, 1998.
• Hay, Louise. *You Can Heal Your Life.* Hay House, 1984.
• Blackstone, Judith. *Belonging Here: A Guide for the Spiritually Sensitive Person.* Sounds True, 2012.
• Sadhguru. *Inner Engineering: A Yogi's Guide to Joy.* Spiegel & Grau, 2016.
• Wilber, Ken. *The Spectrum of Consciousness.* Quest Books, 1977.
• Radha, Swami Sivananda. *Kundalini Yoga for the West.* Timeless Books, 1978.
• Bentov, Itzhak. *Stalking the Wild Pendulum: On the Mechanics of Consciousness.* Destiny Books, 1977. *(Bridges*

physics and meditation — Ajna's scientific correspondence.)
• Grey, Alex. *The Mission of Art.* Shambhala, 1998. *(Visionary interpretation of consciousness through imagery and sacred geometry.)*

Message From The Author

By the time you've reached this sixth book in the *Chakra 101 Series*, your energy has traveled far — from the depths of the body to the horizon of the mind.
You have opened the Heart — awakening unconditional love and divine awareness.
You have grounded that love through the Root — creating stability and trust in the material world.
You have allowed it to flow through the Sacral — embracing emotion, creativity, and connection.
You have ignited it in the Solar Plexus — transforming will into purposeful action.
You have given it voice through the Throat — expressing truth with clarity and compassion.

And now, you arrive at the Third Eye Chakra — the Seat of Vision and Intuition.

Here, sound becomes light.
Perception becomes wisdom.
You no longer seek truth outside of yourself — you *see* it within everything.

The Third Eye invites you to refine not what you *say*, but what you *see*.
It teaches that insight is not imagination, but revelation — the moment when awareness transcends thought and glimpses the pattern behind all creation.
This is the awakening of intuitive intelligence, where mind and spirit merge in luminous understanding.

Through Ajna, the soul perceives without judgment, interprets without distortion, and remembers that true sight is born of stillness.
In the quiet between thoughts, wisdom arises — not as words, but as light.

As you explore these teachings, may you learn to trust your inner vision as the language of Spirit.
May your intuition become the compass of clarity that guides your choices with grace.
May you see through the eyes of compassion — discerning truth beyond appearance, and recognizing the divine pattern in all things.

And above all, may you remember that awakening the Third Eye is not about gaining sight — it is about *remembering* that you have never been blind.

With love, light, and infinite awareness,
Dr. Constance Santego

About the Author

Dr. Constance Santego, Ph.D., DNM, is a bestselling author, teacher, and natural medicine doctor with over twenty-five years of experience in energy healing and holistic wellness. A Grand Reiki Master and founder of multiple wellness and educational programs, she has trained thousands of students worldwide in Reiki, holistic therapies, and intuitive development.

Her passion is to translate ancient wisdom into practical, modern tools for healing, transformation, and self-discovery. Dr. Santego has authored more than forty books — including the *Reiki Wisdom* series, *Secrets of a Healer* guides, and the

Nine Spiritual Gifts novels — each uniting spirituality, science, and story to awaken the soul's potential.

Blending Eastern philosophy, Western natural medicine, and modern energy science, her teachings emphasize compassion, awareness, and self-empowerment as the foundation of all true healing. Her work invites readers and students alike to explore the subtle dimensions of energy, perception, and consciousness — the very essence of the Third Eye's awakening.

Dr. Santego's mission is to help others connect with their inner wisdom, awaken their intuitive gifts, and live with balance, joy, and love. She lives in beautiful British Columbia, where the serenity of nature continues to inspire her writing, her practice, and her lifelong devotion to Spirit.

ALSO AVAILABLE

For additional information on

Constance Santego's

wide range of Motivational Products, Coaching Sessions,
Spiritual Retreats,
Live Events and Educational Programs

Go to

www.ConstanceSantego.ca

Follow on Instagram - Constance_Santego and
Facebook - constancesantegoo

Subscribe and receive Free Information and Meditations on her
YouTube Channel - Constance Santego

Secrets of a Healer, Magic of Reiki

ISBN: 978-1-7772220-0-0

Secrets of a Healer, The Reiki Master's Manual

ISBN: 978-1-990062-34-6

www.ingramcontent.com/pod-product-compliance
Lightning Source LLC
Chambersburg PA
CBHW060142150626
46550CB00014B/55